CW01501718

TO:

_____

FROM:

_____

MESSAGE:

_____

_____

_____

LIVING
GOD'S WAY

ANGUS BUCHAN

CHRISTIAN ART
PUBLISHERS

Published by Christian Art Publishers
PO Box 1599, Vereeniging, 1930, RSA

© 2023
First edition 2023

Designed by Christian Art Publishers
Cover designed by Christian Art Publishers
Images used under license from Shutterstock.com

Unless otherwise indicated, all Scripture quotations are taken from the
New King James Version®. Copyright © 1979, 1980, 1982 by Thomas Nelson, Inc.
Used by permission. All rights reserved.

Scripture quotations marked NLT are taken from the Holy Bible, New Living Translation,
copyright © 1996, 2004, 2015 by Tyndale House Foundation.
Used by permission of Tyndale House Publishers, Inc., Carol Stream, Illinois 60188.
All rights reserved.

Printed in China

ISBN 978-0-638-00111-2

© All rights reserved. No part of this book may be reproduced in any form without
permission in writing from the publisher, except in the case of brief quotations in critical
articles or reviews.

23 24 25 26 27 28 29 30 31 32 – 10 9 8 7 6 5 4 3 2 1

Now may the God of **PEACE**—
who brought up from the dead our **LORD JESUS**,
the great **SHEPHERD** of the sheep,
and ratified an **ETERNAL COVENANT** with His blood—
may He **EQUIP YOU** with all you need for doing **HIS WILL**.
May He **PRODUCE** in you,
through the **POWER** of Jesus Christ,
every good thing that is **PLEASING** to Him.
ALL GLORY to Him forever and ever!
AMEN.

HEBREWS 13:20-21

HAPPY NEW YEAR

As it is written: "Eye has not seen, nor ear heard,
nor have entered into the heart of man the things
which God has prepared for those who love Him."
1 CORINTHIANS 2:9

In this new year, we must walk by faith and not by sight (see 2 Corinthians 5:7). We must remember that Jesus will be a standing guarantee for us—He will back us all the way. Now remember, Zig Ziglar said that if you aim at nothing then you are sure to hit it every time. I hope you have something that you are aiming at this year, because where there is no vision, the people perish (see Proverbs 29:18).

We really need to focus on the vision that we ask God to give us. Habakkuk 2:2-3 says, "Write the vision and make it plain on tablets, that he may run who reads it. For the vision is yet for an appointed time; but at the end it will speak, and it will not lie. Though it tarries, wait for it." Remember, if your vision doesn't scare you, it is not big enough.

I want to close with a quote from John Wesley: "Do all the good you can, by all the means you can, in all the ways you can, in all the places you can, at all the times you can, to all the people you can, as long as ever you can."

May Jesus bless you this year. Keep your eyes fixed on Him as you pursue His vision for your life.

THE GOOD BOOK

*Your word is a lamp to my feet
and a light to my path.*
PSALM 119:105

Do you know that the Bible is the Book that comforts us? It is our mediator in family squabbles. It is our guide for life. It tells us right from wrong. It is also the joy of our hearts; in fact, it is our ultimate hope for this year.

I don't really believe in New Year's resolutions because none of mine ever work! But the word *resolution* is a great word because it means to make a firm decision. I want to encourage you to make one good New Year's resolution this year: to make a firm decision to place the Bible at the center of your decision-making for the year. You will be pleasantly surprised at how wise and successful you will become.

If you read the Bible and pray every single day, first thing in the morning, it will set you up for the day. Start with the book of John and read it through, then carry on in the New Testament. You can also read the Psalms for daily inspiration. Or you can work through a daily devotional and write down what God says to you in a journal.

I want to tell you, it will see you through the year. I have been doing it for over 40 years and God speaks to me daily through the Good Book.

A PRAYING PEOPLE

"Pray without ceasing."

1 THESSALONIANS 5:17

Prayer must become the fiber of our very being. When we get up in the morning, we put our clothes on for the day and in the same way we must cover ourselves in prayer every morning. We have to become a praying people. What was Jesus doing at the most critical time in His life when He was in the Garden of Gethsemane? He was praying. Prayer was the focal point in Jesus' life and remains so to this day. In fact, He is interceding in heaven right now on our behalf.

Remember when the five thousand people had nothing to eat and the disciples came to the Lord and said, "What must we do?" (see Matthew 14:13-21). The Lord prayed over two small fish and five loaves of bread and this fed five thousand men. This is not even including the women and children who were there.

When I was still a young Christian, there was a fire on our farm. A strong wind was blowing and the fire was about to set my neighbor's pine plantation alight. It would have meant absolute devastation for us. Our neighbors were helping us try to put the fire out, but we were not succeeding. Then I got on my knees, in front of everybody, and I prayed. The wind from the north miraculously died down and a cool wind came up and gentle rain fell on that fire and put it out.

This year let us become a praying people. There is great power in prayer.

GROUNDWORK FOR FREEDOM

For I am not ashamed of the gospel of Christ,
for it is the power of God to salvation for everyone
who believes, for the Jew first and also for the Greek.
For in it the righteousness of God is revealed from
faith to faith; as it is written, "The just shall live by faith."

ROMANS 1:16-17

You might wonder to yourself, *How can I increase my faith?* Well, Romans 10:17 says, "So then faith comes by hearing, and hearing by the word of God." In other words, you get faith by reading your Bible!

I recently read a beautiful quote by Horace Greeley: "It is impossible to enslave, mentally or socially, a Bible-reading people. The principles of the Bible are the groundwork of human freedom." Isn't that beautiful?

So if you are full of fear today, read 2 Timothy 1:7 (NLT), where it says, "For God has not given us a spirit of fear and timidity, but of power, love, and self-discipline." If you have sinned and need to repent turn to 1 John 1:9 that reads: "If we confess our sins, He is faithful and just to forgive us our sins and to cleanse us from all unrighteousness."

Do you see how the Bible is the key to setting us free? John 8:36 says, "Therefore if the Son makes you free, you shall be free indeed." This year let us read the Word of God. It will keep us successful and at peace. It will set us free.

NOT FORSAKEN

The LORD went before them by day in a pillar of
cloud to lead the way, and by night in a pillar of fire
to give them light, so as to go by day and night.

EXODUS 13:21

For forty years God never abandoned the Israelites in the wilderness and He is not about to abandon you now. That desert, that wilderness the Israelites wandered in, reaches temperatures of up to 46°C and drops below freezing at night.

The cloud of God kept the people from the heat by day while a pillar of fire kept them warm at night. The pillar of cloud and of fire not only kept the Israelites safe but also gave them direction. By following the cloud they went where God was leading them.

We need direction. You know, in East Africa, in the great plains of the Maasai Mara, there are herds of wildebeest, tens of thousands of them, that follow the rain clouds at the end of the dry season, as the wet season begins. They watch the clouds because they know that those clouds are full of rain and where the rain falls, the grass will grow very quickly. Now, if the animals know that what about you and me?

We need to follow the great Rainmaker and Creator of the clouds and we do that through reading the Bible. Reading His Word nourishes us and guides us in the right paths.

BE HUMBLE

*"God resists the proud,
but gives grace to the humble."*
1 PETER 5:5

Always remember, pride comes before a fall. How many times have we seen an arrogant person brought low because of pride? Just look at the mighty Titanic, the ship they said was unsinkable. On its maiden voyage it sank. But God gives grace to the humble. Remember, humility is controlled strength, it is not weakness.

Many years ago, I was preaching in Scotland. I was in a little country village, in the Community Hall. Before the meeting, we were having tea and cucumber sandwiches when the organizer introduced me to a middle-aged man. I asked him, "Sir, what do you do for a living?" He said, "I am a part-time farmer and a soldier."

After the meeting, the organizer came to me and said, "That gentleman you were having tea with, do you know who he is?" I said, "Yes, he said he was a soldier." Then the organizer told me that the man was a Commander General of one of the biggest military forces in Europe. Just a soldier indeed! This man showed humility when he could have been arrogant and full of himself.

Humility is a wonderful thing so "clothe yourself in humility" as Paul says in Colossians 3:12 and go out today and be humble and God will raise you up.

SUCCESSFUL PEOPLE

*"Though your beginning was small,
yet your latter end would increase abundantly."*
JOB 8:7

Job was successful. Why? Because he never wavered. Successful people are not superstars or perfect in everything they do. They make a difference because they carry on through thick and thin. I remember when I went to Ladysmith, at the start of the first campaign I ever organized. I went to the first church in the town and knocked on the door. The man said, "You can come here if you want but peoples' hearts are as hard as the rocks and the thorn trees in this town." I went to the second guy and he said, "This place has been over-evangelized." I went to the third guy, who said: "Maybe God sent you here to bend you a little bit."

I went and parked underneath a thorn tree, just like Elijah, and I said, "Lord, what am I doing here? I am a successful farmer; I don't have to do this." And I felt the Lord saying, "Are you going to go through with it or not?" And like Job, I persevered. I went to another minister's house and he said, "Angus, we are waiting for you. We have been praying for revival in this town for six months." And that was the first campaign we ever had. Probably the smallest one but it was incredibly successful.

Obedience is better than sacrifice. Get out there today, like Job, and keep on keeping on for Him!

YOUR FRIEND, JESUS

Now when Herod saw Jesus, he was exceedingly
glad; for he had desired for a long time to see Him,
because he had heard many things about Him,
and he hoped to see some miracle done by Him.

LUKE 23:8

Without a doubt, Jesus Christ is the most popular Man who ever lived on earth.

Many years ago, there was a little boy named Thoko who lived in the little children's home (that closed many years ago) just across the road. My dear wife, Jill, used to read him Bible stories; his favorites were always about heaven. I often used to take my horse Snowy over to give little Thoko a ride. He would just sit quietly in front of me on the saddle.

Sadly, Thoko had a terminal disease and did not live long. One day he told me that his Friend, Jesus, was going to come on His big white horse and take him home to heaven. Shortly afterwards, Jesus came and took Thoko home.

I want to ask you today, do you know Jesus as Thoko did? Is He real to you? Herod was so excited when he knew that he was going to meet with the Son of God. How excited are you to meet the Son of God one day?

SEVENTY TIMES SEVEN

"Nevertheless in Your great mercy You did
not utterly consume them nor forsake them;
for You are God, gracious and merciful."

NEHEMIAH 9:31

Time and again the Israelites sinned against the Lord, forgot about Him and turned their backs on Him, but He constantly forgave them and was merciful towards them. In Matthew 18:21-22 (NLT) Jesus speaks about forgiveness to Peter, "Then Peter came to Him and asked, 'Lord, how often should I forgive someone who sins against me? Seven times?' 'No, not seven times,' Jesus replied, 'but seventy times seven!'"

That is a lot of forgiveness! But it is actually for our own sake that the Lord says we must forgive. You know if we carry an offense, in an attitude of unforgiveness, it will eventually eat us up and completely destroy us. Many times, the person you are hateful towards is not aware of it and it doesn't even affect them. Unforgiveness wears us down. Rather lay it down today at the foot of the cross and leave it there. Revenge belongs to the Lord, let Him deal with it.

They say that unforgiveness and bitterness are like drinking poison and hoping the other person dies. Let's not be like that. Ask God to help you "be kind to one another, tenderhearted, forgiving one another, even as God in Christ forgave you" (Ephesians 4:32).

A CHEERFUL GIVER

"Will a man rob God? Yet you have
robbed Me! But you say, 'In what way have
we robbed You?' In tithes and offerings."

MALACHI 3:8

Remember, the tithe belongs to the Lord—the full 10%. Offerings and gifts come after that. We will never be able to "out-bless" the Lord. He is a giver by nature; He gave His very life for us. Now I can hear you saying, "But where do we tithe?" Well, you tithe to the place where you receive your spiritual food. When you tithe, remember that God loves a cheerful giver (see 2 Corinthians 9:7). We are also not just speaking here about finances only, but also time given to God each day.

How much time are we giving to the Lord each morning? How much time are we giving to our family? What about time given to helping widows and orphans? They need us to help them. And what about time given to yourself? Do you spend a bit of time on your own doing sport, exercising, or maybe even gardening?

Give God the first fruits of everything that you have, let us not give it to Jesus as our leftovers. Put Jesus first and then everything else will fall into place. As Matthew 6:33 says, "Seek first the kingdom of God and His righteousness, and all these things shall be added to you." Let's be cheerful givers of our money, time and talents.

BE CHILDLIKE

"Therefore whoever humbles himself as this little child is the greatest in the kingdom of heaven."

MATTHEW 18:4

If we want to be the greatest, we must be prepared to become the least in God's kingdom. Father God works in the opposite way to the world's system. The world is looking for the strongest, most powerful, most talented and the most intelligent person to be their leader. But Jesus said that it is better to be as loving, trusting and humble as a little child.

He told His disciples that they must receive the kingdom of God like a little child, "Then they brought little children to Him, that He might touch them; but the disciples rebuked those who brought them. But when Jesus saw it, He was greatly displeased and said to them, 'Let the little children come to Me, and do not forbid them; for of such is the kingdom of God. Assuredly, I say to you, whoever does not receive the kingdom of God as a little child will by no means enter it.' And He took them up in His arms, laid His hands on them, and blessed them" (Mark 10:13-16).

You see, Jesus wants us to be completely trusting in Him. A little child can do nothing on its own. It has to depend on its parent. We must be the same. We must trust Jesus.

As you go about your day, be like that little child, totally trusting in the Lord. He will not fail us and He will never let us down.

CAN YOU SEE HIM?

The women were terrified and bowed with
their faces to the ground. Then the men asked,
"Why are you looking among the dead for someone
who is alive? He isn't here! He is risen from the dead!"
LUKE 24:5-6 NLT

Our Lord and Savior Jesus Christ is not just some famous person who used to live on the earth and is now dead. I can take you to Jerusalem and the Old City. I can take you to the grave of King David and I can show you where his bones are buried, but I cannot show you Jesus' bones. No, because He is still very much alive!

In fact, this very morning, I was having a hot cup of tea with Him in my prayer room and that is not a joke. I can honestly say it and mean it: Jesus Christ is not a figment of my imagination.

The many times He has been so close to me are not when I have seen Him move in great signs, wonders and miracles, but rather when I have been going through my deepest, darkest valleys.

I see Him in the morning sunrise or after a shower of rain. I see him in the newly sprouting crops and in the fish eagle's majestic call. Jesus is all around us, we simply have to open our eyes and our ears. Please speak with Him today, He is waiting to hear from you!

SIMPLE FAITH

And their words seemed to them like
idle tales, and they did not believe them.
LUKE 24:11

When the women came back from the tomb and told the disciples that it was empty, they did not believe them. The women's words seemed like nonsense to the disciples.

In Luke 17:5 the disciples ask Jesus to, "Increase our faith." You see, without faith we are not going to make it. We need childlike faith. That is the only way that we are going to complete this race here on earth.

You know, if I was to take my son, Fergie, when he was still very small, out in the evening to show him a big full moon and say, "Fergie, that moon is made out of cheddar cheese," he would have believed me. Even if he was to meet Neil Armstrong after that, and Neil told him, "Fergie, the moon is not made of cheddar cheese. I have walked on the moon. It is made out of rock and dust." Fergie would say, "No, Sir, my dad said it is made out of cheddar cheese." This is the kind of childlike faith God expects from us.

We need to have simple faith, simple believing faith. Without faith, we can't please God. Go out today and believe what God has told you. It will change your life.

THE RIGHT PRIORITIES

"But seek first the kingdom of God
and His righteousness, and all
these things shall be added to you."
MATTHEW 6:33

What are your priorities today? In this rat race we are living in our priorities can get skewed. That is why we have to get back to basics. Now, this is how our priorities should be: God first; secondly, your spouse; thirdly, your children and your extended family; lastly, your career, your ministry, your vision and whatever else is important to you.

Yes, we have to reach out to others and show care and concern to others but not at the expense of our marriage. We have to take care of as many people as we can but not at the cost of our children. We have to work hard and do our best in everything but not at the cost of our relationship with the Lord. First your relationship with God before anything else.

The disciples looked for Jesus and when they found Him asked, "Where were You, Lord? The crowd is waiting for You." Jesus replied, "I am with My Father. I am up the mountain to hear from Him and spend time with Him." Spend time today and get your priorities in order. Only when you seek Him first will everything else fall into place.

ENCOUNTER JESUS

Suddenly, their eyes were opened,
and they recognized Him. And at that moment
He disappeared! They said to each other,
"Didn't our hearts burn within us as He talked with
us on the road and explained the Scriptures to us?"

LUKE 24:31-32 NLT

On the road to Emmaus two disciples had an encounter with Jesus. They were filled with joy and excitement. Oh, let us cherish that first encounter with the Savior of the world. Let us never forget it! Do not allow the business of this world to rob you of that moment. Do not waste precious time because of the mediocre, mundane and wasteful things that this life has to offer.

I remember going to Jerusalem and walking with Jill, my wife, to the Church of the Holy Sepulcher. I sat down and all of a sudden, I had an encounter—an encounter with the living Christ. I broke down and I wept. I will never forget that experience.

What about you? In Revelation 3:20, Jesus says, "Behold, I stand at the door and knock. If anyone hears My voice and opens the door, I will come in to him and dine with him, and he with Me." Now, remember, the handle of the door is on the inside. Why don't you open the door, invite Him in and have an encounter with the living Christ today?

LOVE YOUR WIFE

Wives, submit to your own husbands, as to the Lord.
Husbands, love your wives, just as Christ also
loved the church and gave Himself for her.
EPHESIANS 5:22, 25

We need to clearly understand that the marriage institution, the life-long covenant between one man and one woman, is not just a good idea—it is God's commandment and holy ordained by Him. It is for the benefit of the whole family for parents to be married and to love one another. I am thinking particularly of children who get so upset when mom and dad just cannot get along. It breaks down a marriage quicker than anything else.

A wife who doesn't submit to her husband causes division. On the other hand, husbands should not make it hard for their wives to submit to them. If a husband doesn't provide for his family or if there is no discipline in the home, it will be extremely hard for his wife to submit to him.

Love your wife by looking after her and protecting her, providing for your children and making sure they respect their mom. Then, all of a sudden, things will change completely. You see the more you love and cherish your wife, the more she will willfully submit to you, and most importantly, the children in the home will flourish.

What can you do to show your wife love and respect today?

BE CONTENT

Now godliness with contentment is great gain.
1 TIMOTHY 6:6

King David had everything. He had money and he was a very handsome man. He could do whatever he wanted. He had the most beautiful women in the world. He had fame and power and yet in Psalm 27:4 he said, "One thing I have desired of the Lord, that will I seek: that I may dwell in the house of the Lord all the days of my life, to behold the beauty of the Lord, and to inquire in His temple." David was satisfied with what he had and only desired to be in God's presence.

You and I need to be content and we need to be satisfied with what God has given us. We have a little window box made out of brick and cement, which my wife filled with the most beautiful pansies a while back. Then we had a terrible hailstorm and it wiped out every single flower.

But as I walked out some weeks later and looked at that little window box, I saw the most beautiful pansy. It was growing out of the wall on the side of the window box. The Lord just said to me, in my heart, "You see, Angus, that little pansy is so content. It blooms beautifully just where it is."

Let us be as content as that little pansy today. Spend time in God's presence and thank Him for all that He has given you.

BE STILL

"Be still, and know that I am God;
I will be exalted among the nations,
I will be exalted in the earth!"

PSALM 46:10

In Mark 6:30-31, we read that the disciples were so busy telling Jesus of all the miracles and the healings that had taken place that they did not have time to eat. So Jesus said to them, "Come aside by yourselves to a deserted place and rest a while."

A few years ago the Lord spoke to me almost audibly and do you know what He said? He said, "Your busyness is making Me tired." I tell you what, that was a wake-up call. God is not impressed by your busyness—He wants you to Himself.

I love to ride my horse Snowy. He is an Appaloosa and he talks to me probably more than a lot of people. If I am in a hurry and I just want to have a quick ride before I have to go, that horse of mine becomes very agitated.

He becomes naughty sometimes. He doesn't listen to what I am saying because he thinks that there is trouble. He thinks that Angus is too uptight and needs to slow down. We need to relax and we need to be still and know that the Lord Jesus Christ, He is God.

Take some time to be still today and pray to the God of peace and serenity.

OBEDIENCE IS KEY

Now Esther had not revealed her family
and her people, just as Mordecai had charged her,
for Esther obeyed the command of Mordecai
as when she was brought up by him.

ESTHER 2:20

Esther was obedient to her uncle Mordecai and this action saved her life. You see, the King of Persia was captivated by Esther's beauty.

She was a very beautiful young Jewish maiden but her uncle told her: "Do not tell them that you are Jewish." Esther obeyed her uncle and listened to what she had been taught when she was a little girl. Because of this, she was safe and would later go on to save many lives (see Esther 4-9).

Discipline is so very important. Discipline your children when they are young and when they grow up, they will not depart from the ways of the Lord (see Proverbs 22:6). It is for the sake of the child and for their own protection that you need to discipline them and they need to obey you.

Hebrews 12:11 (NLT) is a hard verse but it is for our own good: "No discipline is enjoyable while it is happening—it's painful! But afterward there will be a peaceful harvest of right living for those who are trained in this way."

We need to accept God's discipline and obey His Word; it will bring us safety and security.

JESUS IN PRINT

In the beginning was the Word, and the Word was with God, and the Word was God. He was in the beginning with God. All things were made through Him, and without Him nothing was made that was made.

JOHN 1:1-3

Who is John speaking about? He's speaking about Jesus. Yes, Jesus is the Word. Now, if we go to 1 John 5:7-8, it says, "For there are three that bear witness in heaven: the Father, the Word, and the Holy Spirit; and these three are one." So who is the Word? That's right, it is Jesus!

Now, if anyone says to you, "Show me this Jesus you're always talking about," give them a Bible. Why do you think I've written on the front of my Bible: "My Agricultural Manual." There's a reason for it: This Holy Book, when I was an active farmer and even to this day, is my daily direction finder.

The Bible is a friend when you're lonely. It's a compass when you are lost and it's a lawgiver in times of dispute. It never ages and it never changes—it's the same yesterday, today and forevermore. Mathew 24:35 says, "Heaven and earth will pass away, but My words will by no means pass away." The Bible stands the test of time.

Spend time studying the Book of Life today and I tell you what, your life will become so much more simplified and so much more fulfilled.

A GOOD AMBASSADOR

"Now then, we are ambassadors for Christ,
as though God were pleading through us:
we implore you on Christ's behalf, be reconciled to God."

2 CORINTHIANS 5:20

We have been called to represent Jesus and the ideal example of an excellent ambassador was none other than John the Baptist. If we look at John 1:19-20, they asked him: "'Who are you?' He confessed, and did not deny, but confessed, 'I am not the Christ.'"

He was the bravest of men. He was so outspoken and he was a godly man but he was also very humble. In John 1:27 (NLT), he says, "I'm not even worthy to be His slave and untie the straps of His sandal." He was talking about Jesus.

Be careful you don't draw people to yourself; draw people to God. What are the credentials of an ambassador of Christ? Well, the fruit of the Spirit: "…love, joy, peace, longsuffering, kindness, goodness, faithfulness, gentleness, self-control" (Galatians 5:22-23).

Often we get called to a drought-ravaged area and we are asked to please pray for rain. And sometimes, we will get sarcastic comments like: "Oh, so you think you are the rainmakers do you?" No, we are not the rainmakers, we are the Rainmaker's sons and daughters. The Lord always comes through for us when we pray.

Be a good ambassador for Jesus today.

RAISING CHILDREN

Direct your children onto the right path,
and when they are older, they will not leave it.
PROVERBS 22:6 NLT

I heard a very disturbing story: A young schoolteacher, whom we know well, phoned up her mom and said, "I feel like giving up teaching. I have been given a class of small children who are totally undisciplined, unruly and very bad-mannered." It made me so sad.

It takes time and effort for parents to bring up their children. It is not the responsibility of the schoolteacher, nanny or domestic worker. It is Mom and Dad's responsibility.

Remember, your little boy or girl will not do what you tell them, they will do what you do. If you love your spouse, they will love their wife or husband when they grow up. If you have quiet times with the Lord every morning, that little child will do exactly the same. If you work hard, they will be hardworking when they grow up.

You see, that little child has to go out into an unforgiving world where they will be treated very severely for a lack of discipline and respect for others. So, Moms and Dads, bring up your children correctly and they will do well in the world.

HE UNDERSTANDS

And the Word became flesh and dwelt among us,
and we beheld His glory, the glory as of the only
begotten of the Father, full of grace and truth.

JOHN 1:14

Sometimes the worst thing you can say to somebody who is going through a bad time is: "I understand." Maybe you are going through one yourself at the moment—bankruptcy, the loss of a child or maybe you are going through an ugly divorce. If somebody comes to you and says, "I understand," when in fact they have no idea what you are going through, it just makes you feel even more alone in your situation.

The good news is that Jesus really knows what you are going through because He has been there. In Isaiah 53:3-4, the Bible says, "He is despised and rejected by men, a Man of sorrows and acquainted with grief. And we hid, as it were, our faces from Him; He was despised, and we did not esteem Him. Surely He has borne our griefs and carried our sorrows." So yes, He understands.

Have a good heart-to-heart chat with Him today, because He really understands and most of all He loves you. He can help you get through the toughest times.

A HUNGRY BEGGAR

Andrew went to find his brother, Simon, and told him,
"We have found the Messiah" (which means "Christ").
JOHN 1:41 NLT

What is evangelism? Daniel T. Niles said it right, he said, "Evangelism is one hungry beggar showing another hungry beggar where he can find bread." That is all it is. That is exactly what Andrew did: he brought his brother and introduced him to Jesus.

You can't do it without zeal and belief. You see, unless you have been hungry yourself, you will never understand what it means to show somebody where to find bread.

Have you seen the movie *Ordinary People*? It is the story of different people and their experiences surrounding the Mighty Men conferences. One of those stories, a true story, is about a hijacker who tried to hijack two men on their way to a Mighty Men conference. They overpowered the hijacker, put him in the back of their vehicle and took him to the conference. And what happened? That hijacker got saved and the last I heard, he was preaching the gospel in his hometown.

Go out today and introduce somebody to Jesus, the King of kings. Show another beggar where to find the true Bread of Life.

DO GOOD

Let us not grow weary while doing good,
for in due season we shall reap if we do not
lose heart. Therefore, as we have opportunity,
let us do good to all, especially to those
who are of the household of faith.

GALATIANS 6:9–10

I believe the Lord is telling us not to give up. Do not grow weary, you don't know how close you are to victory. With that rebellious child in the house, keep on persevering; keep on loving that child and they will come through.

In that relationship at work, you say, "Angus, I can't work with that guy anymore." Keep on and don't grow weary. Keep putting your best foot forward and God will do the rest.

Hebrews 13:6 says, "The Lord is my helper; I will not fear. What can man do to me?" Remember, it took the Israelites forty years in the wilderness. God was getting them ready for the Promised Land. It doesn't happen overnight.

Don't grow weary and miss the opportunity to do good. See this year as a new beginning, a new opportunity to do good to one another. Don't lose heart.

Remember, if Christ is for you, there is no man that can ever stand against you (see Romans 8:31).

DO WHAT HE SAYS

His mother said to the servants,
"Whatever He says to you, do it."
JOHN 2:5

There was a wedding feast at Cana and they had run out of wine. Mary said to the servants, "Just do what Jesus tells you to do." Now, remember, faith begets faith. In other words, the more faith you exercise, the more faith you receive.

Hebrews 11:1 says this about faith: "Now faith is the substance of things hoped for, the evidence of things not seen." But how do we get more faith? By spending time with the Lord in prayer and Bible study.

The more time you spend with Jesus, the more faith you will receive. You see faith is a verb, it is not a noun. It is an action word and involves doing something.

Faith requires action. Those servants were told to fill six stone water jars with water, which would have been about 75-100 L of water per jar.

Can you imagine what those servants must have thought? "Is He mad…We have run out of wine, not out of water!" But what happened? The water was turned into the finest wine that they had at the wedding feast. Just do what the Lord tells you to do and He will do the rest.

A GOOD CHAT

When the time came, Jesus and the
apostles sat down together at the table.
LUKE 22:14 NLT

You and I need to have a good talk with our loved ones. And where do we do that? The same place that Jesus did it—at the dinner table. In today's busy world, we have less and less time to speak to each other. But we really do need to chat to each other.

Dad, do you know why your little boy doesn't like school? "No, well, I didn't like school when I was young either." No, that is not the point. Maybe it is because he is getting bullied at school and he doesn't know what to do about it.

Mom, your teenage daughter is under severe peer pressure at the moment, do you know that? She needs help; she needs counsel.

Just like Jesus spoke to His disciples at the Passover meal and told them what was going to happen to Him—how He was going to be crucified but on the third day He was going to rise from the dead—we need to talk to our families. We cannot have any secrets; we need to work through challenges together.

Today, sit down and have a good honest chat with one another, and Jesus will do the rest.

YET WILL I TRUST HIM

Then the LORD said to Satan, "Have you
considered My servant Job, that there is none
like him on the earth, a blameless and upright
man, one who fears God and shuns evil?"

JOB 1:8

I think that Job is one of God's favorite men—an incredible man of integrity. Now this is the quality that the Lord Jesus is looking for in us as well—especially when we are under extreme pressure.

No matter what happens, even if your loved ones will not support you because of what you are going through, you have to be a man of integrity like Job.

In Job 2:9, his wife told him: "Do you still hold fast to your integrity? Curse God and die!" But Job just said, "Though He slay me, yet will I trust Him...He also shall be my salvation." (Job 13:15-16).

We need to do the right thing today. Pay your accounts, be no man's debtor. Honor your marriage vows. Respect your loved ones. Do your best work for your employer.

Stand tall for God and God will see you through. Do the right thing today and honor God then He will honor you.

PERSONAL BODYGUARD

The angel of the LORD encamps all around
those who fear Him, and delivers them.

PSALM 34:7

Do you believe in angels? We find them throughout the Bible so I definitely believe in angels. They fight for us against the forces of darkness. Do not ever feel, as a follower of Jesus Christ, that you are alone. You are never ever alone.

Many times we have attempted something that is humanly impossible. Like the time we catered for 5,000 hungry men at a Mighty Men conference, but then 7,500 men arrived for the weekend. The ladies were in a panic in the kitchen and came up to me and kindly said, "Angus, please tell the men just to go easy on the food."

And of course, I got up there and said to the starving men: "I have a message for you from the kitchen: Eat as much as you can!" You know, we picked up 36 baskets of leftovers after the men had eaten as much as they wanted. That can only be a miracle!

So remember, God has put an angel right next to you. You have a special angel looking after you all day. When you are afraid, know that the angel of the Lord will deliver you.

A FRESH START

Jesus answered and said to him,
"Most assuredly, I say to you, unless one is
born again, he cannot see the kingdom of God."

JOHN 3:3

In order to get anywhere in life we need to make a fresh start. There has to be a defining moment in our lives when we have to say, "Lord, I can't do it anymore. I am handing it over to You. I really want to start again." We are talking about a relationship with a living God—His name is Jesus Christ.

You know I asked my dear wife, Jill, once, "Remember the time that we surrendered our lives to Jesus Christ in that little church on Main Street in Greytown? What was the first thing that you encountered?" She said, "Hope."

Up until then, she had no hope for the future and that day when she gave her life to Christ, hope came into her heart. For me, it was a burden that fell off my shoulders. It was like I was carrying a 50 kg bag of cement and that morning I laid it at the foot of the cross.

What about you? Maybe this is the day that God is going to change your life forever. Pray and give your life to God anew. Make a fresh start and see your faith grow.

THE BATTLE OF SELF

*"After this Job opened his mouth
and cursed the day of his birth."*
JOB 3:1

Your biggest enemy is you. You might be thinking: "I can't take it anymore, Lord." And that is exactly what Job was thinking when he lost everything—his family, his farm and his house. He was sick and he was humiliated. He was sitting in ashes, full of painful boils from the top of his head to the very soles of his feet.

But you and I need to do what Job did. We need to stand up, dust ourselves off and get back into the fight. After everything that happened to Job, he stood up and said, "For I know that my Redeemer lives, and He shall stand at last on the earth" (Job 19:25).

We need to keep on keeping on but the good news is that we are not alone because Jesus is walking with us every step of the way. You say, "But we have messed up." Well, welcome to the club. If you look in the Bible, Moses was a murderer, David was an adulterer and Peter was a liar. But what did they all have in common? They repented. They said sorry, got up again and carried on—just like you and I are going to do today.

Now let's carry on with the race. Let's not look behind us; let's look ahead and I am telling you, Jesus will see us through.

FAITH IS BELIEVING

God did not send His Son into the world
to condemn the world, but that the world
through Him might be saved. "He who
believes in Him is not condemned."
JOHN 3:17-18

The most important thing in the Christian faith is to believe. It has nothing to do with our effort or our good works, but simply acknowledging Jesus Christ as the Son of God.

Some might say that they are not ready to give their lives fully to the Lord because they first have to get rid of that bad habit or that unforgiveness and hatred in their hearts. Only then will they come to Jesus. But Jesus says to you today, "Come as you are, just as you are, with all your warts and all your mistakes."

Matthew 11:28 reads: "Come to Me, all you who labor and are heavy laden, and I will give you rest." It is all about faith, which is the absolute opposite of fear, worry, anxiety and stress.

We need to give everything to God in faith. You see, it is Jesus who heals, delivers and sets us free. All we have to do is to let Him do it.

Simply believe today that Jesus Christ is the Son of God and you will be saved.

A HUMBLE HEART

"For I say, through the grace given to me, to everyone
who is among you, not to think of himself more
highly than he ought to think, but to think soberly,
as God has dealt to each one a measure of faith."

ROMANS 12:3

We need to be careful to not think too highly of ourselves. I always say, my biggest enemy is not the devil because his neck was broken on the Cross of Calvary; my biggest enemy is me, myself and I.

Now, John the Baptist, he was the opposite. In John 3:30, he says, "He must increase, but I must decrease." And that is why John the Baptist is such an amazing person. He is one of my heroes in the Bible—a humble man.

We are not here on earth to promote ourselves; we are here to promote Jesus. Solomon had everything that money could buy. He was handsome and the wisest man who ever lived. He had everything he wanted and yet, what did he say at the end of his life? He said, "I have seen all the works that are done under the sun; and indeed, all is vanity and grasping for the wind" (Ecclesiastes 1:14).

You and I today need to strive to serve the living God and not ourselves. Go out today and lift up the name of Jesus. Put others before yourself and give Him all the glory.

DRINK DEEPLY

"...whoever drinks of the water that I shall
give him will never thirst. But the water that
I shall give him will become in him a fountain
of water springing up into everlasting life."
JOHN 4:14

Have you ever been thirsty, I mean *really* thirsty? All you want is clear, pure, cool water to drink. Not tea, not coffee or soda—just water! But, of course, Jesus is not speaking here of physical water. He is speaking about spiritual water. Just like a human being cannot live without water, so too the person who does not drink from the fountain of life, Jesus Christ, will also die spiritually.

Many years ago, I attempted to run the mighty Comrades Marathon. I had prepared for it and ran my qualifier of 42 km, another slow 68 km race with my daughters and completed many 21 km runs. I thought I was ready. But I did not drink enough water. All I wanted to do was to finish that grueling 90 km race.

Just 14 km before the end the tarmac started moving in front of my eyes! I woke up in an ambulance with a drip in my arm. I was completely dehydrated. If we don't drink from God's Holy Word and pray every day, we will not make it. Let's drink deeply from the Water of Life; it's free and you will never thirst again.

THE PRAYER OF FAITH

The effective, fervent prayer of a righteous man
avails much. Elijah was a man with a nature like ours,
and he prayed earnestly that it would not rain;
and it did not rain on the land for three years and
six months. And he prayed again, and the heaven
gave rain, and the earth produced its fruit.

JAMES 5:16–18

We need more faith just to make it through one day at a time, don't we? Now, the Lord says that we need to pray the prayer of faith and He will supply our needs—not our wants, but our needs.

I want to ask you today, can God not answer your prayers like He answered Elijah's? Can He not supply your needs, too? You see the Bible tells us that Elijah was just a man like you and me. There was nothing supernatural about him, but he prayed the prayer of faith.

He prayed that it would not rain and it did not rain. Then when he prayed for rain three years later, it rained. You see, God does not answer just any prayer, He answers the prayer of faith.

So pray the prayer of faith today and ask God to increase your faith to believe Him for the miracle that you are waiting for. And then once you have asked Him, start thanking Him and let the Lord do the rest.

COUNT YOUR BLESSINGS

"Bring all the tithes into the storehouse, that there may be food in My house, and try Me now in this," says the LORD of hosts, "If I will not open for you the windows of heaven and pour out for you such blessing that there will not be room enough to receive it."

MALACHI 3:10

Wow, too many blessings to count! Even Job in his difficulty said, "I would seek God, and to God I would commit my cause—Who does great things, and unsearchable, marvelous things without number" (Job 5:8-9). We need to be thankful today. We need to be full of gratitude for the goodness of God towards us.

You know, it makes me sad when I see so many people in the world being so ungrateful. They are always complaining about not having enough or that nothing is going right. We need to understand that the blessings of God towards us are so abundant that they cannot even be numbered.

A good exercise is to sit down with that cup of coffee or tea and count your blessings. Name them one by one. We have got so much to be grateful for. Philippians 4:19 says, "And my God shall supply all your need according to His riches in glory by Christ Jesus."

Thank the Lord Jesus for His faithful provision and constant care.

FALSE ACCUSATION

You shall hide them in the secret place of
Your presence from the plots of man; You shall keep
them secretly in a pavilion from the strife of tongues.
PSALM 31:20

Has anyone accused you lately of something that you didn't do? Well, the man who wrote this psalm was David and he knew all about false accusations.

It can be very painful, especially when someone accuses you of something or says something about you that just isn't true. But the Lord Jesus Christ has promised us that He will hide us from all the attacks on our character. The real question today is: How does one handle untrue accusations or people who twist your words?

Well, we handle it the very same way that Jesus did. If we go to Matthew 27:13-14, it says, "Then Pilate said to Him, 'Do You not hear how many things they testify against You?' But He answered him not one word, so that the governor marveled greatly." Not one word…

We need to seriously pray for our accusers; often they are speaking out of a heart of fear, jealousy or envy. If we don't have anything good to say about someone then rather say nothing.

Remember, Jesus loves you, so try to love those who have a go at you because, at the end of the day, the truth always comes out.

THE THINGS WE DO NOT OWN

"I have been crucified with Christ; it is no longer
I who live, but Christ lives in me; and the life which
I now live in the flesh I live by faith in the Son
of God, who loved me and gave Himself for me."

GALATIANS 2:20

Today, I want to say that it is in dying to self that we live. I have always said: Our worst enemy is ourselves. You see, when you hand over everything you have to Jesus, everything you do not own, then freedom comes.

Hand it over to Him today and He will lighten your load. First Peter 5:7 (NLT) says, "Give all your worries and cares to God, for He cares about you."

When we realize that the responsibility is God's anyway, it gives us great joy, peace and confidence. It is His responsibility. You see your wife belongs to God—she is not yours. You didn't create her. That little baby that is a tremendous gift is not yours. God has given you that little child to take care of on His behalf.

Do you see the freedom there? That is why we hand over to God the things that we don't own and thank Him for it. We don't have to take care of them, He will! Pray about everything and then leave the rest to God.

OUR FOOD

Jesus said to them, "My food is to do the will
of Him who sent Me, and to finish His work."
JOHN 4:34

W e cannot live without food. Food is life, if you don't eat, you die. That's a fact. Many people walking around today are dead; their hearts might be pumping but there is no life in them. For a Christian, food is to do the will of Jesus Christ and to finish His work. That is the most important part.

The Lord is not interested in good starters, He wants good finishers. If you are a truck driver reading this, I want you to drive that truck for Jesus today. If you are a shop assistant, put a smile on your face today and let the people know who you belong to. That is your food. If you are a sports coach, you can do it; you can encourage people.

I want to tell you about June. June translates the Word of God. I met her in Mozambique many, many years ago when I was using the big yellow Seed Sower to preach the Gospel.

She was living by herself in a very small little home with very few amenities. She was translating the Bible so that the local people could read God's Word. Nobody knows about her but she is still doing it, even today. We need to do the will of Him who sent us and to finish His work.

NO GREATER LOVE

*"Greater love has no one than this,
than to lay down one's life for his friends."*
JOHN 15:13

No greater gift can you and I give to our friends than to die for them. That is what we call extreme kindness and love. Jesus did that for us.

Now, if you want to have a friend you must become a good friend. A good test of who your friends really are is if they stay around when things are tough. Jesus unfortunately also found that out in the Garden of Gethsemane when the high priest's soldiers came to arrest him. The Bible tells us that all the disciples forsook Him and fled. But you know, just before that, Jesus said, "…since I am the one you want, let these others go" (John 18:8 NLT). That is indeed an incredible friendship.

There is a man in the Bible that we don't hear much of, his name was Joseph of Arimathea. When Jesus died on the cross, Joseph went and asked for the body of Christ. He took the horrible nails out of Jesus' hands and feet, washed His body and wrapped it in brand-new, clean linen. He then placed Jesus' body in a tomb that he had dug out of solid rock. He did it because he loved Jesus.

I want to encourage you today to go out and be kind to people. Be a friend to those who do not have any friends because this is what the Lord Jesus Christ requires from you and me.

LIKE VAPOR

How do you know what your life will be
like tomorrow? Your life is like the morning
fog—it's here a little while, then it's gone.

JAMES 4:14 NLT

You know right next to our farm there is a big valley. Often early in the morning when I go for my bike ride, it is shrouded in mist and when I come back from my ride an hour later it is clear; the sun is shining and you can see the whole valley. That is how brief our lives are. Today, we need to get our priorities in order.

Remember, Jesus only did what His Father told Him to do. He did no more and no less. Let's not put off for tomorrow what we can do today. Jesus did it all in about 33 years on this earth. It's not about seeing how long we can live on this earth; it's about maximizing the time that we have here.

Jesus is coming for us at exactly the time that He has planned—not a day early, not a day late. So we must live like He's coming today but we must plan like He's coming in a hundred years.

So today, let's get our priorities in order. Tell your wife that you love her. Tell your children that you love them. Keep short accounts with God and people.

THE WORD MADE FLESH

Jesus said to him, "Go your way; your son
lives." So the man believed the word that
Jesus spoke to him, and he went his way.

JOHN 4:50

First John 5:7 says, "For there are three that bear witness in heaven: the Father, the Word, and the Holy Spirit; and these three are one." It is not the Father, the Son and the Holy Spirit; no, it's the Father, the *Word* and the Holy Spirit that bears witness. So who is the Word? The Word is Jesus.

You see, in John 4, a nobleman came to Jesus. He said, "My son is dying, please pray for him." Jesus prayed for the son, who wasn't even there, to be healed. The nobleman left because he believed the Word of God and his servants came running up the road saying, "Your son lives."

The nobleman said, "When did he get better?" They said, "Yesterday, at the seventh hour." That was the exact time that Jesus prayed and said to the nobleman, "Your son lives." Jesus is the Word!

You and I need to believe the Bible because it is Jesus Christ in print. Believe the Word!

PEOPLE

Jesus said to him, "Rise, take up your bed and walk."
And immediately the man was made well, took up
his bed, and walked. And that day was the Sabbath.
The Jews therefore said to him who was cured, "It is
the Sabbath; it is not lawful for you to carry your bed."

JOHN 5:8-10

The Jews were looking at an absolute miracle! This man had not walked for 38 years and now he was walking. Yet they were more concerned that he was carrying his bed on the Sabbath because they were not supposed to do any work on the Sabbath. That is so sad and I see the same thing happening today.

You know two young girls came to our church a few years back. They were very suggestively dressed. After the church meeting, a visiting church leader approached us and said, "This is the House of God. How can you allow this kind of dress code in your church?" They were visitors, two young girls seeking to find Jesus. They were coming to our church for the first time.

Be very careful to take the plank out of your own eye before you try and take the splinter out of your brother's eye (see Matthew 7:3). Today, let us spend time with people. People are a priority; people were a priority to Jesus, too.

Yes, we have to obey the law. That is what it is there for, but remember, it has been put there to benefit people, not to criticize or hurt them.

THE NAME OF JESUS

*"And when I am lifted up from the earth,
I will draw everyone to Myself."*
JOHN 12:32 NLT

What a name, the name of Jesus. There is power in this name; there is life in this name. There is healing in this name; there is peace in this name. There is salvation for the lost soul in this name and there is a future in this name.

It is not the name of an organization. Oh no! It is the name of my Friend and, I trust, your Friend, too. He is the Friend of sinners; He is the Comforter of those who are bereaved. He is the Teacher for those who are trying to find the way. He is the Son of God.

Polycarp was one of the early church fathers. He was an old man who was arrested by the Romans. They took him to the arena. They were going to burn him at the stake but just before they did, they said to him, "Just deny the name of Jesus and honor the gods of Rome and we will let you go home and die a peaceful death." But that old gentleman said, "Eighty and six years I have served Him, and He has done me no wrong." So they killed Him.

It is that name, Jesus, that Polycarp was willing to die for. What does that name mean to you and me today?

THE ALMIGHTY

He said to them, "But who do you say that I am?"
Peter answered and said to Him, "You are the Christ."

MARK 8:29

We need to ask ourselves a question: Who do we say the Carpenter from Nazareth is? Isaiah 45:5 says, "I am the LORD, and there is no other; there is no God besides Me." Yes, He is indeed Immanuel, God with us.

I want to say to you that our heavenly Father is not to be trifled with. He is not the man upstairs; He is not just another one of my mates—He is Almighty God.

When Moses went up Mount Sinai to receive the Ten Commandments from the Lord, no human being or even animal could touch the base of that mountain for fear of death (see Exodus 19).

This Mighty Creator of the universe created everything that we see with one word. In the beginning was the Word. He came down from heaven to earth in the form of a little defenseless baby. Why? Because He wanted to have fellowship with you and me. In fact, He cares so much about you that He even knows how many hairs are on your head. Isn't that amazing?

Bring all your fears to Him today and all your inadequacies. Why? Because He is bigger and stronger than your greatest fears!

HE UNDERSTANDS

"Look!" he answered, "I see four men loose,
walking in the midst of the fire; and they are not hurt,
and the form of the fourth is like the Son of God."

DANIEL 3:25

Jesus understands what you're going through because He has been there before. He didn't take Meshach, Shadrach and Abed-Nego out of the fiery furnace. No, He was in the furnace and went through the fire with them. He has never promised us that He will take us out of the fire. What He has promised us is that He will never leave us and He will never forsake us (see Hebrews 13:5).

Maybe today you are feeling forsaken. Well, Jesus understands; He has been there. In the Garden of Gethsemane, all the disciples ran away and left Him. Maybe you are feeling betrayed by a loved one. Well, Jesus' right-hand man, Peter, betrayed Him three times and said, "I never knew Him."

I want to say something very important: Never say to a person that you understand what they are going through when they are hurting badly if you have never been there yourself. You can't do it. You have to have been through it.

You know what you can do? You can get into the fire! You can put your arm around that person who is mourning or hurt and you can weep with them. Just love that person like Jesus did for you and me.

THE WAY HE MADE YOU

Know that the LORD, He is God; it is He who
has made us, and not we ourselves; we are
His people and the sheep of His pasture.

PSALM 100:3

Remember, God does not make mistakes! He has created us in His very own image. God does not make junk; you cannot be dissatisfied with yourself. You are one of a kind. Do you know that there is no one in the whole world who has the same fingerprints as you?

God knows our finest details. He knows our strengths and our weaknesses. So why do we continually go to every Tom, Dick and Harry when we have a problem? Why not go to the Manufacturer for help?

Proverbs 8:17 says, "I love those who love Me, and those who seek Me diligently will find Me." Let's go to the Creator of our very selves today and ask Him to sort out the problem that we are facing—whether it be physical, spiritual or mental.

Why is it that we are always so dissatisfied? Ladies with curly hair always want straight hair and ladies with straight hair always want curly hair. People with blue eyes want brown eyes and those with brown eyes want green ones. Short men want to be tall and tall men want to be shorter. We need to be satisfied with the way God has made us.

THE EARLY BIRD

"Behold, I am coming as a thief. Blessed is
he who watches, and keeps his garments,
lest he walk naked and they see his shame."
REVELATION 16:15

The early bird catches the worm…You know, my wife always says to me, "It is just as easy to be early as it is to be late." It's an absolute fact. It is a good habit to be early. You see, if you are late starting off, you just don't seem able to catch up, do you? You are just late all day long.

Jesus was never late for an appointment; He was also never early for an appointment. He was always spot on time! Often the disciples were looking for Jesus early in the morning because the crowds had already gathered. And where was He? He was up the mountain having fellowship with His Father.

What about your quiet time? When do you get up for your quiet time? You say, "Oh well, I don't have time at the moment." You can't afford not to have time.

When I was a young man in Scotland, I used to walk down the little village roads and a farmer would hang over the fence. He would always have time to speak. Do you know why? Because he was an early riser. He had done most of his work early in the morning. Always have time to speak to Jesus. He is never too busy to speak with you.

WISDOM AND UNDERSTANDING

"And to man He said, 'Behold,
the fear of the Lord, that is wisdom,
and to depart from evil is understanding.'"
JOB 28:28

We must not waste valuable opportunities, especially spending time with people who have lots of wisdom that they want to give us for free. There is an African proverb that says, "When an old man dies, a library burns to the ground." We must never waste the opportunity to learn from people who have walked the road. But then again, it is not so much about age, is it? No, it is more about a person who knows God.

We must spend time learning. We shouldn't keep going around that mountain when we don't have to; we don't have that kind of time left. There are a lot of people, full of wisdom, that would love to share it with us, but we just don't seem to have time to talk to them.

I remember an old man, a farmer, who used to drive up and down the country roads in his pickup truck. He was a most delightful old gentleman and an absolute encyclopedia on beef cattle. He was a former Farmer of the Year in Kenya and yet he looked so lonely to me. He never seemed to have anything to do. Where were the young farmers? Why weren't they asking him questions?

Never stop learning. Learn from God's Word and other Christians. Grow strong in wisdom and in faith.

BREAD OF LIFE

"I am the bread of life."

JOHN 6:48

You know, if you don't eat, you die. Now if a man does not eat good, wholesome food, he cannot do the work. When I was young, my dad would always say to us, "What you save on the grocery bills, you pay out on the doctor's bills." So true.

In South Africa, we enjoy our biltong and will take some with us as a snack to a rugby or cricket game or to work. We need protein if we are going to work. It is the bottom line; if you don't eat, you cannot operate.

In the same way, if we don't eat the Bread of Life, we will die. I am talking about the Bible. I am talking about spending time in the presence of Almighty God, every single morning.

We need to pray, read our Bible and meditate on it each morning before we go to work. And then when we are at work, yes, during our lunch hour, we need to spend time just reading the Word of God. Then, of course, before we go to sleep at night, preferably with the whole family, we spend time reading God's Holy Word again.

When you do that, it will protect you. It will energize you and strengthen you. Jesus is the Bread of Life and if you feed on His Word, you will never hunger and you will never thirst.

IN REMEMBRANCE

...When He had given thanks, He broke it and said,
"Take, eat; this is My body which is broken for
you; do this in remembrance of Me." In the same
manner He also took the cup after supper, saying,
"This cup is the new covenant in My blood. This do,
as often as you drink it, in remembrance of Me."

1 CORINTHIANS 11:24-25

This is a very solemn reminder of what Jesus Christ has done for you and me. Remember now, with this wonderful act of God there is no one who is exempt. All who love the Lord Jesus Christ can come to the table—that is the only qualification you need to come to Jesus.

Jesus had communion with His disciples at the last supper. I have been to the Upper Room in Jerusalem where the Bible says the last supper took place. I had a wonderful experience there with God. Fortunately, there is no specified place, no specified time, that we are told to have communion today. You can partake in the Holy Communion in a hospital, a jail, at university or at work, down a mine or on a farm.

When you partake in Holy Communion there is healing that takes place. There is healing, freedom, the forgiveness of sins, liberty and, most of all, there is salvation because when we remember what Jesus Christ did for us the devil has got no more hold over us.

A MEASURE OF DAYS

*"Since his days are determined, the number
of his months is with You; You have appointed
his limits, so that he cannot pass."*
JOB 14:5

Our days on this earth have been appointed to us even before we were born. You cannot lengthen and you cannot shorten your life. It is in God's hands alone. Now, there are exceptions: King Hezekiah prayed to God on his deathbed (see 2 Kings 20). He was weeping bitterly and he asked God to increase his life by 15 years, and God answered his prayer.

The sad thing is some people are obsessed with trying to prolong their lives and in so doing live miserable, sad lives. It is not the length of time that we have on this earth that counts; it is what we do with the time that God has given us that counts. You know, Paul said, "For to me, to live is Christ, and to die is gain" (Philippians 1:21). In other words, you can't frighten a Christian with heaven. If we live, we live for Jesus; if we die, we are going home.

Robert Murray M'Cheyne started a massive revival in Scotland. He died at the age of 30. Jim Elliot took the Gospel to the Amazon jungle. He died at the age of 28. Remember, he said, "He is no fool who gives what he cannot keep to gain what he cannot lose." That's right! Enjoy the day that the Lord has given you and do what you can to help your fellow man.

A RUSHING WIND

And there was much complaining among the people
concerning Him. Some said, "He is good"; others said,
"No, on the contrary, He deceives the people."

JOHN 7:12

We need to make a decision: Do we believe that Jesus Christ is indeed the Son of God? I am sitting in my prayer room thinking about what happened to me in 2012 when I was invited to be the speaker at the Feast of Tabernacles at Ein Gedi near the Dead Sea in Israel. It was a very warm evening. Now, remember, it is the lowest point on earth, it doesn't rain there and the wind never blows there.

I went up onto the platform and started reading from Acts 2:2-3, which says, "And suddenly there came a sound from heaven, as of a rushing mighty wind, and it filled the whole house where they were sitting. Then there appeared to them divided tongues, as of fire, and one sat upon each of them."

When I had finished reading I felt so excited. I was in Jesus country…and then it happened—a rushing mighty wind came as I had never seen before. It was incredible!

Now, I want to ask you a question today: Was that a coincidence or was that a God-incidence? We need to understand one thing: Jesus Christ is coming back very soon and we need to believe and we need to be ready.

PREACH THE GOSPEL

"For the Holy Spirit will teach you in
that very hour what you ought to say."
LUKE 12:12

When we spend time in the presence of God, the Holy Spirit becomes our teacher and the Bible becomes our compass. You see, spending time studying without the Holy Spirit makes us mere history students. If you haven't met the Man from Galilee, that's all you become. Memorizing Scripture without knowing the Author of the Book has no reward. In fact, you can even teach a parrot to do that.

Do you know that not one of the disciples was a Bible teacher, a priest or even a scribe? Peter, James and John were fishermen. Matthew was a tax collector. Paul, who wrote two-thirds of the New Testament, was a tentmaker. And Jesus Himself was a carpenter. I am not saying that it is a waste to study. I would have loved to go to a Bible college. I wanted to be a preacher, but thought I had to go to university for seven years. And I gave up. I should have pressed on with the vision and the passion that I had to tell people about Jesus.

Today, you might feel that you want to tell people about Jesus but you think you have lost the opportunity. Never, never—there is no time like the present. Go out today and just tell people about Jesus. You might be a farmer or a shopkeeper…just tell people what Jesus means to you, that is what God wants us to do.

HE WANTS US

"Many will say to Me in that day, 'Lord, Lord, have we not prophesied in Your name, cast out demons in Your name, and done many wonders in Your name?' And then I will declare to them, 'I never knew you; depart from Me, you who practice lawlessness!'"

MATTHEW 7:22-23

The Lord is not interested in our good efforts. No, He wants us. Just like your wife wants you, not all the gifts that you can bring her. Just like your daughter wants you, not what you can give her. God wants us not because of what we can do for Him. He created you and me to have fellowship with Him.

John Wesley sailed all the way to America where he preached his heart out to the people but said, "I went to America to convert the Indians; but, oh, who shall convert me?"

On his way back, the ship encountered a huge storm and was about to sink. As he looked up, he saw a group of German Moravian Christians, who were singing hymns and worshipping God. He came to know and to have fellowship with Jesus Christ, and then God used him to start one of the biggest revivals the world has ever seen.

Today spend time with your loved ones, spend time with God. Do not focus on what you can do for Him; just spend time with Him.

JOB'S COMFORTER

*"I have heard all this before.
What miserable comforters you are!"*
JOB 16:2 NLT

The phrase *Job's Comforter* refers to someone who makes a person feel worse about what they're going through when trying to comfort them. You see, Job's friends were supposed to comfort him but they didn't really, did they?

Now, I want to say to you today, we need to encourage one another. When your wife cooks you that beautiful meal, don't get up from the table to say: "That was very nice. It's a pity that you burned the potatoes." Or when your husband brings you a lovely bunch of flowers, don't say, "Darling, thank you, but they are not really my favorite flowers." What does that help? We need to build each other up. There is enough pain in this world, we don't need to add to it.

The Lord has called us to be encouragers. Build people up. Phone somebody today and say, "Listen, I just want to tell you, I really appreciate your friendship." When you see a lady walking by you say, "I really love that dress you are wearing." And that will make that lady's day. Help that elderly person across the road.

Sit down and spend time with somebody today. Be an encourager; don't be a Job's Comforter.

THE GREATEST ORATOR

The officers answered,
"No man ever spoke like this Man!"
JOHN 7:46

The greatest orator who ever lived was Jesus! An orator is someone good at public speaking. Now, remember the soldiers were told by the High Priest to arrest Jesus and they didn't. When the High Priest asked, "Why didn't you arrest Him?" They said, "No man ever spoke like this Man."

I want to talk to you about extempore preaching. Do you know what that means? Extempore preaching is what the great preachers of the old times used to do. They would take a verse and preach, open-air, no notes, for hours non-stop. You see, if it is not inside you then it is not coming out of you. These men spent time with God.

You know, as a young man I was so desperate to preach after I gave my life to the Lord. I would go into the middle of my maize fields and when nobody was looking, I would jump on the back of the pickup truck and preach my heart out to the maize plants. And then at the end of the message, I would say, "Let's bow our heads in prayer," and the Lord Jesus would send a gentle breeze and all the maize plants would bow their heads!

Go and read the Sermon on the Mount (see Matthew 5). It is a magnificent message. And then go out and tell people about the greatest Man who ever lived. No man ever spoke like this Man!

AMAZING GRACE

"For the Son of Man did not come
to destroy men's lives but to save them."
LUKE 9:56

You know that there is nothing you and I can do to make Jesus love us more and there is nothing we can do to make Him love us any less. The Lord has not come down to earth from heaven to condemn us but to forgive us and to give us a brand-new life.

One of my favorite Scriptures is found in Romans 8:1, which says, "There is therefore now no condemnation to those who are in Christ Jesus, who do not walk according to the flesh, but according to the Spirit."

You know what I love? Jesus has got a bad memory when it comes to our mistakes...Oh yes, because when He forgives us, He forgets. In 1 John 1:9, the Lord says, "If we confess our sins, He is faithful and just to forgive us our sins and to cleanse us from all unrighteousness."

Just say sorry today to the Lord and then move on with your life. Leave it at the foot of the cross. Remember, Jesus died for sinners! He didn't die for good people, He died for sinners like you and me.

Go out today, knowing that your sins are forgiven. Jesus says, "Go and sin no more" (John 8:11).

FROM THE ROOFTOPS

"What I tell you now in the darkness, shout abroad
when daybreak comes. What I whisper in your
ear, shout from the housetops for all to hear!"

MATTHEW 10:27 NLT

This is not a time for you and me to be quiet. We need to be more vocal now about our faith than ever before. Jesus has told us that we need to shout it out from the rooftops. Like never before in the history of the world, people need the Lord.

Jesus is never caught by surprise. He knew everything that was going to happen 2,000 years ago and He knows what is still to come.

We need to speak it out in the workplace, in schools, hospitals and on the farm. People are asking questions. It is time to tell them about a friend who will never leave them nor forsake them.

This is a time to tell people about Jesus. On July 30, 1956, Dwight Eisenhower, then President of the United States of America, signed a law that said "In God We Trust." This was to be America's official motto. Later, on his deathbed, he invited his friend Billy Graham to talk to him about the assurance of salvation.

This is the time to tell people about the Savior of the world.

SETTLE YOUR DIFFERENCES

*"...do not let the sun go down on
your wrath, nor give place to the devil."*
EPHESIANS 4:26-27

Don't let the sun go down on that argument, settle it before
you go to sleep. We need to settle our differences. Don't keep
grudges because they just fester and grow into something ugly.
Don't hold on to unforgiveness—learn to say sorry. I can hear
someone saying, "But it is not even my fault." It doesn't matter,
just say sorry. It is the quickest way to diffuse an argument. We
don't have time to hang on to bitterness and our own personal
opinion. Let us be peacemakers.

You know, I once heard a very sad story about a couple who
really loved each other but the man had a drinking problem.
One night, his wife was lying in bed unable to sleep because
she was worried about her husband who had not come home.
In the early hours of the morning, he staggered into the bedroom and passed out. She was so angry that she said, "I wish
you would die!" The next morning, she woke up and wanted
to say sorry, but her husband had died in his sleep. She was
devastated. It took a long time for her to accept the fact that
the Lord forgives if we apologize.

Don't let that happen to you. Don't let the sun go down on
your unforgiveness. Settle your differences today.

TRUSTING OUR REDEEMER

"For I know that my Redeemer lives,
and He shall stand at last on the earth."
JOB 19:25

There is a big difference between hoping and knowing. Despite what Job suffered (and did he ever suffer) he could still say, "I know that my Redeemer lives." Our faith can never be based on feelings. There is no place in God's kingdom for fair-weather Christians.

What does that mean? Well, when the sun is shining, we love the Lord but when the dark, black clouds come over, we turn our backs on Him. In these last days, Jesus is looking for unconditional loyalty and faith in Him. You see, Job said, "Though He slay me, yet will I trust Him" (Job 13:15). Wow, that is commitment and we need to exercise that commitment in our lives today.

You know that even before Jesus came down from heaven to earth the first time, Job was already talking about the second coming, because he said, "He shall stand at last on the earth." What a wonderful thing to realize.

Now, how do you find that kind of trust? Well, it is by knowing someone; it is by spending time with that person. Do you and I know God? Spend time with Jesus today so that you can get to know Him better.

A FAIR JUDGE

...For He is coming to judge the earth. He will judge
the world with justice, and the nations with fairness.

PSALM 98:9 NLT

If we look around, we see gross injustices in the world. You turn on that television and you see violence. You might say, "It is not fair. How can they get away with it?"

Well, Judgment Day is coming and remember, judgment belongs to the Lord. He says in His Word: "Vengeance is Mine, I will repay" (Romans 12:19).

Every single one of us is going to give an account of our life here on earth (see Romans 14:12). Each of us will be judged according to what we have done on this earth. We really need to get our lives in order, and we need to leave revenge and judgment in the hands of a fair and impartial God.

This is not a time to take judgment into our own hands. This is not a time to start making out that you know who is guilty and who is not. We need to pray for our enemies. You say, "Come on, Angus, that is going a bit too far." No, that is what Jesus did on the cross. In Luke 23:34, He said, "Father, forgive them, for they do not know what they do."

Today, let the Lord be the judge and live your life according to His principles.

ABUNDANT LIFE

"Therefore if the Son makes you free,
you shall be free indeed."
JOHN 8:36

We need to turn our eyes upon Jesus. Focus on Him and the things of the world will grow strangely dim. The things of this world do not last. They lose their luster and their glamor but when we meet the Master, that is when life really begins. There is nothing else in this world that makes you more excited about the future than when you become a Christian.

Think of the CEO who has been working all his life, running a large organization and saving up his money. His dream is to have his own beach cottage and to go out fishing every day. Eventually, he retires, gets his beach cottage, and goes out every morning to fish, but soon he gets bored. He starts driving his poor wife around the bend.

When we meet Jesus, however, He sets us free. We still enjoy fishing, but it is no longer the main reason we get up in the morning.

You see, Jesus sets us free from ourselves. When we take our focus off ourselves and put it on Jesus the sun suddenly shines brighter when we wake up in the morning. After Jesus sets you free, you can start living a life that is full of purpose and joy.

THE GREAT I AM

And God said to Moses, "I AM WHO I AM."
And He said, "Thus you shall say to the
children of Israel, 'I AM has sent me to you.'"
EXODUS 3:14

Why did they kill Jesus? Jesus was not a murderer; He was not an adulterer or a thief. He never did anything wrong. So, why did they kill Him? Because He said, "I AM." He said, "If you have seen Me, you have seen the Father because the two of us are one Person" (see John 14:9).

Who do you say Jesus is? Many years ago, I had the privilege of going to Great Britain to the Welsh Agricultural Show. I asked if I could film in the shed where they were preparing the bulls for the finals.

The stockmen were brushing the bulls furiously. I began preaching my heart out to the camera that was filming and I could see that the men were listening. When I finished speaking one old stockman said, "How can you say that Jesus is the only God?" I said, "Because He is." We spoke for a bit and finally I asked him, "Who do you say He is?" He said, "It is a mystery to me!"

I want to say to you today, it is not a mystery, it is a fact. John 1:1 says, "In the beginning was the Word, and the Word was with God, and the Word was God." So, who do you say He is today?

FEAR OF GOD

"Can anyone teach God knowledge,
since He judges those on high?"
JOB 21:22

It is ludicrous to question God and yet we always do it, don't we? We are always questioning God and we always have a better solution. It has got to be the absolute height of arrogance to question our Creator when we are merely a creation.

I have a very beautiful little granddaughter who has her grandfather wrapped around her little finger. She comes down to my house and she has a tea party with all her dolls. Now, can you imagine that little girl arguing with Albert Einstein about physics? No, that would be ridiculous! Now wanting to argue with God who is in heaven is even more ridiculous.

In Job 38 we see that God gets tired of Job asking so many questions. God says, "Where were you when I laid the foundations of the earth? Who shut the sea with doors when it wanted to burst out of its seams? Can you make the sun come up? Have you entered the springs of the depths of the sea where the water comes from? Can you determine life or death?" Of course not.

I want to leave you with one very important Scripture passage: "The fear of the LORD is the beginning of wisdom, and the knowledge of the Holy One is understanding" (Proverbs 9:10). Fear God and you will grow in wisdom and understanding of His ways.

PRINCE OF PEACE

"Peace I leave with you, My peace I give to you;
not as the world gives do I give to you. Let not
your heart be troubled, neither let it be afraid."

JOHN 14:27

Peace only comes to us when we acquaint ourselves with the Prince of Peace, Jesus Christ Himself. They tell me that in the center, in the heart of a vicious tornado or hurricane that is tearing houses and buildings up from their very foundations, there is absolute peace and calm. You see, peace comes from within and not from the outside.

When I was a young man and I had to leave Zambia and sell my farm, my dream was to own a farm one day in South Africa. I thought that if I owned that farm, it would bring me peace. You know, I almost worked myself to death trying to get that farm.

Eventually, I did manage to secure the farm at a tremendous cost. But there was absolutely no peace in my heart; in fact, the opposite was the case, I had come to the end of myself. I then reached out to Jesus and found real peace for the first time in my life.

Maybe you are troubled in your spirit. Maybe you are fearful. Pray that the Lord will fill your life with His peace. Turn to Him and ask Him to come into your life and give you His peace.

A PENCIL PARABLE

Then they said to him again, "What did He
do to you? How did He open your eyes?"
He answered them, "I told you already, and you
did not listen. Why do you want to hear it again?
Do you also want to become His disciples?"
JOHN 9:26-27

You know, there are none so blind as those who refuse to see. We believe whatever we read in the media…in the newspapers, on our devices, on television. We don't question it, but we always seem to doubt a genuine miracle that is performed by God. Even when the person in question confesses that he has received healing, like this young man who was blind from birth, we don't believe.

You and I need to stop questioning God and we need to start simply believing what He has said and what He has done. That is the only way that we can be used by God.

Everyone is like a pencil, created by the Lord Himself for a specific purpose. A special meaningful purpose in our hearts and a daily relationship with Him.

Go out today and believe God, then He will use you to do mighty things for Him.

THE SHEPHERD'S VOICE

"...the sheep hear His voice; and He calls His own sheep by name and leads them out. And when He brings out His own sheep, He goes before them; and the sheep follow Him, for they know His voice."

JOHN 10:3-4

Jesus leads us from the front, He does not chase us from behind. In the Middle East the shepherds lead their sheep and their sheep follow them because they hear and know the shepherd's voice. "How does this happen?" you might ask. Well, because the sheep spend time with the shepherd all day long, not just for five minutes in the morning.

I have a very dear friend, a very successful forester who, when he was running his huge operation, employed hundreds of employees. Even so, he would greet every person by name every day...No wonder they worked so well for him.

In these turbulent times, people just don't know what to believe. They don't know where to go and they don't even know what to do. We need to follow the Good Shepherd. Many of us today are just like Thomas, one of the Lord's disciples. In John 14:5, he asked, "How can we know the way?" In verse 6, Jesus answered, "I am the way."

Involve the Good Shepherd in every single decision you make. Listen to the Good Shepherd and let Him lead you and you won't go wrong.

GOD'S PURPOSE FOR YOU

"The thief does not come except to steal, and to kill,
and to destroy. I have come that they may have life,
and that they may have it more abundantly."

JOHN 10:10

Is that glass half full or is it half empty? Well, that is your decision...the devil says it is half empty. Jesus says it is half full. What do you believe today?

A long time ago, I returned from a preaching tour in Scotland. I had been there for three months. I was tired and I felt the Holy Spirit tell me to take a pencil and an A4 pad of paper and to write my story.

Well, straight away the devil came in and tried to steal my dream. He said, "You don't have a formal education, you have no learning. You don't know how to write a book. No one taught you anything." The Lord said, "Write the story!"

Well, I very nearly listened to the devil and if I had, I would not have started writing books. Do not allow the devil to steal your dream!

Live your dream today and remember, we have a glorious future to look forward to. We are going to spend eternity in the presence of God.

LIFE-GIVING WORDS

By the word of the LORD the heavens were made,
and all the host of them by the breath of His mouth.

PSALM 33:6

The power of the spoken word! We must make sure that our words are sweet because we might have to eat them, as they say! But seriously, a word can be used for good and it can be used for evil. I have seen too many broken families and strong friendships destroyed by a word spoken in the heat of the moment. Sometimes we need to let our words be few but, of course, sometimes words can also heal, forgive, build up and strengthen.

Many years ago, Jill and I knew an elderly couple who had such a beautiful marriage. They had been married for well over 50 years. We said to them one day, "What is the secret to your beautiful, successful marriage?"

They said, "Every Sunday afternoon, after we have had our lunch, we lie on the bed together and we have a good talk about everything…about offenses committed during the week, about not doing things we promised we were going to do. We clear the air, and the most important thing is we encourage each other and we love one another."

That is what we need to do today. We need to speak life and not death.

THE CHIEF PURPOSE OF MAN

"For what profit is it to a man if he gains the
whole world, and loses his own soul? Or what
will a man give in exchange for his soul?"
MATTHEW 16:26

I heard a story of an old businessman who was extremely successful and very wealthy. Somebody came to visit him and sat in his beautiful office and said: "You have done so well." The old businessman's eyes filled with tears as he said, "Yes, I have used all my strength to build up this gigantic business and now I am using my money to try and buy back my health, but it is not working."

I want to say to you today that we need to keep our priorities in order. As Mark 8:36 says, "What will it profit a man if he gains the whole world, and loses his own soul?" You know, according to the Westminster Shorter Catechism, the purpose of man is very simple: It is to glorify God and to enjoy Him forever.

Are you doing that? Because the wisest man who ever lived, Solomon, said very clearly in Ecclesiastes 12:13, "Let us hear the conclusion of the whole matter: Fear God and keep His commandments, for this is man's all."

DON'T RUSH

Trust in the LORD with all your heart, and lean
not on your own understanding; in all your ways
acknowledge Him, and He shall direct your paths.

PROVERBS 3:5-6

We need to be wise these days. It is not a case of "I did it my way…" We have to do it God's way. We have to make quality decisions and we have to do it the way the Lord would have us do it—not impulsively. We must not be quick to act or in a hurry. We have to take our time.

Remember when the Pharisees brought the woman who was caught in adultery to Jesus (see John 8)? He didn't give a decision straight away, did He? No, He bent down and started writing in the sand with His finger. Now a lot of theologians have a lot of theories about why He did that, but I believe He was waiting for instructions from His heavenly Father. Then He stood up and said, "He who is without sin cast the first stone." And what did they do? They put their stones down and they walked away. Jesus said, "Woman, where are your accusers?" She said, "They have left." And He said, "Go and sin no more. Your sins are forgiven."

We must not rush. Remember, anything done in haste is not from God. We really need to remember what the Lord says, "He shall direct your paths." So today, remember that Jesus will direct you.

STUCK IN A RUT

He said to them, "Our friend Lazarus sleeps,
but I go that I may wake him up."
JOHN 11:11

You know, I was in a rut...in a shallow grave. That's right, I was dead and I didn't even know it. Then on a beautiful Sunday morning in a little church, Jesus came and found me. And He woke me up from the dead. He brought me back from the grave.

How are you feeling right now? Just like the Lord said to Lazarus in John 11:43, "Lazarus, come forth!" He wants to say to you and me to come to Him.

I will never forget that morning. I didn't really want to go to church. Reluctantly I went and I want to tell you that morning was resurrection day for me!

My dear friend, He wants to do it for you today. Don't think it is too late. They said that Jesus was too late to save Lazarus when He came to Bethany. But you know, Jesus is never late for an appointment. He is never late, and He is never early—He is just spot on time.

Maybe you are in a rut today and you are saying, "I don't know what to do." Why don't you call upon Him? I promise you won't regret it.

WE NEED COMPASSION

Jesus wept. Then the Jews said,
"See how He loved him!"
JOHN 11:35-36

Great compassion is what the world desperately needs today. Jesus knew that Lazarus was about to come out of the tomb and yet He still felt heartsore for the people mourning.

You know that wonderful man of God William Booth was once sent a telegram from some of his Salvation Army soldiers. They said, "We have tried everything. We are trying to preach the Gospel and the people are not interested." He responded a few days later with just two words: "Try tears." We need to get closer to the people. We need to be more compassionate.

You know, as the story goes, the Queen of France, Marie Antoinette, was totally out of touch with her people, so when she was told that they had no bread to eat, she supposedly said, "Let them eat cake." We need to get to where the people are. We need to have a heart of compassion, a heart that can identify with people who are suffering.

When you go out today, look for people who are hurting and love them like Jesus loves you. Don't preach to them, just put your arm around them and weep with them—that is where healing happens.

SOWING SEED

"Most assuredly, I say to you, unless a grain of wheat falls into the ground and dies, it remains alone; but if it dies, it produces much grain."

JOHN 12:24

It's an amazing paradox, isn't it? In other words, it is in dying that we truly live. Now, farmers understand that principle. You can take precious seed and it can be preserved for hundreds of years if it is kept in a safe climate and a controlled storeroom. But the tragedy about that seed is that it never does anything, it just stays as it is. It does not produce food.

This life is not about seeing how long we can live. No, it's about dying to self. When we start to live for others then we start to produce everlasting life, peace and joy. If we look at Matthew 16:24-25, Jesus says to His disciples: "If anyone desires to come after Me, let him deny himself, and take up his cross, and follow Me. For whoever desires to save his life will lose it, but whoever loses his life for My sake will find it."

It's in dying that you and I live. The greatest time in a Christian's life is when we see the seed we planted in someone's life germinating and then, when we get to heaven one day, hearing from the Lord Jesus, "Well done, good and faithful servant. Come and enter into your rest." Go out today and sow your seed because you can't take it with you to heaven.

REVIVE YOUR SOUL

I don't mean to say that I have already achieved
these things or that I have already reached
perfection. But I press on to possess that perfection
for which Christ Jesus first possessed me.

PHILIPPIANS 3:12 NLT

We have to keep growing in the Lord. You see, we already have His Holy Spirit within us when we are born again. We have His church around us and the Holy Bible with us. We have everything we need but we need to keep growing. The Bible is God's written word, it is our ultimate and absolute teacher. The Bible is our adviser, our peacemaker in the home and our marriages. What does the Bible say…and that is the answer!

The Bible is also our conscience. It tells us when we are doing something wrong or when we are doing something right. The Bible corrects us when we are on the wrong road or when we are making a poor decision. It prepares us for the work ahead and equips us with the right tools. God's Holy Word is alive; it is not dead.

You see Christian growth is what God wants from us. He wants us to grow and that requires reading the Bible and meditating on the Word of God. It requires studying and memorizing the Bible. Don't waste your time anymore, read the Word—it will revive your soul!

SETTLE YOUR DEBTS

"...And forgive us our debts, as we forgive our debtors."
MATTHEW 6:12

You know, we have to pay our debts. Maybe you owe a lot of money. Well, you need to stop buying things you cannot afford. Don't ignore the people you owe money to. You need to sit down with them and explain that you have fallen on hard times, but you will pay them as soon as you can. Even if you have to pay them a mere pittance every month, start paying them. We need to take responsibility for our debts.

The system of this world is, "Buy today and pay tomorrow," and once they have got you then you are in trouble. But this is not God's principle. The Lord says we must be no man's debtor. As soon as you owe something to someone, in a way you become enslaved to them until you have paid back every single cent.

I remember my old dad with great fondness. When he was in hospital, every time I visited him he would ask, "How is the money?" because he gave me power of attorney. I always said, "Dad, there is plenty there. Don't worry, you don't owe anybody anything." And I could see peace come upon him.

Be an honorable person, let the only person you owe a debt to be the Lord Jesus Christ. So do what you can to settle your debts and be free!

KNOWING JESUS

Then he said to Jesus, "Lord, remember me
when You come into Your kingdom." And
Jesus said to him, "Assuredly, I say to you,
today you will be with Me in Paradise."

LUKE 23:42–43

According to the law, that criminal on the cross deserved to die. Yet because he acknowledged and confessed that Jesus Christ is Lord, he was given eternal life. Good people don't go to heaven, believers go to heaven. Now, some people don't like that but I really believe it with all of my heart.

When we come forward to give an account on the day of judgment, Father God will not be concerned about the good works we did on earth. I believe that Father God will turn to His Beloved Son, Jesus, and ask Him one question: "Do You know this person?" If Jesus says, "Yes, Father, I know him," then Father God will answer, "Let him in!" But if Jesus says, "I don't know this man," irrespective of what he has done the Father will say, "Take him away!"

We need to spend time with Jesus. We need to confess Him as Lord and Savior. We need to confess with our mouths and believe in our hearts, that He has been raised from the dead and we shall be saved.

CHILDREN OF LIGHT

Jesus replied, "My light will shine for you just a
little longer. Walk in the light while you can, so the
darkness will not overtake you. Those who walk in
the darkness cannot see where they are going."
JOHN 12:35 NLT

I think you will agree with me that we are living in a very dark
world. But the good news is that Jesus is the Light of the
world! Now, remember, light always overcomes darkness. Walk
into a dark room, strike a match and what happens? The darkness has to leave, because it cannot be where there is light. We,
as children of Jesus Christ, as sons and daughters of light, need
to shine like never before.

We have a thirty-foot cross on the farm and it has a timer
switch attached to it. When it gets dark on the farm, the light
comes on and the whole cross lights up. It is magnificent! There
is an airstrip on the farm next to us and a lot of planes land
there. Often the pilots say, if it is a misty night, they look for
that bright shining cross on the hill, next to the little chapel
that my dad and I built, and then they see their way home.

I want to say to you today that this is the time to shine in
a dark world. People will come to you and you can introduce
them to the Light of the world—His name is Jesus!

CHRISTIAN LIVING

"Truly, God will not do wrong.
The Almighty will not twist justice."

JOB 34:12 NLT

You and I serve a just and righteous God who sees everything, even that which happens behind a closed door. That is why righteous men like Stephen pray for their enemies. While the people were stoning him to death in Acts 7:60, he said, "Lord, do not charge them with this sin." He knew that unless there is repentance, there will be severe consequences. So, don't be concerned about justice taking place; God has promised to take care of it.

Many years ago, before I met Jesus, there was a man who used to visit me with his family around lunchtime every day. They would eat our food with us and he would tell me, "Angus, you have to become a Christian. We are Christians." I was a young farmer then and I'd say to myself, "I will get to heaven before he does because at least I can feed my family."

But what would happen if I got to heaven and I told God, "The reason I have not become a Christian is because this other guy who says he is a Christian has lived a terrible life," and the Lord looks around and says, "But he is not here." Folks, we need to concentrate on our own lives and God will do the rest.

STAND YOUR GROUND

Nevertheless even among the rulers many
believed in Him, but because of the Pharisees
they did not confess Him, lest they should be
put out of the synagogue; for they loved the
praise of men more than the praise of God.

JOHN 12:42-43

People will often do anything to find acceptance in society. You see, many of the rulers believed in Jesus, but for fear of becoming unpopular with the crowd, they did not speak up. In these days of extreme compromise where society says, "All roads lead to heaven," and, "Just do as you please," God is looking for people with courage who will be outspoken about the truth and about righteousness.

I want to say to young people today, stand your ground. Don't lower your standards to fit in with the crowd. Don't compromise because you want to fit in.

Stand up for your beliefs. Stand up for the standards that God has put in place. Remember, people don't have to like you, but they must respect you.

Run with the hare and hunt with the hounds, as they say, but be a righteous person who is not ashamed of the Gospel. Remember, it takes a live fish to swim against the current and it takes a dead one to flow with the crowd.

AN ASSURANCE

"For the promise is to you and to
your children, and to all who are afar off,
as many as the Lord our God will call."
ACTS 2:39

God always keeps His promises, but we need to keep our promises, too. First of all to God, then to our family and finally, to our fellow man. You know, in the old days, a handshake would secure a deal. Even in a big deal like the sale of a business, a farm, or a horse, a man's handshake meant: "I promise to do it." Don't ever break your promise and never make a promise that you can't keep.

I knew an old man who lived in an old-age home. His family had emigrated overseas but they promised him that, when they were settled, they would send for him. Every time I spoke to him, he kept telling me that they were getting settled. They never came to fetch him and he died in the old-age home. But do you know something? He went to be with Jesus, who never breaks His promise even when we do.

In Numbers 23:19, we read: "God is not a man, that He should lie, nor a son of man, that He should repent. Has He said, and will He not do? Or has He spoken, and will He not make it good?"

He can't be untrue to Himself; it is not in His nature. He will keep His promise and you can count on it.

BE A SERVANT

After that, He poured water into a basin and
began to wash the disciples' feet, and to wipe
them with the towel with which He was girded.

JOHN 13:5

Can you believe that the Son of God was washing dirty, stinky feet? And a pair of those feet were about to leave and betray Him for thirty pieces of silver, yet He still washed them. Jesus says to us today, if we want to be the greatest, we have to be prepared to become the least (see Matthew 20:26).

Charles Colson was the right-hand man of President Nixon when he was the president of the United States of America. Colson was a ruthless man. He was known as "the evil genius". They said he would even walk over his own mother's grave to get to the top.

Then the terrible Watergate Scandal broke and Colson went to jail for seven months. But that is where his life really began when he was born again and thereafter founded the non-profit ministry Prison Fellowship. Having met the Greatest Servant of all, Jesus Christ, Colson said, "It is not what we do that matters, but what a sovereign God chooses to do through us. God doesn't want our success; He wants us. He doesn't demand our achievements; He demands our obedience." Today, go out and be a servant of the Lord.

CALL UNTO ME

"Call to Me, and I will answer you, and show you great and mighty things, which you do not know."

JEREMIAH 33:3

Did you know that Jesus' telephone number is Jeremiah 333? If you call on Him, He will answer you! But how can we call someone we do not know and how can we call someone we don't believe in or, even worse, we don't trust? You see, in Hebrews 11:6, the Lord says, "But without faith it is impossible to please Him, for he who comes to God must believe that He is, and that He is a rewarder of those who diligently seek Him."

I want to tell you that we need to know His name. It is all about faith, isn't it? Not faith in faith but faith in a Person. Now St Augustine said, "Faith is to believe what you do not yet see; the reward for this faith is to see what you believe." And that is what I love about it. Can you imagine phoning somebody, dialing the number, and they say, "Yes, can I help you? Who is this man you are looking for? What is his name?" And you say, "Well, I don't know his name…" How can they help you? They can't help you.

Today, we need to get to know the name of the Person we are phoning. The Lord says, "Call unto Me!" So if you pray, "Lord Jesus, please help me today," I tell you what, He will help you! He wants to help you more than you want to call on Him.

LEARNING HUMILITY

Peter said to Him, "You shall never wash my feet!"
JOHN 13:8

Do you know that statement was very pride-filled? It nearly cost Peter his whole ministry because right after that Jesus said: "If I do not wash you, you have no part with Me." First Peter 5:5 says, "God resists the proud, but gives grace to the humble." You see, it is all about Him.

Many years ago, I grew seed maize which is a very technical crop to grow. You have to pull the flowers out before they pollinate otherwise the company will condemn the crop. I got myself into a very tight spot; I had over a hundred hectares and the flowers were coming out so fast I could not get them out in time. The inspectors came to me on a Friday afternoon and said, "If these fields are not clean by Monday morning, we will have to condemn you."

I was a young man and I had limited funds. So I had to humble myself. I phoned a neighbor, an extremely successful farmer, and I said to him, "Can you please help me?" Do you know, that gentleman arrived on the Saturday morning with hundreds of workers and they cleaned up my field.

Sometimes we have to go through hard times to be taught humility. I have never met a man yet, worth his salt, that has not been through fiery trials. Today, ask Jesus and He will give you what you need (see Matthew 7:7).

WHAT IS MAN?

What are mere mortals that you should think about
them, human beings that you should care for them?
PSALM 8:4 NLT

Early one morning, before the sun came up, I went out for a
ride on my mountain bike and I looked up into the sky. What
a beautiful sky, full of stars…the magnificence of the mighty
Southern Cross in the sky and right next to it the two pointers.
It made me realize again, Father God is so faithful, isn't He? He
is so steadfast; He is so reliable and He is just so big!

You know, it reminded me of years ago when I was up in
Central Africa. I was with my team, preaching the Gospel to an
unreached people and right in the middle of the bush, late one
night, I came out of my tent and I looked up into the sky. see
the Southern Cross and the two pointers next to it pointing to
my wife and my little children on a small farm called Shalom.
They were nicely tucked into bed and the Holy Spirit was there
with them. And I felt so at peace.

I want to tell you, I love Him so much. Don't doubt God or
argue with Him. He is in heaven and we are on earth. Just love
Him and appreciate what He has done for you.

FAITH LIKE POTATOES

Then the Pharisees said to each other,
"There's nothing we can do.
Look, everyone has gone after Him!"
JOHN 12:19 NLT

The world has gone after Jesus because He performed miracles as no one else had ever done before. It was not only the sermons that He preached. I believe that it was the signs, the wonders and the miracles that Jesus performed that made people follow after Him.

You know, some people say that miracles stopped happening when the apostles died. I don't believe that at all because in Hebrews 13:8, the Word of God tells us that Jesus is the same, yesterday, today and forever. We have got to have faith. Just believe and stop arguing and you will see many more miracles.

I once stood up at Kings Park Rugby Stadium in Durban and I said, "I am going back to plant potatoes," in a year of severe drought and they said, "Don't plant your marginal fields." I said, "I am going back..." And I planted a crop of potatoes and you know, we had a beautiful crop of potatoes that year. You have got to have faith—faith that you can touch, that you can taste.

Simple faith—that's what we need.

LIFT YOUR HEADS

"Now when these things begin to happen,
look up and lift up your heads, because
your redemption draws near."

LUKE 21:28

I want to tell you today that very soon we will be free, we will be free indeed and forever. It will be not too long before you and I will see Jesus coming in the clouds. That's right, He is coming to take us home to be with Him in heaven! All the signs are there, everywhere we look. Do you know that beautiful Scripture passage in Psalm 121:1-2? It says, "I will lift up my eyes to the hills—from whence comes my help? My help comes from the LORD, who made heaven and earth." And that is exactly what we need to be doing!

I firmly believe that our days were allotted to us on earth before we were even conceived in our mother's womb, so don't be afraid of death. Death simply means that we are going to be with Jesus forever! All we need to be sure of is that we are ready when He calls us home. Keep short accounts with men and keep short accounts with God. Be prepared to travel lightly.

Now let's be encouraged because death has lost its sting. It has no hold over the believer because our Redeemer is coming to take us back home to heaven, where there will be no weeping, there will be no suffering, there will be no pain and we will be reunited with our loved ones (see Revelation 21:3-4).

THE RIGHT PACE

"But those who wait on the LORD shall renew
their strength; they shall mount up with
wings like eagles, they shall run and not be
weary, they shall walk and not faint."
ISAIAH 40:31

We need to wait upon the Lord. Life is so hectic at the moment. We need to be like that majestic eagle (my favorite bird) in the high places. You never see an eagle flapping around, stressing. No, he locks his wings and catches those beautiful wind thermals. We need to mount up with wings, just like that eagle. We need to run and not grow tired. We need to walk and not become faint-hearted.

I think the eagle is one of the most beautiful of the Lord's creations. He is never in a rush, have you noticed that? He catches those wind thermals and is totally focused. When we look at the eagle, we get fresh strength. Just like Jesus gives us strength. We don't get tired, we don't lag behind.

Just take a few minutes every day to have a rest and stop wasting valuable time running up and down dead-end streets. Keep focused on the goal that God has set before you. Wait on the Lord; don't run ahead of Him. We must also savor the promises of God. Enjoy your life in God. By doing this, you will find an endless supply of fresh strength.

POINTING TO JESUS

It shall be established forever like the moon,
even like the faithful witness in the sky.
PSALM 89:37

The psalmist is talking about the moon, the faithful witness in the sky. We are to reflect Jesus, not ourselves—just as the moon reflects the light of the sun. So when you see a full moon, it is actually the sun that is shining on the moon and reflecting in the darkness to us. That is exactly how we are supposed to be as followers of Jesus—a good reflection of Him in a dark world.

Like never before people are looking for hope and they can only see it in us, as representatives of Jesus. Jesus said, "And I, if I am lifted up from the earth, will draw all peoples to Myself" (John 12:32).

We are not to draw people to ourselves but to draw people to the Son of God. That is why the Lord speaks about His cousin, John the Baptist. He says in Luke 7:28, among those born of women, there has never been a greater prophet than John the Baptist. Why? Because he was a selfless man.

It was John the Baptist who said, "He must increase but I must decrease" (John 3:30). I want to say to you today, point people to Jesus, that is the best help you can ever give them.

A NEW COMMANDMENT

"A new commandment I give to you, that you love
one another; as I have loved you, that you also
love one another. By this all will know that you are
My disciples, if you have love for one another."
JOHN 13:34-35

It is the hallmark of the Christian—love. Not power or effort, not even success, but unconditional love. Not just loving those who love us but loving our enemies.

Now, that is not easy, is it? In fact, sometimes we say, "Lord, it is not even fair. How can You expect me to love someone who is lying, being unfaithful or who is cheating?" And I can hear Jesus saying to us, "But I loved you when you were still very much an unbeliever. In fact, not only did I love you, but I even died for you." We must remember that. You see, there is no force on earth greater than love.

There is a story that says the old disciple John would be brought into the meetings on a stretcher and he would say to the people in the room, "Little children, love one another." And they would say to him, "But John, you always say that, why do you always say that?" And then with tears in his eyes, the oldest disciple would say, "Because that is what the Master always said." Love one another with the love of Christ.

TURN YOUR EYES TO JESUS

And at the ninth hour Jesus cried out with
a loud voice, saying, "Eloi, Eloi, lama
sabachthani?" which is translated, "My God,
My God, why have You forsaken Me?"

MARK 15:34

Have you ever felt betrayed or totally alone? Have you ever had to take the blame for something that you didn't do? Jesus knows because He has been there. Jesus took all our sin upon His shoulders, so much so that His own heavenly Father could not even look upon Him while He was dying on the cross. That is why Jesus called out to Him: "My God, My God, why have You forsaken Me?" Remember, if there is no crucifixion there can be no resurrection.

The most famous verse in the whole Bible is John 3:16, which says, "For God so loved the world that He gave His only begotten Son, that whoever believes in Him should not perish but have everlasting life." Jesus did it all for us.

Mary Magdalene loved Jesus so much because when everyone else gave up on her, Jesus didn't. He drove seven demons out of that woman and she was the first to visit His tomb on Easter Sunday (see Mark 16:9).

My dear friend, Jesus Christ has not given up on you either. Stop doing what you are doing, turn your eyes upon Him and He will give you new life.

HE WANTS US

"For who has known the mind of the LORD?
Or who has become His counselor? Or who has
first given to Him and it shall be repaid to him?"
ROMANS 11:34-35

God does not need us; He has everything because He is God. However, He wants us. The Lord made us in His own image so that He might have fellowship with us (see Genesis 1:27). We don't have to do anything; we just have to be there for Him.

Remember the story of the two sisters Mary and Martha? Martha was running around the house trying to get everything organized while Mary was sitting at the feet of Jesus, listening to Him and having fellowship with Him (see Luke 10:38-42). Martha said, "Lord, can't You tell my sister to help me?" He said, "But she has done a better thing."

The Lord wants to spend time with us today. It is much more important to spend time with someone than to keep trying to do something for someone. Dad, your children want you! Mom, your husband needs you! Sometimes you don't even have to say a word, just spend time together before it is too late.

Don't waste time. Spend time with each other. Spend time with Jesus because He is waiting for you.

WITH GOD, ALL IS POSSIBLE

"Is anything too hard for the LORD?"
GENESIS 18:14

It is a fact that nothing is too difficult for God. And yet Sarah, Abraham's wife, laughed when God said she was to have a baby (see Genesis 18:10-15). The Lord said to Abraham, "Why did Sarah laugh? Is anything too hard for the LORD?" Now, I can just imagine you are saying, "My situation is beyond any help, beyond any redemption." The only thing, my dear friend, that stops God from operating in your life is one word: Unbelief.

It ties God's hands; He cannot work with us if we refuse to believe Him and to believe His promises over us. Remember, God specializes in taking "nobodies" and turning them into "somebodies". If God can give a woman who is 90 years old a beautiful baby boy (Isaac), then He can give you the desires of your heart as well.

Just like the disciples of old, let us ask Jesus to please increase our faith. He will do it! He can heal the sick, He can set the captives free, He can give us new life.

Today, go out and trust God for the impossible because there is nothing that is too hard for Him. Remember, "With men this is impossible, but with God all things are possible" (Matthew 19:26).

DON'T LISTEN TO LIES

"The thief does not come except to steal, and to kill,
and to destroy. I have come that they may have life,
and that they may have it more abundantly."

JOHN 10:10

We really need to understand something: The devil has no power. He is a liar and a thief. He is the father of all lies. Don't listen to his lies.

We were once called to the Eastern Cape to pray for rain. People had been writing to us for weeks, "Please hold a prayer meeting for rain." Well, we left early that Saturday morning to catch our plane from Durban to Port Elizabeth. The plane was delayed.

The team prayed in the departure lounge. We got on our knees in front of everybody and we prayed. Eventually, we got onto the plane. Now we were already running late. I was supposed to be on the platform in an hour, but we still had a three-hour journey ahead of us. The devil told me, "You will never make it."

Well, we arrived in Port Elizabeth and do you know what we did? We found a helicopter! We got to the venue and I walked onto the platform spot on time. We prayed, we worshiped God, we believed God! Three days later the rain came! Don't listen to the lies of the devil.

ASK ANYTHING

"If you ask anything in My name, I will do it.
If you love Me, keep My commandments."
JOHN 14:14-15

Wow, what a promise of God! If we ask anything in Jesus' name, He says He will do it for us. But He expects us to obey His commandments and to keep them. He is not going to give you a big Mercedes Benz car just because you want it! He is going to do anything that you ask Him in His name if you obey His commandments.

Many years ago, I had a great desire to meet a certain Christian gospel singer who lived in Ireland. I loved his music. I had come back from overseas and I was very tired. So, even though I was supposed to preach at a church in Kwazulu-Natal, I phoned them and canceled. Then I got an invitation to a city-wide campaign in South Africa and this international singer was going to be there too! Now, that was the same weekend I had just said I could not go and speak at this other church.

This was the chance of a lifetime, but I felt the Holy Spirit say, "You refused to go to the other church, you can't make this appointment." I was really, really gutted. A few weeks later we got a phone call, that very singer was in Durban and he wanted to sing for us in the service. I couldn't believe it! God says anything that you ask in His name, He will do for you if you obey His commandments.

THE HELPER

"But the Helper, the Holy Spirit, whom
the Father will send in My name, He will
teach you all things, and bring to your
remembrance all things that I said to you."
JOHN 14:26

Jesus did not leave us alone. No, the Holy Spirit is our Protector, our Confidante, our Advisor and most of all, He is our Friend! We never need to be lonely—He is always with us. Jesus promised us before He went to heaven that He would not leave us alone. That is why He sent His Holy Spirit to guide us, love us and protect us.

When I was a little boy, my dad would take us to watch a rugby match on the weekend. When we walked into that rugby stadium with all the people jostling around, it was amazing how, when my brother and I walked in the front, people just seemed to move aside for us. We thought we must be very important. It was only many years later that we realized that they were not moving aside for us but for the big, strong Scottish blacksmith walking right behind us!

We have the Holy Spirit who is walking behind us today, and in us and around us, and we have nothing whatsoever to fear! So remember that you are never alone. Just ask Him and He will help you. He will speak to you through the Word, through another Christian and He will speak to you in your heart.

PLANTED BY THE RIVER

Oh, the joys of those who...delight in the
law of the LORD, meditating on it day
and night. They are like trees planted along
the riverbank, bearing fruit each season.

PSALM 1:1-3 NLT

Spending time with God each day is our number one priority. We need to get up early in the morning and delight ourselves in the Lord's Holy Word—it's like fresh manna from heaven every day. We need to be like that tree planted by the river, always bringing forth fruit in season and out of season because the roots are focused and fixed in the river.

Christians, by the way, are not exempt from trouble. Jesus walks with us through the fire, He doesn't take us out of the fire. We need to understand that. We are here in this world, which is a fallen world, but the Lord says that if we spend time with Him, we will succeed. Our lives will not crumble when the heat is on; on the contrary, we will prosper because God is with us.

I want to say to you today that you need to look at that glass of water: is it half full or is it half empty? Well, that depends on who you are spending time with. If you are spending time with doubters, they will tell you that the glass is half empty. The person who is spending time with the Lord, who continues to meditate on the Bible, will tell you it is half full.

SHALOM

You will keep him in perfect peace,
whose mind is stayed on You, because he
trusts in You. Trust in the LORD forever,
for in YAH, the LORD, is everlasting strength.
ISAIAH 26:3-4

Another word for peace is *shalom*. Do you know that is one of the fruits of the Spirit? That is what we should display; people should recognize us by the peace that is in us. Our peace does not come from the world, it comes from knowing the Prince of Peace. This world is filled with stress, fear, depression and anxiety. This is the time for Christians to display the fruit of the Spirit—peace.

I remember reading a story many years ago of a young man who was a mountain climber. He went to the doctor and the doctor said, "You have got a rare heart disease. Go home and make yourself comfortable because you will die within the next few years." He went home and thought, "You know, I have nothing to lose." He bought a ticket to South Africa and started to climb the mountain peaks of the mighty Drakensberg range. Some of those peaks are sheer walls of stone. He had nothing to fear because he thought he was going to die anyway, so he scaled most of them. But you know something? That man lived to grow old and died peacefully.

Always keep your eyes on the Prince of Peace. He has not given us a spirit of fear, but of power and of love and of a sound mind (see 2 Timothy 1:7).

THE VINEDRESSER

"I am the vine, you are the branches. He who
abides in Me, and I in him, bears much fruit;
for without Me you can do nothing."

JOHN 15:5

Jesus says, "Without Me you can do nothing." I wish I had known that as a young man because I struggled. I worked and I did things in my own strength, but they never amounted to anything. When I handed everything over to Jesus, things started coming together.

Every time I preach, I get down on my knees and I pray before the Lord, "Lord, that You would watch over the words of my mouth and the meditation in my heart, for I ask it in Your precious name." And then I preach. If I don't do that, there is no power at all.

Now, the Lord is the One who prunes the branches of the vine, isn't He? He says that the branches that bear the most fruit, He prunes the hardest because He wants more fruit from us. Remember though, that the pain of the pruning is much more painful for the Vinedresser than it is for us.

Let Him prune you today. Ask Him and always say, "Lord willing, we will do this today or tomorrow..." not, "I will do it." No, "Lord willing."

SHIELD OF FAITH

In addition to all of these, hold up the shield
of faith to stop the fiery arrows of the devil.
EPHESIANS 6:16 NLT

The shield of faith is what will hold off, quench and put an end to the fiery darts, the accusations, of the devil. We must remember that the devil cannot harm us physically. He is a liar, he is a thief and that is why he will attack us with his lies. That is why we need the shield of faith.

How do we overcome these lies, these fiery darts of the devil? Well, there is only one way and that is the same way that Jesus used to defeat the devil in the desert. That's right, Jesus said, "It is written, 'Man shall not live by bread alone, but by every word that proceeds from the mouth of God'" (Matthew 4:4).

Every single morning before my wife and I get out of bed, we put on the armor of God—the whole armor of God and then we face the day together.

We start off with the helmet of salvation and then we put on the breastplate of righteousness. We put the belt of truth around our waist and we clad our feet with the gospel of peace. We take up that same shield of faith and then we take up the sword of the Spirit, which is the Word of God. Then we go out with the joy of our Lord, which is our strength.

ENJOY GOD

"The joy of the LORD is your strength."
NEHEMIAH 8:10

Enjoy time spent with the Master because that's where our strength lies. Remember, we cannot earn our way to heaven; we are going to heaven through God's grace. Ephesians 2:8 says, "For by grace you have been saved through faith, and that not of yourselves; it is the gift of God."

We have to enjoy the time God has given us on this earth. Enjoy exercising—some people love running, others swimming. Some love riding their mountain bikes, as I do, others enjoy sailing. We have to enjoy our time with the Lord because that is where our strength lies. What hobbies do you have? Some people love photography, others carpentry and some love riding horses. I love riding Snowy as often as I can but most of all, I enjoy spending time with the Lord Jesus Christ.

You say, "But I battle to keep awake when I am praying." Well, start walking when you pray. Some of you are saying, "I struggle to read the Bible and concentrate." Well, get a translation that you can understand. Some say, "Well, I just can't find the time." You need to discipline yourself and have a fixed time each day to spend alone in His presence.

Without a doubt, I want to say to you, my dear friend, that the most favorite time of the day for me is spending time enjoying God.

LOVE AND PROTECTION

"O Jerusalem, Jerusalem, the one who kills the
prophets and stones those who are sent to her!
How often I wanted to gather your children together,
as a hen gathers her brood under her wings,
but you were not willing! See! Your house is left to
you desolate; and assuredly, I say to you, you shall
not see Me until the time comes when you say,
'Blessed is He who comes in the name of the LORD!'"

LUKE 13:34-35

Jesus wants to tell us today that He is here to love and protect us, just like the mother hen protects her little chicks. I heard a beautiful story many years ago. In the mighty Drakensberg mountains, men were burning firebreaks to stop fire from spreading. They were walking along the firebreaks they had burnt and it was just black and charred.

As they were checking to see that nothing was left smoldering before going home, they saw the burnt remains of a wild bird lying in the path. It had been caught in the fire. Its wings were spread out and it was lying there dead. When they turned it over, there was a little clutch of chicks alive and well. She had protected her chicks with her very life.

Oh, my dear friend, that is what Jesus wants to do for you and me. Today, allow Him to protect you and to look after you.

STARTING AGAIN

"You did not choose Me, but I chose you and appointed you that you should go and bear fruit, and that your fruit should remain, that whatever you ask the Father in My name He may give you."

JOHN 15:16

He chose us, we didn't choose Him. What an incredible privilege but of course, with it comes an incredible responsibility. Even as Jesus called the disciples, He is calling us this morning. If we look at Matthew 4:19 (NLT), we will see that Jesus called the disciples and said, "Come, follow Me, and I will show you how to fish for people!"

Does that mean that we need to give up our occupations? Not necessarily but we do need to bear fruit where God has put us. You say, "There was a time when I walked very close to the Lord but the pressures of this life have taken me far from God. Is there maybe any hope left for me?" Yes, indeed. If Jesus could still call Peter after he denied the Lord three times, then He can give us a second chance as well. All we need to do is to say sorry, dust ourselves off and get straight back into the race.

Right through the Bible, we see that men messed up regularly. They really did and God persisted with them because He had called them. He didn't give up on them and He won't give up on you or me today. What we have got to do is to say sorry and get started again. God is calling you and me today. Let's respond and follow Him.

JESUS KNOWS

"He is despised and rejected by men, a Man
of sorrows and acquainted with grief...He was
despised, and we did not esteem Him."

ISAIAH 53:3

Jesus did not sit on His throne in heaven and dictate operations on earth. Oh no! He got His hands dirty. He came down to earth and He got involved, that's why He knows how we feel. You see, Jesus was despised, rejected and stricken by grief; He was even betrayed and that is why we can take our problems to Him. He really does understand. He says, "Come to Me, all you who labor and are heavy laden, and I will give you rest. Take My yoke upon you and learn from Me, for I am gentle and lowly in heart, and you will find rest for your souls. For My yoke is easy and My burden is light" (Matthew 11:28-30).

You always know when someone understands what you have been through because that person does not speak a lot, he doesn't give a lot of advice. He is quick to weep with you, comfort you, to sometimes sit in the gutter with you and put his arms around you. He doesn't tell you to pull yourself together, read some Scripture verses and get going. Jesus is exactly the same; He identifies with us because He has been there before.

Jesus knows exactly what we are going through, so today, take your problems, your fears and your pain to Him.

NO GREATER LOVE

"Greater love has no one than this, than
to lay down one's life for his friends."
JOHN 15:13

This verse describes the greatest act of love ever shown in the history of the world! We need to understand that the Lord Jesus Christ paid the ultimate price for you and me. And we really need to take time out today maybe just to sit and meditate a while on the great and wonderful gift that He gave to us when He took our place. Jesus died about 2,000 years ago so that we could live forever. What a gift!

I am a beekeeper—I love bees very much. They are wonderful little creatures; they make honey that is pure, clean and medicinal. Do you know that the little honeybee will defend its hive, its home, at all costs? Yes, when a little honeybee stings you, it is quite painful for a while, but it won't kill you. However, every time a bee stings someone, it dies. They leave the sting in you and they go and sit somewhere and die. That is what Jesus did for you and me—He died to save us so that we might live.

In my prayer room, I have a little cross. I put this cross in my hand when I am praying and I squeeze it tightly. The corners cut into my fingers and they remind me of the pain that Jesus suffered so that my sins could be forgiven.

Jesus loves you and me so much that He died for us. Today, let's spend time in His presence.

GLORIOUS VICTORY

My soul, wait silently for God alone,
for my expectation is from Him.
He only is my rock and my salvation;
He is my defense; I shall not be moved.

PSALM 62:5-6

Are you feeling disappointed? You need to ask yourself: Where am I putting my expectations—in man or in God? You see, it is not fair to put your hope or your expectations on a person because that person cannot fulfill your dream, only Jesus can.

Now the disciples went through this very thing. For three years they had walked with Jesus—they even saw Him walk on water, raise the dead, heal the sick, cast out demons and even change the weather. They used to sit together and argue about who was going to sit next to Him in heaven and then everything collapsed, right in front of their very eyes. Jesus died, was crucified and buried in a tomb.

Maybe today you feel like that as well. Maybe you are dealing with a broken relationship or a business deal that failed miserably. Maybe your child has disappointed you or you have just come back from the doctor and the diagnosis is not good. I have good news for you, it is not over yet, do not give in!

Jesus is in the habit of turning a potential disaster into a glorious victory—only believe! Wait for tomorrow, it's on its way!

NEW LIFE

And as they went to tell His disciples, behold, Jesus met them, saying, "Rejoice!" So they came and held Him by the feet and worshiped Him. Then Jesus said to them, "Do not be afraid. Go and tell My brethren to go to Galilee, and there they will see Me."

MATTHEW 28:9-10

He is alive, He is not dead! The tomb is empty. Death has lost its sting once and for all! You know there are many religions in the world and many gods. You can go to their graves, you can go to their tombs and you can see where their bones are buried…but not Jesus! The tomb is empty. I've been there and the grave is empty! Why? Because He is not dead. He is alive. Now, if you can believe that's true, you too will never die. That's why Jesus said to the women at His tomb: "Rejoice!"

Maybe you are reading this, but you feel dead inside. Your heart is still pumping but there's no life in you. Ask Jesus to give you a new life. Romans 8:11 says, "But if the Spirit of Him who raised Jesus from the dead dwells in you, He who raised Christ from the dead will also give life to your mortal bodies through His Spirit who dwells in you."

That same Spirit that raised Christ from the dead can give you new life today, a new beginning. So, ask the Lord to come into your heart and give you new life today.

PATIENTLY WAITING

The Lord is not slack concerning His promise,
as some count slackness, but is longsuffering
toward us, not willing that any should perish
but that all should come to repentance.

2 PETER 3:9

The Lord is tarrying because He does not want one person to go to a lost eternity. He wants everyone to have the opportunity to hear the gospel. He doesn't want anybody to perish.

You know, I remember it like yesterday, I had just come to know the Lord and I was at a polocrosse game. I was watching the game and a friend of mine was standing next to me. He said to me, "Angus, you have changed. You are different." I smiled and he said, "I want what you have." I said, "I will see you tomorrow afternoon at 4 o'clock in my maize field."

Well, you know, that afternoon, I didn't know what to say. I was so nervous. I had never told anyone about Jesus. I said, "Jill, I just don't know what to say." She said, "Just tell him what Jesus means to you." One hungry beggar showing another hungry beggar where to find bread! My friend gave his life to Christ in that maize field! We wept, we cried, we hugged each other and a few years later he went to be with the Lord.

You know, on that same field, many years later, I had the privilege of praying that same prayer and telling people about Jesus—tens of thousands of men, in fact! Isn't God amazing! Go out today and tell others what He means to you.

STEP OUT IN FAITH

And the Scripture was fulfilled which says,
"Abraham believed God, and it was accounted to him
for righteousness." And he was called the friend of God.
JAMES 2:23

Abraham was called God's friend. Why was that? It is because Abraham believed God. Abraham obeyed God and that is why He is known as the friend of God. What an amazing thing! Don't you and I want to be known as the friend of God, too?

Romans 1:17 says that the just, the righteous, shall live by faith. God is not interested in our efforts; He is not even interested in our good works. He is only concerned about us trusting in Him. Why? Because it glorifies His Son, Jesus. Hebrews 11:1 says, "Now faith is the substance of things hoped for, the evidence of things not seen."

You might ask, "How do you access that kind of faith?" It is very simple; it is found in Romans 10:17, which says, "So then faith comes by hearing, and hearing by the word of God." That's right, it is by reading your Bible and believing the promises of God.

We have a saying here at Shalom: You must attempt something so big that if it is not of God, it is doomed to fail. Why? Well, if it works, God gets all the glory because people will know that no man could have done it.

Today, step out in faith and believe in the promises of God. He will reward you.

MINDFUL OF YOU

What are mere mortals that You should think about them, human beings that You should care for them? Yet You made them only a little lower than God and crowned them with glory and honor. You gave them charge of everything You made, putting all things under their authority...

PSALM 8:4-6 NLT

The Lord loves us so much that He has put all creation under our authority. God cares for you, my dear friend, and He cares for me. In Matthew 8:25 the disciples were in the boat. It was sinking but Jesus was sleeping. They woke Him up and they said, "Lord, save us! We are perishing!" They thought that they would drown in the storm but Jesus saved them and He wants to save you today.

You know, Peter had so disgraced himself that he never thought that Jesus would ever have anything more to do with him. Remember, after saying to the Lord that he would die for Him, he denied Him three times. The Lord knew that and when He sent the angel to tell the disciples in Mark 16:6-7 to go to Galilee, He specifically mentioned Peter: "Do not be alarmed. You seek Jesus of Nazareth, who was crucified. He is risen! He is not here...go, tell His disciples—and Peter."

He knew that Peter would not come because he felt so terrible so He said, "Tell the disciples—and Peter." That is how much the Lord Jesus Christ loves us. He loves us and He cares for us.

HE KNOWS THE WAY

The LORD is my shepherd; I shall not want. He makes
me to lie down in green pastures; He leads me beside
the still waters. He restores my soul; He leads me
in the paths of righteousness for His name's sake.

PSALM 23:1–3

There is nothing worse for me than to see a sheep lost in a field. We used to keep sheep. They are beautiful animals but they are so vulnerable. It is one animal that cannot protect itself and to see a sheep running around in a paddock, not knowing where it is going, is very sad to me. John 10:11 tells us that Jesus says, "I am the good shepherd. The good shepherd gives His life for the sheep." Jesus is our Shepherd.

Many years ago I studied agriculture in Scotland. There was a student there who was a shepherd and he was the only student who received permission to go home. He lived in a very mountainous area and he had permission to go and bring his flock of sheep down to the lowlands where they could give birth to their little lambs in safety. Why? Because he was the only one who knew the way to bring them down from those high mountains.

I want to say to you today that Jesus knows the way. He says in John 14:6, "I am the way, the truth, and the life. No one comes to the Father except through Me." Today, look to the Good Shepherd and He will lead you home.

REAPING IN JOY

"Therefore you now have sorrow; but I will
see you again and your heart will rejoice,
and your joy no one will take from you."
JOHN 16:22

How are you feeling today? Do you feel like giving up? Well, please don't even go there…Jesus has promised that He is coming back for us. You know, He talks about childbirth. He says that when a woman is having a baby, it is very painful indeed (see John 16:21-22). But what joy when that baby is born! The pain disappears even though she has gone through a very torrid time.

Now, let me just say that if giving birth were left up to us men, this world would be extinct! That's right because we could never handle that much pain! I salute all women who endure that amount of pain for the birth of that little blessing from God!

We need to keep on, keeping on for Jesus. We need to keep focused because the Lord is coming back sooner than we think and we need to be ready for Him. You say, "But it's so hard." I know it is, I really do know exactly what you are feeling. Psalm 126:5 says, "Those who sow in tears shall reap in joy." When Jesus meets us on that wonderful day, all the pain and suffering will disappear.

A SAFE PLACE

The LORD also will be a refuge for the
oppressed, a refuge in times of trouble.

PSALM 9:9

Have you got a safe place? Is there somewhere in the house, business, school or hospital…a place where you can find refuge from the trouble of this world? Remember, the Lord says to us not to run from Him but rather to run towards Him. We must not be like the disciples in the Garden of Gethsemane when they all fled and left Jesus on His own. The only person in the whole world that could have saved them—and they ran away from Him. We must be careful that we don't do that.

You know that great English preacher Charles Spurgeon had no formal education, but he knew the Man from Galilee. Now the way he got saved was one night in a tremendous snowstorm. He was trying to get out of the storm so he went into a little country church where he heard a substitute lay preacher read Isaiah 45:22, "Look to Me, and be saved, all you ends of the earth! For I am God, and there is no other." It changed Spurgeon's life. He had found his safe place.

Jesus went up the mountain. Many times the disciples said, "Where are You, Lord? We can't find You. The multitudes, the crowds are waiting for You." But Jesus was in His safe place. He was hearing from His Father in heaven. What about you today? Where is your safe place? Go there and let the Lord strengthen you, too.

THE WINNING SIDE

"These things I have spoken to you, that in Me you
may have peace. In the world you will have tribulation;
but be of good cheer, I have overcome the world."

JOHN 16:33

Jesus has overcome the things that are going wrong in this world. You might say, "But it doesn't seem like it. It seems like evil is abounding. The poor are getting poorer and the rich are getting richer." Then go straight to Proverbs 24:19, which says, "Do not fret because of evildoers, nor be envious of the wicked."

We see corruption, we see abuse. We see people taking advantage of the poor and the defenseless. But the Lord has told us that this world will be filled with hardship and tribulation because the devil is going around like a roaring lion, seeking whom he may devour (see 1 Peter 5:8).

Some of us are getting so bent out of shape that we are losing our joy, even our very own faith because we see what is going on. Don't do that! That is exactly what Satan wants.

Let's understand one thing. We are on the winning side. Let the Lord Jesus Christ deal with all the corruption and injustice. Let God be the judge. He has told us that in Him we will have peace.

APRIL 25

FINISHING WELL

*"I have glorified You on the earth. I have finished
the work which You have given Me to do."*

JOHN 17:4

God is not interested in good starters; He is only interested in good finishers. We need to finish the task that has been set before us by our Lord.

I remember when I was actively farming, sometimes I would prepare the land for a beautiful crop of maize and tend to it with tender loving care. Then a drought would come and the maize would start taking strain.

In the past, some of my neighbors have put the plow in and said, "We will start over again." But I always felt, "No, I must finish what I have started." So I tended to my field and I looked after it as best I could. Yes, the rain came and the crop grew. Often, it was the best crop that I had ever planted because no one else had any corn and the price went up so we got a good price for our crop. But I finished the job. We need to finish the job that the Lord gives to us.

You see, it is not how you start, it is how you finish. I want to say to you today, get up and finish your race. Whether it be your marriage, your business, your degree or your ministry, finish what you have started and Jesus will rejoice with you.

AVOID FLATTERY

Help, LORD, for the godly man ceases! For the
faithful disappear from among the sons of men.
They speak idly everyone with his neighbor; with
flattering lips and a double heart they speak.

PSALM 12:1-2

Flattery is a dangerous thing; we are not supposed to flatter people. We are supposed to encourage people, even rebuke people in love if necessary, but never flatter anyone. Don't listen to flattery, it will not help you one little bit! Concentrate on the truth—Jesus Christ is the Truth! He says to us clearly in John 17:17, "Sanctify them by Your truth. Your word is truth." Encourage people but never flatter them.

I remember a dear friend of mine in Australia, who personally knew and grew up with one of the most famous actors in the business. This actor once said to him, "I want you to come with me to a movie premier. I want you to walk ten paces behind me on the red carpet when all the paparazzi and the cameras are flashing, and listen to what people say," so he did exactly that. As the actor arrived the people shouted, "Wow, it's fantastic! What an amazing movie! What an amazing actor!" Once the actor had walked past them, his friend who was walking ten paces behind him, heard the people say, "You know something, he is not as tall as I thought he was. He is starting to lose his hair…" Flattery gets you nowhere.

Be truthful. Always be gentle with people and be loving. Most of all, remember, sanctify one another with the truth of the Word of God.

GOD'S RICHES

"And my God shall supply all your need
according to His riches in glory by Christ Jesus."
PHILIPPIANS 4:19

What a promise! You know, if you get a deposit made into your bank account, it is usually dated. It can be drawn or spent, you can bank on it…Excuse the pun! The national bank is your guarantee. You can't see it, but you believe it is there.

We need fresh faith every single morning to believe God's promises. Like a young businessman who believes that he can make a huge investment work…He persuades the bank to lend him the money and then the test comes to see the dream materialize. That takes raw, undiluted God-given faith.

In 2008, we believed God. We believed that God gave us a vision to stage a Mighty Men Conference on the farm and to feed thousands of men for an entire weekend for free. The bank did not guarantee that meeting, but God did! I remember we slaughtered over 40 oxen for just one meal.

We cut steel drums in half and used them as pots for cooking. We built big fires underneath them and then cooked the meals for the men. Who paid? The Bank of Heaven paid!

Today, find out what God wants. Get confirmation from Jesus and then with childlike faith, go and do it. God will not disappoint you; He has never ever disappointed me once in my life.

SHOWING KINDNESS

"Then the righteous will answer Him, saying,
'Lord, when did we see You hungry and feed You,
or thirsty and give You drink? When did we see
You a stranger and take You in, or naked and
clothe You...?' And the King will answer and say to
them, 'Assuredly, I say to you, inasmuch as you did it to
one of the least of these My brethren, you did it to Me.'"
MATTHEW 25:37-40

My wife and I once visited a very quaint little coastal town in the Southern Cape. It was a lovely day and so I decided to go downtown to buy some fish and chips—much easier than cooking I walked into this little fish and chip shop and I placed my order.

While I was waiting for our food, I looked up at the wall and there was this beautiful inscription. It was a quote by William Penn and it read, "I expect to pass through life but once. If therefore, there be any kindness I can show, or any good thing I can do to any fellow being, let me do it now, and not defer or neglect it, as I shall not pass this way again."

And I want to tell you that those words sobered me up right away. Let's take our eyes off the carnage and world politics taking place. We can't do anything about that, can we? No, we can't but we can pray and we do. But let's also go out today and be Jesus' hands and feet to those who cannot help themselves.

Do something today for someone who can't pay you back.

OUR LIVING GOD

The fool has said in his heart, "There is no God."

PSALM 14:1

We can go into the darkest reaches where people have never seen or heard of a Christian missionary and we can ask them if there is a God and they will tell you that there is a great being, that there is a Creator. A man who can't read, a man who can't write knows there is a God because God has put eternity into the heart of men. They asked Albert Einstein, who is regarded by some as probably the greatest scientist of all time, and he said he definitely believes there is a God.

Some might wonder where God is. I want to tell you, my dear friend, I see my Lord in the early morning as the sun rises. Oh, yes, as I plant that crop of maize and I see it coming through the ground, the miracle of new life, I know that my Redeemer lives. When I see a couple who have just fallen in love and I see how they look at each other in absolute amazement, I can see the Creator.

Oh, my dear friend, there is no doubt about it. We have a God and He walked on this earth. That's right, He lived on this earth to show us and to prove to us that He's a friend who sticks closer than a brother and He's coming back very soon to take us to be with Him in paradise. Today, go out and thank God for what He's done for you.

A THREEFOLD CORD

Though one may be overpowered
by another, two can withstand him.
And a threefold cord is not quickly broken.
ECCLESIASTES 4:12

There are no lone rangers in the kingdom of God. Jesus desires that we get on together, even as He and His Father in heaven work together. We need to stop fighting each other and start helping each other. God never designed us to be loners; He put us together in families for a reason. A three-fold cord is not easily broken, the Bible says. Jesus is in the middle of your friendship, your relationship and in the middle of your marriage.

Many years ago, I went to Australia. I was working on a ranch and I had to find accommodation in the local town. Now, I could have easily found a hotel but no, I found a family. They were wonderful people but very poor and they needed the extra income, so they took me on as their border. Why didn't I stay in the hotel? I had the money, but I was homesick. I was lonely and I needed a friend.

Jesus is a friend who sticks closer than any brother. We need to spend time together. We need to say sorry if we have offended each other. We need to really put family, loved ones and friendship right at the top of our list. We need to put Jesus at the very top because He will never leave us and He will never forsake us.

THE RACE

"He who overcomes shall be clothed in
white garments, and I will not blot out his name
from the Book of Life; but I will confess his name
before My Father and before His angels."
REVELATION 3:5

The Bible often speaks about overcoming. We are busy running a race that has been set before us and we must run it until we reach our final destination. Philippians 3:12 says, "Not that I have already attained, or am already perfected; but I press on, that I may lay hold of that for which Christ Jesus has also laid hold of me."

The good news is that we are not running this race alone. Our Savior is running this marathon with us. Just like the bus driver that you will find on an ultra-marathon. He sets the pace. Now it is not an actual bus; it is a group of people who run with someone they trust. He puts a little reed in his belt with a flag on it and the group follow him. He is the one who tells the group when to walk, when to jog, and when to stop and have a rest. If the group listen to the bus driver, he will get them over the finish line.

Now, Jesus is also our bus driver. He says, "If you obey Me, I will get you home. If you obey Me and My statutes, you will be overcomers." And He will help us to make it right to the end.

SOMETHING SWEET

*"Out of the eater came something to eat,
and out of the strong came something sweet."*
JUDGES 14:14

This was a riddle Samson put forward to the men and said: "If you solve my riddle during these seven days of the celebration, I will give you thirty fine linen robes and thirty sets of festive clothing. But if you can't solve it, then you must give me thirty fine linen robes and thirty sets of festive clothing" (Judges 14:12-13 NLT).

Now earlier Samson was walking down the road when a young lion attacked him. He killed the lion with his bare hands. Remember, Samson was the strongest man who ever lived. He came back a while later and a swarm of bees had gone into the carcass of the lion. He put his hand in there and took out some sweet honey. So that was the riddle: Out of strength comes forth sweetness.

Out of Jesus' death came new life; out of pain came the sweetness of salvation. I just want to say thank You, Lord Jesus, for dying for a sinner like me and sinners like us.

Remember, He loves you. And as you look to the cross, hope, love, life and sweetness will emanate.

OPPORTUNITY

"For I am not ashamed of the gospel of Christ, for it
is the power of God to salvation for everyone who
believes, for the Jew first and also for the Greek."
ROMANS 1:16

Do not be ashamed of the Gospel of Christ! People do not have to like us, but they must respect us. Peter must have felt so wretched when he said, "I am not," in John 18:17, when the servant girl asked him if he was not one of Jesus' disciples. Yet that same very big, outspoken fisherman who denied Jesus three times before the rooster crowed (just as the Lord said he would), when filled with the Holy Spirit in the upper room, went out into the streets and unashamedly preached the Gospel and 3,000 souls were saved.

This is not a time for us to hold back. We must speak up. The Lord Jesus tells us to open our mouths wide and He will fill it (see Psalm 81:10). Do not miss the opportunity today, for some poor lost soul it might be their last chance to hear the Gospel before they die.

Today, don't waste an opportunity, don't be afraid. Just open your mouth and tell people about the love of Christ. Like never before in the world people are desperate to hear the truth.

PASSING THROUGH

Jesus answered, "My kingdom is not of this world."
JOHN 18:36

We mustn't become too comfortable here on earth, this is not our permanent home. We need to be careful that we do not spend all our time and all our money on our temporal dwelling here on earth and nothing on our heavenly home.

Like a story I heard of a rich lady and the maid servant who worked in her mansion. Both of them were Christians but had different value systems. The rich lady spent all her money and time making her home very beautiful. But the maid spent most of her spare time in prayer and service towards the Lord by helping the poor folk. Eventually, the maid grew old and she went to heaven. A few years later, the rich lady also died and went to heaven.

St Peter was waiting at the pearly gates to show the rich lady where her home was in heaven. So they walked down streets of magnificent homes built on both sides of the road. St Peter showed the rich lady a beautiful home, he said, "That is where your maid lives." The rich lady was so excited. They then arrived at a little shack made with tin and poles. The rich lady said, "There must be some mistake. What has happened?" St Peter said to the rich lady, "That is the only material you sent to us for building your home here in heaven."

This is just a story but we must remember one thing very clearly. We are only passing through in this life. Heaven is our permanent home.

OUR LIGHT IN DARKNESS

"Do not rejoice over me, my enemy;
when I fall, I will arise; when I sit in darkness,
the LORD will be a light to me."
MICAH 7:8

Maybe we are sitting in a dark place this morning. Maybe our enemy is laughing at us. Well, the Bible says that weeping may last for a night but joy comes in the morning (see Psalm 30:5). We may be knocked down but we are by no means knocked out of the fight. Why? Because Jesus Christ is on our side! So, no matter how dark the situation may be, He is with us in our time of extreme testing.

You see, Jesus has been there. He was in the Garden of Gethsemane where He was left all alone while His disciples slept. Jesus was in absolute darkness and despair. The Bible tells us that He was sweating blood (see Luke 22:44). He was taken to the High Priest's house and was put into a pit. He knew what was coming—death on a cross!

Oh yes, He has been through what you and I are feeling right at this very moment and much worse. But I want to say to you, my dear friend, Jesus says in Psalm 34:19, "Many are the afflictions of the righteous, but the LORD delivers him out of them all." Jesus truly is a Friend who sticks closer than a brother.

WHAT OTHER PEOPLE SAY

Then Jesus came out, wearing the
crown of thorns and the purple robe.
And Pilate said to them, "Behold the Man!"
JOHN 19:5

Jesus was totally humiliated and mocked by His very own creation! It wasn't the Roman soldiers, no! It wasn't the Jewish High Priests. It was our sin that led to this! Yours and mine… and yet we never learn as we continue to mock others today.

Have you ever been mocked? Have you ever been made a fool of by your peers, maybe at school or at work, or on the sports field? Like the little boy who goes to Sunday school with his brand-new pair of bright, shiny brown shoes his mom bought for him. He is so proud of them. He sits in a row with all the other little boys only to find out that they have all got white shoes on and they mock him. I have seen it so many times, children can be very cruel.

When Jesus returns, He will not be wearing a crown of thorns; He will not be beaten and humiliated. No! He will be the most handsome and the most dignified Man that we have ever seen.

Today, go out and be encouraged. Don't worry about what people say about you. Jesus loves you and He created you in His own image!

QUIETENING YOUR SPIRIT

Let the words of my mouth and the meditation
of my heart be acceptable in Your sight,
O LORD, my strength and my Redeemer.
PSALM 19:14

We have to think before we speak. We have to adhere to this statement and obey it. If we do, we shall make fewer mistakes in life. The Lord Jesus Christ impressed this beautiful verse upon me many years ago.

The Lord Himself only spoke when He had to. He stood before Pontius Pilate and Pontius Pilate said, "Have You nothing to say?" But He only spoke when the Lord God, His Father, gave Him the words to speak. In Proverbs 10:19, it says very clearly: "In the multitude of words sin is not lacking, but he who restrains his lips is wise."

In other words, only speak when the Lord gives you the words to speak. Before I speak at a big meeting, wherever it might be, what I do is get on my knees and humble myself before God and before the people in prayer. Then my spirit is quietened to focus on what I need to be speaking about. It prevents me from speaking about irrelevant things.

We need to pray more and speak less. Today, quieten your spirit. Spend time in the presence of the Lord. He will give you His peace.

WHO CAN WE TRUST?

"Some trust in chariots, and some in horses; but we
will remember the name of the LORD our God."

PSALM 20:7

Who can we put our trust in during these troubled days? Can we put our trust and our faith in education? We thank God for education but I know many young people who are well educated who can't get a job.

Can we put our trust in the economy? One day it's up and the next it is down. Can we put our trust in our health? I am a man who exercises. I ride my horse and my mountain bike, and I do press-ups but still I can't put my trust in my health.

There is only One who will never, ever fail us and His name is Jesus Christ. He is totally trustworthy and He has promised us: "I will never leave you nor forsake you" (Hebrews 13:5).

His word is dependable and sure. You can stake your life on it and indeed, the lives of your loved ones. You see, Jesus has got an unblemished track record—He has never failed. Everything that He has promised us He has given us. His track record goes right back to the beginning of time itself.

Your investments might fail you and men may let you down with empty promises but Jesus will never fail you! So keep putting one foot in front of the other, trust God, and watch what He will do for you.

CELEBRATE YOUR MOTHER

When she speaks, her words are wise, and she
gives instructions with kindness. She carefully
watches everything in her household and
suffers nothing from laziness. Her children
stand and bless her. Her husband praises her:
"There are many virtuous and capable women
in the world, but you surpass them all!"

PROVERBS 31:26-29 NLT

We must never take our mothers for granted. Never forget that Father God chose a woman to nurture, raise, teach and protect His only Son, Jesus, when He came down from heaven to earth in the form of a defenseless baby.

You know, I would give a million dollars to be able to sit down and have a cup of tea with my mom again. Oh, I really am looking forward to seeing her in heaven! I want to say to the young men and women, don't waste valuable opportunities to be close to your mom. She won't be with you forever. Give her a phone call, tell her you love her because she is the one who is responsible for raising you.

John Wesley, the great revivalist, said, "I learned more about Christianity from my mother than from all the theologians in England." Listen to your mom. Remember, she has been there before and she will give you good, godly advice.

A FRIEND OF SINNERS

For "whoever calls on the name
of the LORD shall be saved."
ROMANS 10:13

You know, many of us are dead. We are walking around and our hearts are pumping blood but we are dead in our spirits. The Gospel of Luke says, "I say to you that likewise there will be more joy in heaven over one sinner who repents than over ninety-nine just persons who need no repentance" (Luke 15:7).

Jesus came for sinners, just like me and just like you. He is known by many titles but the title I love the most is the "Friend of sinners." Some of the greatest sinners have become God's greatest ambassadors. Therefore, we must never give up on a lost sheep, on a lost soul.

One of them was Saul of Tarsus, that's right! Remember, he became Paul the apostle when he was knocked off his horse on the road to Damascus while he was seeking to murder Christians (see Acts 9:4-5). The Lord Jesus said to him, "Saul, Saul, why are you persecuting Me?" And he said, "Who are You, Lord?" The Lord answered, "I am Jesus." You know, after that he went on to write almost two-thirds of the New Testament. He took the gospel all over the world.

Remember, good people don't go to heaven, believers go to heaven. Romans 10:9 says, "If you confess with your mouth the Lord Jesus and believe in your heart that God has raised Him from the dead, you will be saved."

STANDING FOR JESUS

"The LORD is my helper; I will not fear.
What can man do to me?"
HEBREWS 13:6

Charles Spurgeon, that great English preacher, said, "He who fears God has nothing else to fear." If God is standing behind you, the devil won't come near you and it also won't make the slightest difference even if the biggest threats of man are made against us.

Yes, we will be mocked and even made fools of by the world because we stand for Jesus. That is a given—Jesus told us to expect that. But if Jesus is our helper, He makes us very bold so that when we are teased by the world, it doesn't have to bother us.

I remember a little boy who loved Jesus very much. He was an excellent shofar blower. He was probably not the most popular boy amongst his peers because of his undivided stand for Jesus. His father contacted us and asked us if this young boy, I think he was about twelve or thirteen years old at the time, could blow the shofar at our National Prayer Meeting in Bloemfontein a few years ago. We agreed. That little boy came up onto the stage and he blew that shofar so beautifully in front of over one million people.

Today, stand up for Jesus and He will protect you, guide you and deliver you.

A WIN-WIN SITUATION

"For to me, to live is Christ, and to die is gain."
PHILIPPIANS 1:21

We are in a win-win situation. If we live, we live for Christ and if we die, we go home to be with Christ in heaven forever…You can't frighten a Christian with heaven, so what are you afraid of?

Some people might say, "But I need Him now. Where has He been?" Remember the old poem *Footprints in the Sand*? The man says, "I noticed that during the saddest and most troublesome times of my life there was only one set of footprints. I don't understand why, when I needed You the most, You would leave me." And God answers, "When you saw only one set of footprints, it was then that I carried you." Yes, the Lord has never forsaken us. Those of us with grey hair can testify to that fact. Remember one thing, Jesus will never forsake you, He loves you so much!

A lot of young people write to me from overseas—they have had to go overseas to find employment but their old folks are still here in South Africa. They write and ask, "Please, could you take care of them, we are worried about them." I want to say to you today that you have nothing to worry about. Just trust the One who has looked after them from birth; Jesus will continue to look after them in their old age. So today, remember, if Christ is for you, there is no man who will ever stand against you.

QUIET TIME

You will keep him in perfect peace, whose
mind is stayed on You, because he trusts
in You. Trust in the LORD forever, for in YAH,
the LORD, is everlasting strength.

ISAIAH 26:3-4

Just a couple of weeks ago I was privileged to speak to a large group of students at one of South Africa's prestigious universities. It was an evening service and it was packed. The praise and worship was amazing, and I knew that I was speaking to Christians. I asked them a question: "How many of you had a quiet time this morning? How many of you spent time reading your Bible, praying and spending time in the presence of Jesus today?" The place went quiet. I said, "I want you to be honest with me. If you did not have a time with Jesus this morning, can you please put up your hand."

My heart broke. Over 80% of those students had not had a quiet time that morning. I said, "How can you trust God for revival if you don't spend time with Him?" Well, the pastor, who is one of my spiritual sons, told me that his daughter who was also at the meeting couldn't find a place where she could have a quiet time the next morning because everybody was up, spending time with Jesus.

So before you go out today, spend time with Jesus and learn to trust and obey Him, because there is no other way to be happy in Jesus but to trust and obey!

DECLARE HIS NAME

"I will declare Your name to My brethren; in the
midst of the assembly I will sing praise to You."
HEBREWS 2:12

This is not a time for us to hold back. We must speak up about
our faith in God. Remember, that beautiful verse in Mark
11:22, "Have faith in God." An easy one to remember!

When I first started preaching the gospel, I had the privilege
of addressing the main congregation in our local church. I was
so nervous. I had spent about six weeks preparing the message.
I got into the pulpit and opened my Bible, took out the first
page, which was the introduction to welcome all the people
and turned the page over. There was the last page! Thirteen
pages of my sermon had gone missing. Well, I tell you what, I
was absolutely shocked.

But it was decision time. Was I going to declare the name of
the Lord to the brethren or not? We had a little band from our
local coffee bar that we used to run, Jill and I, and they had just
sung a song, "Here comes Jesus, walking on the water." The
Holy Spirit just about audibly, said to me, "Are you going to
walk on the water or not? Are you going to speak up for Jesus
or not?" I said, "Lord, I am going to do it." And I have never
stopped since.

Go out today and tell people that Jesus loves you and that
He is a Friend who sticks closer than a brother.

LIVING EPISTLES

Let not mercy and truth forsake you;
bind them around your neck, write them on
the tablet of your heart, and so find favor and
high esteem in the sight of God and man.

PROVERBS 3:3-4

In 2 Corinthians 3:3, Paul says, "…clearly you are an epistle of Christ, ministered by us, written not with ink but by the Spirit of the living God, not on tablets of stone but on tablets of flesh, that is, of the heart."

As Christians, we are to display mercy and truth, and to wear it around our necks like a necklace of fine jewels. It should be written on our hearts, not with ink but by the Holy Spirit of the Living God. We should be an epistle, a living letter of Christ, so that people can see the love and mercy of Jesus through us. Don't tell people that you love them, show them that you love them! That is what Jesus did.

When the disciples were all sitting around the table, Jesus took a basin filled with water and He washed their feet (see John 13:1-17). Now, you know, that physical act spoke louder than any number of seminars or sermons. The world is starving for love, kindness, mercy and truth. Let's be a band of foot-washers today.

Actions speak louder than words. Go out today and be a living epistle of Jesus Christ.

THE POWER OF PRAISE

"Don't be dejected and sad,
for the joy of the LORD is your strength."
NEHEMIAH 8:10 NLT

The power of praise! We don't always feel like it, do we? But we need to praise God because the joy of the Lord is our strength. John Henry Jowett said, "Let us sing even when we do not feel like it, for in this way we give wings to heavy feet and turn weariness into strength." Of course, the devil hates it when God's people start worshiping Him in songs and praise.

Many years ago, I had the privilege of preaching in Wales. Now, I think the Welsh people can sing like no other nation on earth. Even when they speak, it sounds like they are singing. Their words are so beautiful.

I was speaking to a thousand Welsh farmers and their wives and children. That evening they sang a song, one of the old revival songs from the famous Welsh revival. I just stood there and wept. It is very hard to preach after that. That is the power of worshiping God!

Today, worship Him. Sing songs to Him in your pick-up truck, in the car, wherever you are, give Him praise and He will lift your spirits up to a new level.

PEACEMAKER

"Blessed are the peacemakers,
for they shall be called sons of God."
MATTHEW 5:9

Jesus was sent down to earth by His Father to be a peacemaker. John 20:21 says, "So Jesus said to them again, 'Peace to you! As the Father has sent Me, I also send you.'" Today, He sends you and me out into the world as peacemakers, not troublemakers. There are more than enough troublemakers in this world, aren't there? But remember, it takes two to fight. God has called us to bring peace. It takes a much stronger person to turn the other cheek.

To be a peacemaker you have to be at peace with yourself. An angry, bitter, hurting person can never display the fruit of peace, the peace that Jesus is asking us to produce today. We need to forgive just as we have been forgiven. We need to love, just as we have been loved.

Our farm is called Shalom, which means peace. Whenever Jesus came into a home, the first thing he said was, "Shalom," which means, "Peace be in this home." But you know, you can't earn peace, you can't do a course in peace, you can't get a degree in peace, no! You have to let peace come into your heart. Jesus says, "Behold, I stand at the door and knock. If anyone hears My voice and opens the door, I will come in to him and dine with him, and he with Me" (Revelation 3:20). Remember, the handle of the door is only on the inside. We need to invite Him in.

NOT BY SIGHT

The other disciples therefore said to him,
"We have seen the Lord." So he said to them,
"Unless I see in His hands the print of the nails,
and put my finger into the print of the nails,
and put my hand into His side, I will not believe."
JOHN 20:25

Well, what can we say? There are none so blind as those who do not want to see. But you know, without faith it is impossible to please God (see Hebrews 11:6). We have to start walking more by faith and not by sight (see 2 Corinthians 5:7). Even the disciples said to Jesus in Luke 17:5, "Increase our faith."

We are living in perilous times and my dear friend, if you are suffering from depression, anxiety, stress or fear, you have to start believing the promises of God. You have to start to believe the Word of God and you have to stop listening to the lies of the devil.

You see, without faith, you cannot even be a Christian. Because it takes faith to believe that Jesus Christ was born of a virgin, that Mary never knew a man and she was impregnated by the Holy Spirit. It takes faith to believe that a man was raised from the dead and that Jesus is coming again in the clouds.

Today, let us walk by faith and not by sight.

FORGIVENESS AND GRACE

God's law was given so that all people could see how
sinful they were. But as people sinned more and more,
God's wonderful grace became more abundant.

ROMANS 5:20 NLT

You know, one of the hardest things for a sinner to do is to forgive himself and to accept that God has truly forgiven him. We have to accept that the Lord has paid, in full, for our sin. Peter said to the Lord when He wanted to wash His feet: "You shall never wash my feet," and Jesus says, "If I do not wash you, you have no part with Me" (John 13:8).

A young man once told my son that he wanted to give me his horse—not just any horse but his best horse—as a gift. This horse was worth a lot of money and it was fully trained. And he wanted to give it to me as a gift.

Another young man wanted to make me a handmade saddle. Initially, I said, "I can't take it from these boys. It is too great a gift; it is part of their livelihood." But my son said to me, "Dad, if you don't take it, you will hurt their feelings." And so reluctantly and graciously I accepted their gifts, which meant so much to me.

Now, Jesus paid a tremendous price for you. All you have to do is to say, "Lord, thank You for dying for me on a cross." Accept His gift today.

HIS SECRET COUNSEL

For the perverse person is an abomination to
the LORD, but His secret counsel is with the upright.

PROVERBS 3:32

God will not share His close, personal issues with a devious person. He will not allow them to enter into that private place with Him. He only shares His intimate relationship with those of an upright spirit. Secret counsel is found between God and His people. His personal friendship He shares with only those who love and respect Him.

Have you noticed that when you're involved with something you know is wrong, God seems so far away from you? God's guidance, blessing and friendship are only with those who love and honor Him. When we are invited to a questionable place, we need to ask ourselves a question: "Could I take the Lord into this place with me?" If the answer is, "No, I would be embarrassed to take the Lord there," then you need to leave immediately.

Many years ago, I was invited to a huge gathering in a major city in South Africa. They asked me to be one of the speakers. When I arrived, I immediately felt uneasy, they took me up onto the platform in front of multitudes of people. I looked around and I saw people on the platform with me from different faiths, worshiping different gods. Straight away I felt the Holy Spirit saying to me, "What are you doing here?" Well, I had a choice to make…I was most embarrassed but I stood up and walked straight off the platform. Please don't compromise your special relationship with Jesus just to make other people happy.

OUR MIRACLE-WORKING GOD

"For with God nothing will be impossible."
LUKE 1:37

What a beautiful promise from God! The Gospel of John says, "Simon Peter went up and dragged the net to land, full of large fish, one hundred and fifty-three; and although there were so many, the net was not broken" (John 21:11). Wow! Well, I tell you what, we serve a miracle-working God and we need to remember that.

Nothing is too hard for the Lord and nothing is impossible for Jesus. If ever we needed to remember that, it is in these times in which we are living.

Therefore, let us press onward on the road that the Lord Jesus has appointed for us and always remember that He has gone ahead of us. You see, it is not for us to question or to try and reason. We simply have to keep moving forward and He will do the rest.

It is God's work and so He will see that it shall not fail. All we have to do is to believe in a miracle-working God. We cannot do it in our own strength, therefore it is not for you and me to reason with Him. We must just let Jesus do it. And you know something? He wants to do it.

THE RIGHT CHOICES

*"And if it seems evil to you to serve the LORD,
choose for yourselves this day whom you will serve...
But as for me and my house, we will serve the LORD."*
JOSHUA 24:15

You know, life is full of choices. You can choose life or death. Obeying the statutes and the commandments of God will bring life. Doing things in our own selfish ways will bring death.

I heard the story of a man who walked out of the courthouse after having divorced his sixth wife and the remark he made was, "She tried so hard to make me happy." How selfish and self-centered! Marriage is not a 50/50 commitment. No, marriage is a 100% commitment and covenant from both sides. There is no such thing as the perfect marriage or the perfect family. By the grace of God and our own decision, we have to work on our marriages and our family relationships.

There is one Scripture verse that I really need to leave with you today. Ecclesiastes 4:9-12 says, "Two are better than one, because they have a good reward for their labor. For if they fall, one will lift up his companion. But woe to him who is alone when he falls, for he has no one to help him up. Again, if two lie down together, they will keep warm; but how can one be warm alone? Though one may be overpowered by another, two can withstand him. And a threefold cord is not quickly broken." We need to make the right choices and serve God in our family and in that way choose life.

THROUGH THE STORM

Though I walk in the midst
of trouble, You will revive me.

PSALM 138:7

The last thing that Jesus said before He went to heaven was: "I am with you always, even to the end of the age" (Matthew 28:20). So we don't need to be afraid.

If I look back on my Christian walk, my fondest memories are of when I was in my greatest times of turmoil and trouble because those have been the times when I felt Jesus pressing in the closest to me. Therefore, we need not be afraid or fearful of hard times, it is in times like these that we can truly be changed for the better.

I would rather be in a small dinghy with Jesus at the helm, going around Cape Horn in South America, facing huge waves that literally blot out the sun, than to be in a luxury liner on a calm lake without any waves but also without Jesus.

Today, we need to face our storms; we need to face our troubles. All we need to do is to make very sure that the Lord Jesus Christ is at the helm of our boat. Don't be afraid of trouble. But know that the Lord said that He will be with us even to the very end of the age.

Keep your eyes fixed on the Lord and He will take you right through that storm that you are experiencing.

ALL FOR JESUS

One thing I have desired of the LORD, that will
I seek: That I may dwell in the house of the LORD
all the days of my life, to behold the beauty
of the LORD, and to inquire in His temple.

PSALM 27:4

What is it that compels people to give up all they have in order to follow after this Man from Galilee? I think of C. T. Studd who played cricket and came from a wealthy family, yet he gave it all up so he could follow after Jesus. He died in the Congo, having preached the gospel of Jesus Christ to the poorest of the poor.

What about Eric Liddell? He was a Scottish sprinter. He came back from the Olympic Games with a gold medal and yet he chose to go to China as a missionary for Jesus.

You know, people often talk to me about the crowns that they imagine they'll receive when they get to heaven. But I am not really interested in crowns. Like David, I just want to be a doorkeeper in the house of the Lord all the days of my life.

Shouldn't you and I rather take time out, even today, to sit at the feet of Jesus to learn from Him? He will give you peace and He will give you the joy that you are looking for. He will give you that confidence that you have that there is nothing you need to fear if Jesus Christ is in your heart!

LET HIM LOVE YOU

"Can a woman forget her nursing child, and not
have compassion on the son of her womb?
Surely they may forget, yet I will not forget you.
See, I have inscribed you on the palms of My hands."

ISAIAH 49:15-16

Have we ever seen a stronger bond than a mother and her suckling child? Definitely not and Jesus tells us clearly today that His bond with us is even stronger than that! Maybe today, you are feeling lonely. Maybe you are feeling deserted or maybe you feel that nobody cares about you…I want to tell you there is One who cares about you very much.

Have you ever seen the loving, doting eyes of a mother holding her newborn baby in her arms? The absolute wonder of it and the love—it's so beautiful to see. I remember visiting my daughters in the hospital after they'd given birth. When they were holding their little bundles of joy in their arms, they were so proud of their babies.

Jesus loves us even more than that. He says, "Look at the nail scars in my hands, that tells you how much I love you. I died for you!" He loves us so much that He died in our place. John 15:13 says, "Greater love has no one than this, than to lay down one's life for his friends." And that is exactly what He did for us. Now today, speak to Him and let Him love you.

RETURNING ON THE CLOUDS

...And while they looked steadfastly toward heaven
as He went up, behold, two men stood by them in
white apparel, who also said, "Men of Galilee, why do
you stand gazing up into heaven? This same Jesus,
who was taken up from you into heaven, will so come
in like manner as you saw Him go into heaven."

ACTS 1:10-11

Every morning I wake up and I look outside at the clouds, and I say, "Lord, are You coming back today?" because He has promised us that He will return on the clouds. What a wonderful day that will be! I am sure you will agree with me, it couldn't be soon enough.

He is coming back to set the record straight. All the injustice in the world, all the immorality, the corruption…those who stick their tongue out and say, "Where is this God that you are always talking about?" Yes! Everyone will be judged, and every knee will bow and every tongue will confess that Jesus Christ is Lord. And that is why we need to pray.

We need to pray even for our enemies because the Bible says it is a terrible thing to fall into the hands of a Living and Holy God. You and I need to keep short accounts with man and God for the time is very short. Today, remember, the Lord is not dead. He is alive and coming back for you and me very soon.

CONSECRATED

"'Take, eat; this is My body which is broken for
you; do this in remembrance of Me.' In the same
manner He also took the cup after supper, saying,
'This cup is the new covenant in My blood. This do,
as often as you drink it, in remembrance of Me.'"

1 CORINTHIANS 11:24-25

You know, when we consecrate everything we have to the Lord Jesus, He blesses and even multiplies what we have as He did with the two fishes and the five barley loaves of bread (see Mark 6:30-44).

Every morning when we have breakfast together we break bread. That is right, we have Holy Communion, every single day. God blesses what we eat and also what we do. We say our grace before we sit down and eat, then we eat our food heartily.

We need to get into the habit of thanking the Lord for everything that we do. You know, before we travel, we give thanks to God, saying, "Lord, please protect this trip." Before we do a business deal, we pray over it. Before somebody gets employed we pray over them and then God multiplies and He consecrates it. Today, get used to committing every aspect of your life to the Lord and He will do the rest.

PRAISE HIM

"But He answered and said to them,
"I tell you that if these should keep silent,
the stones would immediately cry out."
LUKE 19:40

There is power in praise. Jesus said to the Pharisees, "If these people don't praise Me, the very rocks will praise Me." We don't praise God for the situation necessarily, but we praise Him in the situation.

If you are going through a hard time at the moment, you say, "But, Angus, how can I praise God—my business is going bankrupt, my child is sick or my future is uncertain?" You praise Him *in* the situation. You don't praise Him *for* the situation because He is the One who makes us overcomers through our hardship and our tribulation. Praise takes our eyes off of ourselves and puts our focus back on the Lord. It takes our eyes off of the problem and puts our focus back on the Problem-Solver.

You know, some of our prayers are like shopping lists. That is all we do: "Give me, give me, give me! Lord give me this, give me that. Help me here!" We concentrate on ourselves instead of praising and worshiping the Lord. Praising Him for who He is and not for what He can do for us. We have got to take our eyes off of ourselves, put them on Jesus and praise Him for who He is.

VOICE OF THE LORD

The voice of the LORD is powerful;
the voice of the LORD is full of majesty.
PSALM 29:4

How does God speak to us? He speaks to us in many different ways. He speaks to us through His creation, but we need to listen. People have oftentimes asked me if I have heard the voice of God. The answer is many times, but never audibly. Not many people have. So how does He speak to me? Well, He speaks to me in my quiet times. He speaks to me through reading my Bible. He speaks to me through other faithful believers. Oh yes, the Lord speaks to me through the weather, probably because I am a man of the land.

I remember like it was yesterday, I was preaching at an open-air meeting in Tennessee with a beautiful, responsive crowd of people but it was extremely hot. The sun was beating down and I prayed aloud. I said, "Lord, please can you place a cloud over the sun to shelter these people that are getting burnt from the sun." You know, the Lord put a cloud over that sun! It stayed there until the end of the meeting.

You might think, "Oh Angus, that was just a coincidence." Funny you should say that because the other clouds on either side were sailing past merrily but that cloud remained, covering the sun and sheltering God's people. Yes, the Lord hears us and He speaks to us. Speak to Him today and then listen to what He has to say to you.

YOUR STAFF

"The LORD is my helper; I will not fear.
What can man do to me?"
HEBREWS 13:6

Jesus Christ is our rod and our staff (see Psalm 23:4). He is our protector and our comforter, especially in tough times. You know, Moses had a staff. He used that staff, which the Lord told him to take with him when he confronted Pharaoh, and he told Pharaoh to let God's people go. He used that staff for miracles.

Remember, he threw the staff down and it turned into a snake (see Exodus 7). Then he picked the snake up by the tail and it turned back into a staff. He opened the Red Sea by stretching out his hand holding the staff.

A staff is also used as a support when hiking in the mountains. On long, tough journeys you need a staff. You know, I love to carve sticks. I sit quietly with a knife, and I contemplate and meditate. I carve staffs that I then give to people as gifts. We get the wood from the thornbushes in Zululand because they grow very slowly, and are heavy and very strong. We need to carry our staff wherever we go to support us along the way.

Today, when you go out, take your staff with you—I am talking about Jesus—and don't go anywhere without Him.

SAVED!

"Whoever calls on the name
of the LORD shall be saved."
ACTS 2:21

What a beautiful promise for sinners like us! Romans 10:13 says exactly the same thing. "Whoever" means anybody. That's right!

Billy Bray was one of those who called upon the name of the Lord. Billy was a self-confessed drunkard. He was a tin miner from Cornwall. He could not pass a pub or a bar without going in and getting drunk, spending all his hard-earned money on alcohol. Then Billy Bray met Jesus and his life was instantly transformed…he never touched a drop of alcohol again.

You know, the Lord spoke to me once so clearly, He said, "You have forsaken your first love" (see Revelation 2:4). Maybe you have done that today. It is no good saying, "In 1965, I gave my life to Christ." Are you full of the joy of the Lord today? Is Jesus as real to you as He was when you gave your life to Christ?

Remember, today could be the best day of the rest of your life so remember your first love—the Lord Jesus Christ.

TAKE YOUR TIME

But those who wait on the LORD shall renew
their strength; they shall mount up with
wings like eagles, they shall run and not be
weary, they shall walk and not faint.
ISAIAH 40:31

One of the most difficult things for us to do is to wait. We have been programmed to do everything at full pace—whether it is eating, exercising or making decisions. But this is dangerous! When we do something in haste, it is very often not of God. Now I am speaking from bitter experience. Every bad decision that I have made in my life has been because I rushed it.

Remember the story of Lazarus when he died (see John 11:17-44). His sister Martha said to Jesus, "Lord, if You had been here, my brother would not have died." Still, even after four days, Jesus raised him from the dead. I am a beekeeper and the bees have taught me many lessons about not rushing. You see, when you keep bees, timing is of the essence. If I go to my hives on a cloudy, cool, overcast day the bees are well-behaved. But if I go on a hot, windy day, I am asking for trouble. I also have to be sure that my smoker is working to calm them down and that I put my bee suit on correctly, because if I don't they will sting me.

Today, take your time. Wait on the Lord and He will direct your path. Don't rush into things that you might later regret.

RETIREMENT?

Those who are planted in the house of the LORD
shall flourish in the courts of our God. They shall
still bear fruit in old age; they shall be fresh and
flourishing, to declare that the LORD is upright;
He is my rock, and there is no unrighteousness in Him.
PSALM 92:13-15

There is no such word as "retirement" in the Bible, only pro-
motion! One of my Bible heroes is Caleb. He had a different
spirit in him than the other spies Moses sent to check out the
Promised Land.

When Caleb was 85 years old and the time had finally come
to divide up the Promised Land, Caleb said to Joshua, "Now, as
you can see, the LORD has kept me alive and well as He promised. Today I am eighty-five years old. I am as strong now as I
was when Moses sent me on that journey. So give me the hill
country that the LORD promised me. You will remember that as
scouts we found the descendants of Anak living there in great,
walled towns. But if the LORD is with me, I will drive them out
of the land, just as the LORD said" (Joshua 14:10-12). And he
did. Remember, your attitude determines your altitude.

Don't waste a single precious moment in your life. Go out
today and live it for Jesus and also for your fellow man no matter your age.

SAYING SORRY

"If we confess our sins, He is faithful
and just to forgive us our sins and to
cleanse us from all unrighteousness."

1 JOHN 1:9

I want to tell you, my dear friend, there is immense power and freedom in just saying sorry. It simply defuses everything. You see, the devil is very aware of this and wants to stoke the fires of trouble and make things much worse than they already are. He says, "Don't say sorry. You have got your rights. Stand your ground." But Jesus says, "You surrendered your rights when you gave your life to Me."

Now you might be thinking, "But I haven't done anything wrong." Well, Jesus says in Romans 3:23, "…for all have sinned and fall short of the glory of God." That wonderful English preacher, Charles Spurgeon, said, "Sorrow for sin is a perpetual rain, a sweet, soft shower which, to a truly gracious man, lasts all his life long. He is always sorrowful that he has sinned." Isn't that beautiful?

So what stops us from confessing our sins, from saying sorry? Only one thing: pride. Now Jesus says, "Whoever desires to come after Me, let him deny himself, and take up his cross, and follow Me" (Mark 8:34).

Don't let the devil hold you back from saying sorry and getting on with your life.

GENEROUS PEOPLE

"Now all who believed were together,
and had all things in common, and sold
their possessions and goods, and divided
them among all, as anyone had need."
ACTS 2:44-45

You know, it is very hard for a hungry person with a rumbling stomach or a freezing cold person who is shivering to hear the Gospel preached. Their physical needs need to be met before you can tell them about Jesus. James says: "…and one of you says to them, 'Depart in peace, be warmed and filled,' but you do not give them the things which are needed for the body, what does it profit?" (James 2:16).

You see faith is not just talking; it is action. You might think, "But I can hardly feed my own family. I don't have anything to give anyone." But God always takes care of a generous person.

Do you remember the story of the starving widow and her little boy in 1 Kings 17? She only had enough flour and oil to make one cake, then they were both going to lie down and die. But the prophet Elijah came and what did he do? He asked for something to eat and she gave him their last cake! Miraculously the flour and the oil never ran out and they had food right through the duration of that drought. God takes care of His own.

Go out today and help a needy person and you will be helping the Lord.

WORDS OF LIFE

Then He arose and rebuked the wind,
and said to the sea, "Peace, be still!"
And the wind ceased and there was a
great calm. But He said to them, "Why are you
so fearful? How is it that you have no faith?"

MARK 4:39-40

God simply spoke the word! Jesus is the Word as we read in John 1:1: "In the beginning was the Word…" You and I have the word of God on our very lips, why don't we use it more? When Jesus was tempted in the desert by the devil, He used the spoken word against the devil (see Matthew 4:1-11). What you say is what you become.

We need to be so careful how we speak. A negative, hurtful word can literally destroy someone. You need to be very careful how you speak to your children.

Sometimes they test you severely and you say, "You little devils! You'll never amount to anything." Don't say that! That can destroy a little boy or girl; they will remember that for years to come. But a godly, uplifting, wholesome word can restore, heal and build up a person.

Make that phone call today. A kind word might even save a life. Let's be sensitive today and let's speak life to one another.

THE COMFORTER

When the Day of Pentecost had fully come, they were all with one accord in one place. And suddenly there came a sound from heaven, as of a rushing mighty wind, and it filled the whole house where they were sitting. Then there appeared to them divided tongues, as of fire, and one sat upon each of them. And they were all filled with the Holy Spirit and began to speak with other tongues, as the Spirit gave them utterance.

ACTS 2:1-5

Jesus said in John 16:7 that it is to our advantage that He goes back to His Father so that He can send His Holy Spirit to comfort us, guide us in truth and give us His peace.

I personally experienced an encounter with the Holy Spirit visiting us in Israel, at Ein Gedi, when I was speaking to a group of pilgrims who had come from all over the world.

It was an encounter that I shall never, ever forget as long as I live. I had read from Acts 2 and then I said, "Lord Jesus, please do it again," and a rushing mighty wind came from nowhere and just about blew us off the platform!

Oh, my dear friend, He is the Comforter. I want to tell you today, to speak to Him. Allow Him to comfort you, to put His loving arms around you.

THE NAME

*"And His name, through faith in His name,
has made this man strong..."*
ACTS 3:16

When Peter and John had prayed for the lame man and he was healed, the people thought that they had done it. But no, it wasn't them. It was the power in the Name. I want to say to you today that power, hope and freedom are all in the Name. That's right, the name is Jesus! He alone is the Savior of the world. His name means Immanuel: God with us (see Matthew 1:23).

Oh, my dear friend, He is not "the Man upstairs", or your "pal". No, He is God made flesh! The Bible tells us that it is the Name which is above any other name. In fact, very soon every knee shall bow and every tongue shall confess that Jesus Christ is Lord (see Philippians 2:10). Do you know that wars have been started because of that Name? Do you know that millions of people have died as martyrs because they will not deny that Name? That's where the power lies. It is Jesus who is the Miracle Worker.

You know, when I use the Name of Jesus, and I ask Him to bring rain, He brings rain. When I ask Him to heal the sick, He heals the sick. When you mention the Name of Jesus in faith, it is like everything becomes electric. Speak to Him today.

FOR HIS GLORY

...as it is written, "He who glories,
let him glory in the LORD."
1 CORINTHIANS 1:31

Never touch God's glory! Always give Him all the praise and the honor. James 2:5 says, "Listen, my beloved brethren: Has God not chosen the poor of this world to be rich in faith and heirs of the kingdom which He promised to those who love Him?" Our Lord specializes in using nobodies and then He makes them into somebodies.

You see, God will not share His glory with any man. Often, as a new Christian, I used to say, "Lord, why don't You use some famous people, wealthy people or some influential people to do Your work?" And I felt the Lord saying, "No, I don't want anybody to take the glory." You know, God took twelve nobodies and with those twelve nobodies, He changed the whole world.

He took a young teenager to slay a mighty giant. That's right, David killed Goliath when he was still a teenager with nothing more than a sling and a stone…Who got the glory? It was God. Then He took a man who had completely blown it and who was hiding in the desert looking after his father-in-law's sheep. He took him at eighty years of age to deliver an entire nation from slavery. That's right, I am talking about Moses. Jesus can use you and me as well if we can only believe.

God takes nobodies like you and me, and with us, He will change the world.

LACKING WISDOM

"If any of you lacks wisdom, let him ask of God,
who gives to all liberally and without reproach,
and it will be given to him. But let him ask in faith,
with no doubting, for he who doubts is like a wave
of the sea driven and tossed by the wind."
JAMES 1:5-6

Every one of us needs advice in some way. We need advice for the big decisions and the small ones. And how do we get advice? We ask our Father. We pray in faith and He will answer us.

Many years ago, my late dad used to live in a little cottage just behind us. I would go and sit on the porch outside his little cottage, and we would talk. I would ask him for advice and many times he would just say to me, "Son, I don't know. I don't know the answer but…" then he would tell me what he felt and that advice I have never forgotten.

Please do not become too proud to ask for advice. Ask your elders or those you respect and they will help you and give you godly advice. It might not be the advice that you are looking for. You might not even like it at the moment but it will bless you and it will help you in the future. Most important of all, ask Jesus today and He will answer you.

LIVING LETTERS

"The only letter of recommendation we need
is you yourselves. Your lives are a letter written
in our hearts; everyone can read it and
recognize our good work among you."

2 CORINTHIANS 3:2 NLT

We need to walk the talk. We need to be a living epistle, a letter. People need to be able to read us with their eyes when they see us walking down the street. There needs to be a difference in us by our lifestyle and not necessarily by anything else—not by our college degree, our university qualifications or our sporting attributes. No, you see the greatest miracle is the change in a person's life after they accept Jesus as their Savior.

Remember the story of Zacchaeus in Luke 19? He was a terrible man. He was robbing his own people. He climbed up a tree because he was a short man and he wanted to see Jesus. Jesus was walking through town, looked up at the tree and said, "Zacchaeus, I am coming to your house today to have a meal with you." There was a complete and instant transformation in Zacchaeus' life. Can you imagine what the people must have said as he was walking down the street the next day? A thief turned into an angel overnight.

That's what you and I have to do my dear friend. We need to change. People need to read us like a book. They need to say, "You see that man? He was a scoundrel but now he has become a saint. He has had a change in his life. He has met Jesus Christ, the Savior of the world."

BECOMING NEW

Then Peter said, "Silver and gold I do not have,
but what I do have I give you: In the name of
Jesus Christ of Nazareth, rise up and walk."

ACTS 3:6

If you introduce someone to Jesus, then you have given them everything they need. Remember, the beggar who was sitting at the gate? He had been there from birth and he was begging for some money.

Peter said, "We don't have any money but what we do have we are going to give to you." And what did he give to that lame man? He gave him a key. That's right, a key that opens the door to life itself. That is what it did. It gave that lame man healing; he could walk again. It gave him a multitude of blessings, opportunities and new beginnings.

How many testimonies do we hear of folk who have met Jesus and whose lives have been completely changed in an instant? Now I am one of them, that is right! After I responded to an altar call many years ago, my life was changed forever. I went home and I started farming more efficiently. I also became a better, more loving husband and father.

Do you know something? If you do the same thing today, it can happen to you too.

TRUST GOD, NOT MAN

No king is saved by the multitude of an army;
a mighty man is not delivered by great strength.
Behold, the eye of the LORD is on those who
fear Him, on those who hope in His mercy.
PSALM 33:16, 18

Many years ago I was planting a very expensive crop of seed maize. I had all the experts advise me on how to plant it: Put in the right amount of fertilizer; use the right seed spacing; make sure there are no weeds; and don't forget to top dress with fertilizer. I did everything according to the book but I still got it wrong. My calibration for the seed spacing was totally out…

When the maize came up, there were huge gaps in the crop and I really thought I was going to go bankrupt. I was so despondent. Then I remembered that lovely Scripture in John 16:33, which says, "In Me you may have peace. In the world you will have tribulation; but be of good cheer, I have overcome the world."

I put my trust in the Lord. That particular year we had a terrible drought and you know, with those big gaps in between the plants, the maize crops had more room to absorb the moisture and we had a gigantic crop of maize! It didn't make a bumper crop but it covered all my costs. Sometimes we make a mistake and put our trust in man's ability, but it's our trust in God that will see us through.

ONE GENUINE MIRACLE

Then they knew that it was he who sat
begging alms at the Beautiful Gate of the
temple; and they were filled with wonder and
amazement at what had happened to him.

ACTS 3:10

The story of the lame beggar reminds me of one of the Mighty Men Conferences that we had at Shalom years ago. It was a Saturday morning and we were so excited. There were thousands of men gathered together in the presence of God. It was a very hot day and when I finished preaching I suddenly collapsed. My son Andy caught me.

I had a heart attack and then another one. Two heart attacks, and with the second one my blood pressure went down to zero. They got a helicopter to take me to hospital. As the helicopter left the farm, the pilot tilted the helicopter. I was strapped on a stretcher and saw tens of thousands of hands praying for me for a miracle.

And I want to tell you, when that helicopter touched down and the heart specialist examined me, he said, "Mr Buchan, there is nothing wrong with you, you may go home." A miracle had been performed. That Sunday morning, I was preaching… Yes, I felt like I had been run over by a truck but Jesus was there. When I made the altar call, men were weeping all over. Not because of me, but because of the miracle that I was standing there preaching. Jesus is the Miracle Worker! Don't ever forget that.

PRAY FOR YOUR LEADERS

"Look, this day your eyes have seen that the LORD
delivered you today into my hand in the cave,
and someone urged me to kill you. But my eye
spared you, and I said, 'I will not stretch out my
hand against my lord, for he is the LORD's anointed.'"

1 SAMUEL 24:10

When King Saul was trying to kill David, David had an opportunity to kill Saul in the cave but let him go instead. David cut off the corner of King Saul's robe and when Saul was down the hill, he shouted out to him, "Look what I have. I could have killed you but I didn't because I know that I may not touch God's anointed."

I want to say to you today that we are not permitted to touch God's anointed. Instead, we should pray for our leaders. I am talking about Christian leaders particularly. We need to pray that God will keep them safe and accountable. The danger is when men and women get separated and they have no one to stand with them.

I praise God that I have four trustees and these men hold me accountable. I have to tell them exactly what I am doing, where I am going and where I am not going. It gives me a tremendous sense of security. I want to encourage you to do the same. Get men or women around you who can advise you in your day-to-day living and keep you safe.

HOW ARE YOU FEELING?

"Repent therefore and be converted, that your
sins may be blotted out, so that times of refreshing
may come from the presence of the Lord."

ACTS 3:19

How are you feeling today, are you feeling condemned? Are you feeling like you are a loser? Maybe you are suffering from depression and you just can't get out of that bottomless pit? Maybe you are feeling guilty because you did something you know was wrong? Well, I want to tell you today that Jesus Christ wants to set you free.

Romans 8:1 says, "There is therefore now no condemnation to those who are in Christ Jesus." The Lord wants to give us a time of renewal, a moment in our lives when we repent and say sorry.

I remember that time in my own life: It was the most wonderful time I have ever experienced, when I said, "Lord, I can't anymore. I want You to please take over." And I handed it all over to the Master. First Peter 5:7 tells us to cast our cares on Him because He cares for you and me. Why don't you do it today?

It's like driving down the highway and feeling so tired. Just pull over, get out of the driver's seat and let the Master drive the car for you. You will be totally refreshed and full of the joy of the Lord.

ETERNAL SECURITY

*"And I give them eternal life, and they
shall never perish; neither shall anyone
snatch them out of My hand."*
JOHN 10:28

Wow, eternal security! Eternal means valid for all time. It means there is just no end to it! To never perish means we will live forever and ever in the presence of Almighty God! My dear friend, Jesus has got us in the very palm of His hand and no one will snatch us from Him.

The safest place to be is nestled in the loving arms of our heavenly Father. I remember years ago, at a meeting, I felt the Lord say I need to pray for people suffering from insomnia. I drew a picture in my mind for them. I said, "I want you to imagine our heavenly Father sitting in a big easy armchair and He says to you, 'Come up, My child. Come and sit on My lap.' You get up onto His lap and put your head onto His chest. He puts His big strong arms around you and then He just rocks you to sleep." Now that is a lot better than counting sheep!

The next evening one of the ladies I had prayed for never came back to the meeting. Two days later I saw her and she said, "I came back from work. I sat down and remembered what you said. I said, 'Lord, I am in Your hands' and I fell fast asleep. I never even made it to the meeting." Jesus loves you. Today remember He is our eternal security.

HOTLINE TO HEAVEN

"...And if he has committed sins, he will be forgiven.
Confess your trespasses to one another, and pray
for one another, that you may be healed. The effective,
fervent prayer of a righteous man avails much."
JAMES 5:15-16

It has happened that when I drive into town in my truck and I stop at the traffic lights, another farmer pulls up alongside me and says, "Listen, can you send a prayer up to the Man Upstairs and ask Him to send us a bit of sunshine?" Then off he drives with a big smile on his face.

I used to get a little bit angry and think this was being totally disrespectful towards God. Then I felt the Holy Spirit say to me, "No, don't be like that, Angus. That man obviously believes that you hear from Me and that's why he's asking you to pray and send the sunshine." They call it a hotline to heaven.

You've got a hotline to heaven. I know it's always tongue-in-cheek, but I think there's a lot of truth behind that. People really believe that we, as children of the Lord, can hear clearly from God. So let's not be offended by that. Let us take it in our stride and say, "Yes, of course, we will and we are praying for you as well."

NO TURNING BACK

Jesus said to him, "No one, having put his hand to the
plow, and looking back, is fit for the kingdom of God."

LUKE 9:62

As a farmer, if I keep looking behind me to see whether the plow is deep enough into the soil, I'll lose my direction. Instead of plowing a straight line, it'll look like a snake by the time the field is finished. We have got to look forward and put the past behind us.

In 2010, I experienced something on the farm that I shall never forget as long as I live. Thousands of men all came to the farm to join together to hear the Word of God. It was one of the most amazing experiences of my entire life. God said to me almost audibly, "This is going to be the last one. You must pass on the baton to the younger men so they can do it all over the world."

It was extremely hard for me and a lot of people wrote to ask me to keep going. But the Lord gave me a clear word to pass the baton on, which I duly did. And what happened? There are Mighty Men Conferences taking place all over our beloved nation of South Africa and indeed the world. Why? Because it was time to move forward. Today, don't hold onto the past, let it go. God has new plans for you.

IT IS FINISHED

"When God raised up His servant, Jesus, He sent Him first to you people of Israel, to bless you by turning each of you back from your sinful ways."

ACTS 3:26 NLT

Do you know that there has only ever been one Person in the history of this world who can turn us away from our iniquities? His name is Jesus Christ. He is the only One who died for our sins. When He said on the cross, "It is finished!" (John 19:30), He meant it. Jesus paid the full price for our sin. Therefore, because He died for us He has the authority to say, like He has said to millions of people before us, "Your sins are forgiven. Go and sin no more."

A referee has the authority to make the final decision in an international rugby or football match and a high court judge has authority to pass the final ruling. In the same way, Jesus' decision to forgive us is final. If we ask for forgiveness today from our Lord, and sincerely mean it, He is able and willing to forgive us of every one of our sins.

Why don't you ask Him today to set you free? Why don't you lay down that heavy bag of sins you've been carrying on your back for so long? Just say, "Lord, I am sorry. I made a mistake. Please forgive me." And He will do it. Do it today.

JUNE 20

CHRIST IN US

"Now when they saw the boldness of Peter and
John, and perceived that they were uneducated
and untrained men, they marveled. And then
they realized that they had been with Jesus."

ACTS 4:13

There is no substitute for being in the Lord's presence. What caused the religious leaders to marvel at the apostles? It was their boldness. They realized that these men had actually been with Jesus. You see, even though the religious leaders had devoted their lives to studying the Scriptures, they could not heal the lame man sitting at the gate outside the temple. But Peter and John could because they did it in faith and in the name of Jesus Christ of Nazareth. They had spent time in His presence, which made all the difference.

One of my favorite Scriptures in the Bible is Colossians 1:27, which says that it is Christ in us that is the hope of glory. It is not us; it is Christ in us. You and I need to spend more time in the presence of the Lord.

When I was a young farmer, experts would come from the university to tell the farmers how to do certain things. However, they only knew the theory but not the practical. For example, they could not even start the tractor because they had never done it before. We need to roll up our sleeves and get stuck in.

We need to get to know Jesus personally, and then go out and do exactly what He did.

TRUST IN THE NAME OF JESUS

"I will leave in your midst a meek and humble people,
and they shall trust in the name of the LORD."

ZEPHANIAH 3:12

The poor people of this world have no other name to trust in but the name of Jesus Christ. They have little personal reputation to call upon and very few connections in the business world to lean on. That is why they are unlikely to turn away from God, more so than those who are wealthy in this world. What about you and me? Are we trusting in the name of our Lord Jesus or not?

Paul wrote in Romans 5:3-4 (NLT): "We can rejoice, too, when we run into problems and trials, for we know that they help us develop endurance. And endurance develops strength of character, and character strengthens our confident hope of salvation." It was only when Paul was brought down low, according to his fellow religious leaders, that he changed. Even though he had lost all his "friends", he never turned his back on the name of Jesus.

That same Paul wrote a big part of the New Testament under the inspiration of the Holy Spirit. He traveled the world as it was known then, taking the gospel to the Gentiles. He died as a martyr for his faith, never denying Christ. Today, we must be sure that no matter what happens, the Lord remains the most important Person in our lives.

HE WILL GO WITH US

The LORD replied, "I will personally go with you,
Moses, and I will give you rest—everything will be fine
for you." Then Moses said, "If You don't personally
go with us, don't make us leave this place."

EXODUS 33:14-15 NLT

If God doesn't go with us, we don't want to go. The Lord has promised us today that He will go with us. God never gives us something that we can't handle, which is great news for us. This does not mean that there will be no hardships along the way. Just look at Moses when he took the children of Israel into the Promised Land.

When I was a little boy, if my dad went with me, I would go anywhere. I was fearless. I was afraid of nothing because my dad was standing right next to me. Jesus says in Hebrews 13:5 that He will never leave or forsake us. Do we believe that? If we do, we have nothing to fear. It is fear that makes people sick, but the confidence that the Lord will go with us neutralizes all fear.

Remember the story of David and Goliath? You can imagine that nine-foot-tall undefeated giant, with his scarred face and huge spear. When Goliath looked at that little boy and saw the confidence that David had in God, he knew that he was done for. We have nothing to fear but fear itself. Today, let's be like Moses and say, "Lord, if You are not going with us, we are not going."

THE PRODIGAL SON

And the son said to him, "Father, I have sinned
against heaven and in your sight, and am
no longer worthy to be called your son."

LUKE 15:21

This is without a doubt one of the saddest verses in the Bible. The prodigal son came and said, "I want my inheritance and I want it now." His dear father probably had to scramble to get the money. The Bible tells us that his son went off into the far country and lived a life that was wasted.

And when his son returned, what did the father say? "Well, you deserve it!" or, "Get out of my sight, I don't want to see you ever again!" No, he didn't! He said: "Bring out the best robe and put it on him, and put a ring on his hand and sandals on his feet. And bring the fatted calf here and kill it, and let us eat and be merry" (Luke 15:22-23).

We need to lavish a lot of grace on our children and our loved ones. Many of us make mistakes and sometimes we do things the wrong way round. We must always keep the door open so that when the prodigal son or daughter comes home we can love them, put the past behind us and move on.

That is what Jesus did for us on the Cross of Calvary. He paid for our sins and said, "It is finished," and now we need to move on.

STEALING

"You shall not steal."
EXODUS 20:15

A while ago, I was having my quiet time in the bush outside a little thatched cottage that Jill and I had booked, and I was at total peace. It was early in the morning and I was taking in the glory of God, listening to the sounds of the African bush and the beautiful, peaceful creation of God.

Suddenly, a huge monkey pounced on my table. In a flash, he stole a bright yellow banana that I was looking forward to eating. As amusing as this may sound, it broke right through my time of solitary meditation with the Master.

That commandment, "Thou shalt not steal" made a big practical impact on my life. It is not just the stealing, but the infringement on one's privacy that is saddening.

My prayer for you and me today is that we will not do that. And I'm not just talking about stealing physical things, I am talking about stealing other people's ideas, emotions and even attitudes, and most of all, stealing time from our loved ones.

In Matthew 26:40, Jesus was in the Garden of Gethsemane. He came to the disciples and found them sleeping, He said to Peter, "What! Could you not watch with Me one hour?"

Don't steal time from God. He so desperately wants to help and spend time with you.

RESTING

And He said to them, "Come aside by yourselves
to a deserted place and rest a while."
MARK 6:31

A dear lady wrote me a message a while ago. She said, "Please tell people to be careful. My husband lost his family because he was addicted to work..." That is exactly what happened with the disciples. You see, they were so busy telling Jesus all the good things that they had done. But it did not impress the Lord. His response was, "Come and rest a while."

We need to be careful. You know, we always talk about laziness, which is unacceptable to God, but the opposite of laziness is just as bad. I know, I have been there myself. I was caught on that treadmill of work. When my wife would ask, "Angus, when are you going to come home and just be with the children and me?" I would say, "I am doing this for you. I am keeping those fences straight and I am keeping those cattle fat. I am making sure no weeds are growing underneath the maize crop..." But that wasn't for Jill and the children, that was for my ego. I remember the Lord speaking to me once almost audibly. He said, "Your busyness, Angus, is making Me weary. Come aside."

I want to say to you today, take time out and rest otherwise you might lose your very family.

OUR SWORD

And they were not able to resist the wisdom
and the Spirit by which he spoke. And all who
sat in the council, looking steadfastly at him,
saw his face as the face of an angel.

ACTS 6:10, 15

People are not interested in what we say, they want to hear what Jesus says. It's the Word of God that sets the captives free, not William Shakespeare or Sigmund Freud. No, it is the spoken Word of God! That was exactly what Stephen was doing in today's Scripture passage. People are starving for God's Word in these last days.

Stephen spoke the Word of God and he mesmerized the people with all the answers to life that they were looking for. You see, it is all in the Book, that's right! Healing, family, business…All the answers are there and they are very simple. That is why the devil is trying so hard to stamp out the reading of the Bible. He does not want us to quote Jesus.

Ephesians 6:17 tells us that the sword of the Spirit is the Word of God. It is the only weapon that the Christian has. We have got to get it out of the scabbard. It is rusty. It's blunt.

We need to sharpen it up and when the devil comes at us with accusations, we return his accusations with the Word of God—that defeats him every time. Be a soldier armed with the Word and the glory of God will shine through you!

WHAT A PROMISE!

I have been young, and now am old; yet I
have not seen the righteous forsaken, nor his
descendants begging bread. He is ever merciful,
and lends; and his descendants are blessed.

PSALM 37:25-26

This is a promise from God that you can bank on. I can personally bear witness to it. Do it God's way and He will do the rest. Remember, God does not tell lies. Numbers 23:19 says, "God is not a man, that He should lie, nor a son of man, that He should repent. Has He said, and will He not do? Or has He spoken, and will He not make it good?"

Have a good look at your own life and ask yourself an honest question: *Has God ever abandoned me?* Why should He change now? Just keep on planting good seed, like a good farmer and the Great Farmer, Jesus Himself, will bring it to full harvest.

Keep your eyes on the Lord and He will take care of your children and every need that you have. Remember, "He who calls you is faithful, who also will do it" (1 Thessalonians 5:24).

KEEP YOURSELF UNSPOTTED

Depart from evil, and do good; and dwell forevermore.
For the LORD loves justice, and does not forsake
His saints; they are preserved forever, but the
descendants of the wicked shall be cut off.
The righteous shall inherit the land, and dwell in it forever.
PSALM 37:27–29

These days it sometimes appears that evil and corruption are multiplied and the wicked are getting away with it…but that's not true according to our Scripture verse! Jesus tells us to take care of the widow and the orphan, to do good. He will worry about the wicked.

If we look at James 1:27, it says, "Pure and undefiled religion before God and the Father is this: to visit orphans and widows in their trouble, and to keep oneself unspotted from the world." That is what we have got to do. Leave the wicked person unto the Lord, He will sort him out.

When I was a young boy, I left school very early and worked in a tire factory. It was a dirty and tough job, but now and again one of our customers, an old man who owned a fleet of old trucks, would arrive on a very hot afternoon with a big toolbox full of ice cream for every one of us in the factory. He did it out of the goodness of his heart.

Today, do good, dwell in the land and leave the rest to Jesus.

ALL WE NEED

"The LORD is our God, the Lord alone.
And you must love the LORD your God with
all your heart, all your soul, and all your strength.
And you must commit yourselves wholeheartedly
to these commands that I am giving you today."
DEUTERONOMY 6:4-6 NLT

We need to have a good look at our hearts and ask ourselves: "Is Jesus enough?" Matthew 6:33 says, "But seek first the kingdom of God and His righteousness, and all these things shall be added to you." It is not fair to put our trust and hope in our spouse or family because they are mere mortals. We have to put our hope and our expectations in God. He has to come first and He has to be enough.

I remember a few years back I was invited to speak at a conference to a large group of pastors, evangelists and teachers. I asked them a question, "How much do you love Jesus?" Of course they all responded very positively: "With all that we have." And then I asked them another question: "If God told you that He never wanted you to preach another sermon in your life, would you still love Him the same?" I must be honest with you, the whole assembly went very quiet. We need to ask ourselves today: "Is Jesus all we need?"

CATHEDRALS AND TEMPLES

Thus says the LORD: "Heaven is My throne,
and earth is My footstool. Where is the house that you
will build Me? And where is the place of My rest?"

ISAIAH 66:1

We cannot put God in a box. He cannot be housed in a man-made temple. I have been to London, to that magnificent work of art that is St Paul's Cathedral. It is incredible, but too small to house the King of kings and the Lord of lords. You have often heard me speak about my green cathedral—the maize fields on the farm! Walking through those fields as a young man worshiping God…what an experience!

I have visited prisoners in maximum security prisons all over the world and some of these men are there for life. They will never come out. They are sitting in prison where they can hardly see the sun. But you know the amazing thing is that when they meet the living Christ as their Savior, they are more free to worship God than many of us who go into these majestic cathedrals but have never truly found the Lord Jesus Christ as our Savior.

First Corinthians 6:19 says that our bodies are the temples of the Holy Spirit. Today, you might be in a wheelchair, or in hospital, or even in a prison cell, but that will not hold you back because Jesus lives inside your heart. Praise Him because He is worthy.

GOD WITH US

"God will be with you..."
GENESIS 48:21

This is a wonderful reassurance for you and me living in these troubled times. Maybe today you have lost a loved one and you are battling, saying to yourself, "How am I going to cope with life?" Maybe your business has gone bankrupt or your family has immigrated and you feel all alone.

I want to tell you today that Jesus has given us His Holy Spirit, the Helper. Remember, when Jesus went back to heaven, He said, "It is to your advantage that I go away; for if I do not go away, the Helper will not come to you; but if I depart, I will send Him to you" (John 16:7). We are no longer orphans, the Holy Spirit is with you as you are reading this. We need to encourage ourselves with this great news.

In 1 Samuel 17:43, we see a small boy with five stones and a sling take on Goliath. He had said to David, "Am I a dog, that you come to me with sticks?" What was David's response? "I come to you in the name of the LORD of hosts, the God of the armies of Israel" (1 Samuel 17:45).

Today, when you go out, remember that you are not going alone. You are going with the Lord of hosts, the King of kings. His name is Jesus and He will not forsake you.

FIGHT FIRE WITH FIRE

"The thief does not come except to steal, and to kill,
and to destroy. I have come that they may have life,
and that they may have it more abundantly."
JOHN 10:10

Have you heard the saying, "Fight fire with fire"? In the winter when the grass is tinderbox dry, we burn some firebreaks on the farm. One time, my son and I had all the water carts there and the fire fighting equipment should the fire run wild, but when that fire started roaring, there was an absolute wall of fire coming against us. How did we fight it? With water carts and hoses and water? No, what we did was we put fire in and we back-burned it. So the fire put the fire out. You and I need to do the same. The devil is a liar, a thief and a coward…when you stand up against him, he always backs off.

Father God has given us all the weapons that we need to fight the darkness:

1. He has given us His Holy Spirit;
2. He has given us His Holy Word, the Bible; and
3. He has given us the power of faithful prayer.

We must remember that even as Jesus stood up against the powers of darkness when He was tempted in the desert (see Matthew 4), we need to do the same.

DON'T PUT THINGS OFF

LORD, make me to know my end, and what is
the measure of my days, that I may know how
frail I am. Indeed, You have made my days as
handbreadths, and my age is as nothing before You;
certainly every man at his best state is but vapor.

PSALM 39:4-5

Life is but a vapor. That is what the Word of God is telling us. Don't put off something that you can do today. Phone, write or, best of all, visit that person you have an issue with today because tomorrow doesn't belong to us; tomorrow might be too late.

Our farm is situated on the edge of a plateau and there is a huge valley right next to us. Often, very early in the morning, the valley is completely covered in a blanket of mist and you cannot see anything. When the sun rises, it burns off the vapor, that blanket of mist, and in a few minutes it is gone forever. Now Jesus says our lives here on earth are just as short and just as fragile. We do not have time to waste, we need to get our house in order.

You can't keep putting things off. You need to do it today because you may have regrets. Today is the only day that we have; tomorrow might be too late. So today make a definite effort to put everything in order and then, when the Lord calls you, you will be ready to go in peace.

NO TURNING BACK

"You did not choose Me, but I chose you and
appointed you that you should go and bear fruit,
and that your fruit should remain, that whatever
you ask the Father in My name He may give you."

JOHN 15:16

Jesus chose you and me; we did not choose Him. That is great news, isn't it? It takes the heat off. Moses couldn't speak properly. He said to God, "I can't," and God said to him, "You can."

Queen Esther thought she couldn't and Mordecai said, "Yet who knows whether you have come to the kingdom for such a time as this?" (Esther 4:14). When Jesus calls us, He also equips us and He never reconsiders. It is a done deal. That is good news, isn't it?

If we have made a mistake or dropped the ball, say sorry to the Lord, stand up, dust yourself off and get straight back into the race. Get back into the fight. Remember, Jesus appointed us therefore we are qualified to do the job.

A young Jewish maiden saved a nation from annihilation. A so-called failure hiding in the desert took the Jews out of slavery—trust God for what you've been called to do.

PRAISE HIM WHEN IT'S HARD

He has put a new song in my mouth—
praise to our God; many will see it
and fear, and will trust in the LORD.
PSALM 40:3

How are we feeling today? Maybe a bit down? We need to sing a new song just like King David did. He was in a miry pit. He called out to the Lord and God brought him out and set him on a rock, on solid ground. That is worth praising Jesus for, isn't it? There is power in praise.

It is not about your circumstances or about how you feel today, it's about the fact that if we praise the Lord, He lifts us up. I remember sitting at the dining room table in our little house at about 4 o'clock in the afternoon. I was witnessing to an alcoholic. This man had lost everything and I was saying to him, "God will undertake for you."

Just then we heard banging on our tin roof. Massive hail stones were falling down and our beautiful green maize crop that was standing tall was flattened in about five minutes! I was devastated. This alcoholic was watching me and I gritted my teeth and said, "I am still going to praise the Lord, irrespective." I did and we sang praises to Him. Three days later that maize crop stood up and we reaped a massive crop that year. The stalks were a bit bent, but they were full of maize. Praise the Lord!

YOU CAN'T BUY THE GOSPEL

But Peter said to him, "Your money perish
with you, because you thought that the gift
of God could be purchased with money!"
ACTS 8:20

Simon the sorcerer, the magician, thought that he could buy the power of Jesus Christ and he was severely rebuked by Peter, the Lord's apostle. We cannot earn our way to heaven. We cannot buy our way home. So what do we do? Well, we simply say to Jesus, "Thank You for Your loving grace."

The definition of "grace" is undeserved loving-kindness or unmerited favor. It was very difficult for me when I became a Christian. I was brought up in the old-school ways and my Scottish parents taught me: If you can't pay for it, then don't buy it. It was extremely hard for me to accept that Jesus Christ paid for everything I owe, and that is why I love Him so much.

Once I went to a restaurant with Jill and we had a nice hearty meal. When it came time to pay for my meal, the waitress came along and said, "Sir, did you enjoy your meal?" "Yes, I did. Can I please have the bill?" And she said, "Sir, it has already been paid for! There was a gentleman who walked out of the restaurant 15 minutes ago and he paid for your entire meal." That was very humbling. Obviously, I was very grateful, I didn't know who he was and I couldn't thank him. That is what Jesus Christ says, "I have paid for everything. You don't owe a thing." You can't buy the Gospel.

SPEAK UP

I have proclaimed the good news of righteousness
in the great assembly; indeed, I do not restrain
my lips, O LORD, You Yourself know. I have not
hidden Your righteousness within my heart; I have
declared Your faithfulness and Your salvation.

PSALM 40:9-10

There are no secret agents in God's kingdom. We have an obligation to speak up and share the Good News with everyone who will hear us. The Apostle Paul was fearless when it came to speaking up for the Master. He regularly got beaten, stoned and abused, just for telling people that Jesus Christ is Lord. Why? Because His name brings salvation, peace, healing, forgiveness and most of all, love. It brings new life.

Imagine you were lying in a hospital bed in a ward full of people who were dying of a terminal disease. Then somebody arrived with a bottle of tablets and said, "Take one of these tablets and you will be healed." You took the tablet and straightaway your body was completely healed. You got up and looked around at all the other patients who had the same disease as you, who were dying, and you said, "God bless you and keep well," and you walk out. What kind of person would that make you?

That is exactly what happens when we have been saved from eternal damnation and we keep the Gospel to ourselves. This sick and dying world needs us to tell them about the Great Healer.

SEEK AND FIND

And behold, a man of Ethiopia, a eunuch of
great authority under Candace the queen of the
Ethiopians, who had charge of all her treasury,
and had come to Jerusalem to worship.

ACTS 8:27

God has put eternity into the hearts of all men everywhere. It is the way we are made. Jesus died for all men, women, boys and girls.

I have often been invited to speak in Jerusalem at the Feast of Tabernacles, which takes place every year. It is hosted by the International Christian Embassy in Jerusalem. Many nations are represented and they all have interpreters. I was on the platform one night, preaching my heart out, and I was making a very serious point when all of a sudden a group of Chinese people started laughing. I thought, *Why are they laughing? It's not funny.* Then I realized there was a few seconds' delay from the previous comment I made.

You have to really be on the ball when you are speaking to people from all over the world, all coming to Israel for the same purpose as the Ethiopian eunuch—to worship Jesus in Jerusalem. We all know you don't have to go to Jerusalem to worship the Lord but this man was seeking God and he found Him.

What about us today? How desperate are we to know about Jesus? Luke 11:9 says, "Seek, and you will find." He is patiently waiting today. He wants to speak with you.

WHO DO YOU SAY HE IS?

"Also we have come to believe and know that
You are the Christ, the Son of the living God."
JOHN 6:69

Wow! What a confession by Peter, Jesus' disciple. Immanuel! If we look at Isaiah 7:14, written hundreds of years before Jesus Christ was born, He is known as Immanuel, which translated means, "God with us".

There is nothing complicated about being a Christian— either you believe or you do not believe. Jesus is not just a good man. No! He is the Son of God. He is not one of many gods. No! He is the only God. He is the Messiah, the soon-coming King, and I can't wait for that day.

Simon Peter had absolutely no doubt who Jesus was. He walked with Jesus for three years; they lived together, ate together, and walked the whole of Israel together. Peter saw Jesus walking on water, stilling the storm, raising a dead man and multiplying food; He even saw Jesus being transfigured, and speaking with Moses and Elijah on the Mount of Transfiguration. But what about us today? Who do we say He is?

I say He is the Friend of sinners because He saved a wretch like me. I say that He is a Miracle-worker because He has worked so many miracles in my life. I say that He is the most wonderful Savior and Friend who has ever lived, and I say that He is coming back very soon.

DEATH DEFEATED

Then he fell to the ground, and heard a voice saying
to him, "Saul, Saul, why are you persecuting Me?"
And he said, "Who are You, Lord?" Then the
Lord said, "I am Jesus, whom you are persecuting."
It is hard for you to kick against the goads.

ACTS 9:4-5

It is a terrible thing to fall into the hands of the living God. Jesus said in Matthew 10:28, "And do not fear those who kill the body but cannot kill the soul. But rather fear Him who is able to destroy both soul and body in hell."

Some people seem to fear the devil and his demons more than they fear the living God. I want to tell you today that the devil is a mere creation. He cannot even create a storm in a teacup. He had his neck broken on the Cross of Calvary. Don't give him any place in your life.

You see on that road to Damascus, Jesus turned a potential mass murderer into a saint. At that moment, Saul of Tarsus became Paul the Apostle. He did it in mere seconds and He can do it for you and me today. So, please don't allow the devil to fill you with fear.

Paul reminds us in 2 Timothy 1:7 that, "God has not given us a spirit of fear, but of power and of love and of a sound mind." The devil cannot hurt you. He can only tell lies.

JESUS IS THE WAY

"For God so loved the world that He gave His only begotten Son, that whoever believes in Him should not perish but have everlasting life."

JOHN 3:16

I once met a young horse trainer from the USA named Ed Harrison. I had the privilege of spending time with this dynamic young man when he came to South Africa on a trip. His greatest desire was to tell people about Jesus and he made no apologies for his faith. He would open his teaching clinics in prayer and speak unashamedly about his Friend, Jesus. He is not here any longer. He died in Namibia while on a horse-training tour. The question is: Where is he today? We might be honest and say we don't really know.

Thomas asked Jesus the same question in John 14:5, "Lord, we do not know where You are going, and how can we know the way?" And Jesus said to him, "I am the way, the truth, and the life. No one comes to the Father except through Me" (John 14:6). It's not about being a good person. Remember the thief on the cross? Minutes before he died, he said, "Lord, remember me when You come into Your kingdom" (Luke 23:42). He acknowledged Jesus as his Savior and Jesus said, "Assuredly, I say to you, today you will be with Me in Paradise" (Luke 23:43).

Acknowledge the Lord as your Savior and believe that He is the Son of God.

SUFFERING

When He had called the people to Himself,
with His disciples also, He said to them,
"Whoever desires to come after Me, let him deny
himself, and take up his cross, and follow Me."
MARK 8:34

Who is our biggest enemy? It is not the devil; he is a defeated foe. I will tell you who our biggest enemy is—it is ourselves. One thing that always saddens me is self-preservation. It is such an ugly thing.

Do you remember that epic movie *Titanic*? People fought to get a seat on a lifeboat. Yet there were also stories of brave people who denied themselves; men who were safely seated in a lifeboat with their life jackets on who got out and gave their place to someone else. Those are the stories that stir my soul.

One of my heroes is a young American evangelist by the name of Jim Elliot. He was a missionary who gave his life up for the lost. He was murdered by Huaorani Indians, leaving behind a young wife and a baby daughter. But do you know what he said? He said, "He is no fool who gives what he cannot keep to gain that which he cannot lose." Even Paul, who suffered more than all the apostles, said, "For to me, to live is Christ, and to die is gain" (Philippians 1:21). If we live, we live with Jesus; if we die, we go home to be with Jesus. It is a win-win situation!

Today, remember, it is all about Him and He will see us through.

BUT GOD!

Why are you cast down, O my soul? And why are you disquieted within me? Hope in God; for I shall yet praise Him, the help of my countenance and my God.

PSALM 43:5

We need to ask ourselves that question today. Ask yourself, *Why are you so cast down?* Maybe one of the reasons is that we are spending time with negative people. Psalm 42:10 says, "My enemies reproach me, while they say to me all day long, 'Where is your God?'" Remember folks, eagles don't fly around with turkeys. Your attitude will determine your altitude.

Say to your soul this morning, "But God!" It doesn't matter what people say about you. It doesn't matter what your situation looks like, "But God…" The battle is not against the flesh; it is in the mind. Remember how many times in the past our Lord Jesus has pulled us out of the miry pit.

Many years ago I had a total crop failure, an absolute disaster. We had many people working for us and we had no crop to reap. Do you know what happened? We had a snowstorm in this area. It was so heavy that the timber and the forest were broken up and the trees looked like spaghetti.

The forestry companies didn't have enough staff to clear up and they gave us the job. That job saved us! Second Corinthians 5:7 says we walk by faith and not by sight. God is great!

THE RIGHT ROAD

Immediately there fell from his eyes something
like scales, and he received his sight at
once; and he arose and was baptized.

ACTS 9:18

Saul of Tarsus was on the wrong road. He was on his way to Damascus to persecute the Christians. He thought he was doing the right thing. There are none so blind as those who just do not want to see. Paul was clearly on the wrong road and passionately doing the wrong thing.

How many of us today are doing the same? We are saying, "Lord, why are you allowing this to happen to me?" Jesus is saying to us today that He is not prepared to be a rubber stamp of approval on our personal plans. He will not bless them if we are not prepared to listen to His instructions and obey His commands.

Unfortunately, just like Paul, we will be knocked off our horse because we are going the wrong way. Sometimes Jesus allows that disaster in our lives to save us from sheer death. The scales fell off Paul's eyes and then he could see clearly. I want to say to you this morning that we need to open our spiritual eyes.

Pray that the Lord will put you on the right road just like He did with Paul, so that you might live a life that is fulfilled and a blessing, not only to yourself, but to many others.

MOURNING

"Blessed are those who mourn,
for they shall be comforted."
MATTHEW 5:4

Mourning is an important part of a person's life. So often we unintentionally try to stop people from mourning the loss of a very important person in their life. We want to try and cheer them up and help them to get on with their life. That is wrong. There is a time for mourning, when people need to be quiet, to contemplate and to allow the Holy Spirit to comfort them. Jesus knows that only too well.

When Mary and Martha lost their brother, one of Jesus' best friends, they were very sad. They were weeping and beside themselves. When Jesus came into town He was four days late, but He wasn't really. He was spot on time. Of course, the people didn't know that, and Mary and Martha said, "Lord, if you had come in time you would have healed our brother." Jesus knew that Lazarus was about to be raised from the dead and yet in John 11:35 we read, "Jesus wept." Why did He weep? He wept because He had compassion for those who were mourning.

People who are hurting and people who have lost loved ones need to be comforted. They need to be comforted by the love of God because that is the only thing they can hear. The best thing you can do for someone who is mourning is to put your arm around them and weep with them. That will comfort a mourner more than anything else.

CONTENTMENT

"Now godliness with contentment is great gain.
For we brought nothing into this world, and it is
certain we can carry nothing out. And having food
and clothing, with these we shall be content."

1 TIMOTHY 6:6–8

Contentment does not come naturally. It has to be learned. Philippians 4:11 says, "Not that I speak in regard to need, for I have learned in whatever state I am, to be content."

My late dad was a prisoner of war in World War II. As a prisoner, he witnessed extreme hunger and starvation. So, as a rule in our home, we were allowed to eat as much food as we wanted, but whatever we put on our plate had to be eaten. Nothing was allowed to be left over. That golden rule has been handed down to my own children and even my little grandchildren when they come to visit.

It is wise to learn to be content with little and with much. The wisest man who ever lived was Solomon and he said in Ecclesiastes 2:11, "I looked on all the works that my hands had done and on the labor in which I had toiled; and indeed all was vanity and grasping for the wind."

Today, let us be content with what God has given us. Amos 5:6 says, "Seek the LORD and live." If our eyes are focused on God we will be content with what we have in this life.

LEARNING FROM BARNABAS

But Barnabas took him and brought him to
the apostles. And he declared to them how he
had seen the Lord on the road, and that He
had spoken to him, and how he had preached
boldly at Damascus in the name of Jesus.

ACTS 9:27

We don't often hear much about Barnabas, the introducer. Remember, Andrew too was an introducer—He introduced his brother, Simon Peter, to the Lord Jesus Christ. How we so desperately need men and women in these troubled times with a Barnabas character—people who believe in others. You see, Barnabas was not a troublemaker, he was a peacemaker.

Barnabas took Paul under his wing and stood up for him, and then Paul was accepted by the rest of the apostles. Barnabas came to Paul's defense and he gave testimony of how Paul preached so boldly about Jesus in Damascus. He believed in Paul. If it was not for Barnabas, Paul would have found it very difficult to get started and remember, Paul became one of the greatest apostles.

It is all very well to stand up for someone when they are a success because there is no risk involved but to stand up and to trust and believe in someone who has never really done anything is quite another thing. Today, many young folks need a break in life. Let's give them an opportunity to show us what Jesus can do through them.

THROUGH CHRIST

*"...but the people who know their God
shall be strong, and carry out great exploits."*
DANIEL 11:32

If we desire to be used by God we need to spend time with Him. You see, it is Jesus Christ alone who trains us to do great exploits for the Lord. It is He alone who gives us the vigor and the victory—no-one else. It is Jesus alone who gives us strength for the strain. When we get to know the character, power, faithfulness and the love of Jesus, then nothing is impossible to achieve in His name. When we know Him we can risk everything on His behalf. Paul said in Philippians 3:10, "...that I may know Him, and the power of His resurrection, and the fellowship of His sufferings, being conformed to His death..."

When we get to know Jesus, it is He who excites our very enthusiasm and makes us willing to do the impossible for Him. When you spend time with the Lord, it is infectious.

I made an outrageous statement years ago at Kings Park Rugby Stadium in Durban. At the time, I had no irrigation and on the radio farmers were warned not to plant because a terrible drought was coming. But I said, "I am going back to plant potatoes." We reaped a crop of potatoes that year, why? Because we can do all things through Christ who strengthens us.

OUR REFUGE

God is our refuge and strength, a very present
help in trouble. Therefore we will not fear, even
though the earth be removed, and though the
mountains be carried into the midst of the sea.

PSALM 46:1-2

If God is for us there can be no man who can stand against us
(see Romans 8:31). If God is for us then what do we need to
be afraid of?

The devil is like a little mouse running around with a loud-
speaker frightening people to death with malicious lies. Let's
not make the same mistake that the disciples made when they
ran away from the only Person in the whole world who could
help them in their time of trouble (see Matthew 26:56). I am
talking about Jesus. This was in the Garden of Gethsemane
when the High Priest's soldiers came to arrest the Son of God.

It is said that John G. Lake, the evangelist who came to
South Africa and started a mighty revival, would get up in the
morning, get dressed and look in the mirror. He would look at
that person in the mirror and say that God lives in that man.

Go out today knowing that: "The LORD of hosts is with us;
the God of Jacob is our refuge" (Psalm 46:7).

THE STRIKE OF A MATCH

Will You not revive us again, that Your people
may rejoice in You? Show us Your mercy, LORD,
and grant us Your salvation. I will hear what God
the LORD will speak, for He will speak peace to
His people and to His saints; but let them not turn
back to folly. Surely His salvation is near to those
who fear Him, that glory may dwell in our land.

PSALM 85:6-9

Revival is dependent on the saints, not on the unbeliever or the heathen. We need revival—not only South Africa but the whole world. Jesus said, "If My people who are called by My name will humble themselves, and pray and seek My face, and turn from their wicked ways, then I will hear from heaven, and will forgive their sin and heal their land" (2 Chronicles 7:14).

We need to pray. We need to pray for the unbeliever and the backslider; we need to pray for the lukewarm Christian. We need to pray for our prodigal children—it is time for them to come back home. The match is about to be struck.

I have a little fireplace in my prayer room. Sometimes when I try to start a fire, the kindling is a bit damp and the fire smolders, it smokes. But when I take a single match, strike it and throw it on top of that smoldering wood, all of a sudden it bursts into mighty flames…That is what is about to happen in our world. Christian, it is time to stand up.

PRAY ABOUT EVERYTHING

"Is anyone among you sick? Let him call for the
elders of the church, and let them pray over him...
And the prayer of faith will save the sick,
and the Lord will raise him up...pray for one
another, that you may be healed. The effective,
fervent prayer of a righteous man avails much."
JAMES 5:14-16

Do you see how many times the word *prayer* appears in this Scripture passage? I want to tell you, without the prayer of faith nothing will happen.

George Müller started a children's home by faith, he never asked for a penny. When he had a need, he prayed. He was invited across to America and while on the ship, there was a heavy mist. Eventually the captain stopped the ship. George Müller asked the captain: "Captain, why has the ship stopped? I have an appointment tomorrow in America." The captain said, "There's so much mist. We can't see where we are going and there are icebergs. We are afraid that we might hit one of them." So George Müller asked him a question: "Have you prayed about the matter?" They got on their knees and George Müller started to pray. When he had finished praying the prayer of faith, he opened his eyes and said, "Look, the mist has lifted. Let's go."

I want to encourage you today: Pray about every single thing that you need to do and give the Lord an opportunity to help you.

PRAISE HIM

Oh, clap your hands, all you peoples! Shout to God
with the voice of triumph! For the LORD Most High
is awesome; He is a great King over all the earth...
God has gone up with a shout, the LORD with the
sound of a trumpet. Sing praises to God, sing praises!
Sing praises to our King, sing praises! For God is the
King of all the earth; sing praises with understanding.

PSALM 47:1-2, 5-7

Praise the Lord because He is worthy! He is the King of kings; He is the Lord of lords; He is the Worthy One. Our Jesus is the Defender of the weak, the Friend of the widow and the orphan, and most of all, He is the Friend of sinners, just like you and me.

Ian Mackintosh, a very dear friend of mine and former Springbok rugby coach, helped Natal bring back their first Currie Cup win. A few years ago, one of Ian's close friends told me that he had had the privilege of walking onto the field at Kings Park Rugby Stadium with Ian just before the Curry Cup Final. The atmosphere had been electric.

A few years later, he came to one of the Mighty Men Conferences with Ian, and they walked in amongst tens of thousands of men. They were praising and worshiping the living God. This man said he had never encountered the presence of God in such a miraculous way.

Today, praise Him because He is worthy. Praise Him because He loves you and because He is coming back soon.

LOVING HOSPITALITY

And a voice spoke to him again the second time,
"What God has cleansed you must not call common."
ACTS 10:15

Peter had been called to an unbeliever's house and Jews never went into a Gentile's house. But the Lord said that what He had made clean, no man can call unclean. When I travel overseas to different countries and cultures, I tell those who travel with me that we will eat whatever is put in front of us because it has been lovingly prepared for us. It can be so very hurtful and, in fact, insulting to pick at your food when you are at somebody's home.

Peter broke all the rules. He went into that Gentile's home as a Jew. Cornelius was an Italian and an officer in Rome's army, but because of that impartial act of love, the whole household became followers of Jesus.

My youngest daughter's husband is a very big, strong and powerfully built man. He has a huge, healthy appetite and I love taking him with me when I go overseas to people's homes. He gets stuck into his food, eats it all and many a time, he helps me eat my meal as well. But at the end of that meal, the host and the cook gravitate towards my son-in-law.

I want to say to you today, open your home to others and also be willing to cross cultural barriers in order to win people for Christ.

OUR GUIDE

"The LORD will guide you continually, giving
you water when you are dry and restoring
your strength. You will be like a well-watered
garden, like an ever-flowing spring."

ISAIAH 58:11 NLT

This verse is beautiful and a wonderful promise. We must follow Jesus where He leads us. You always follow a guide. You do not walk ahead of someone who is trying to show you the way. We must obey the Guide and do what He tells us to do. We must listen to what the Guide tells us. If we do not, we will cause ourselves unnecessary pain and hardship.

I often watch the horse trainers that come from America. They are mainly senior men who understand how to train horses, and they are the ultimate horse whisperers. I go with my son to watch how these men operate. They charge money because you have to learn the way from them.

One day I saw a young man, who had paid quite a lot of money, and he spent his half-hour telling the horse trainer what he could do. The horse trainer, being a seasoned old man, sat on the stool and listened to him for half an hour, then took his money. That youngster still didn't know anything about training the horse!

Let's start to listen today. Let's start to obey and let's start to follow. We will find that life is a lot sweeter and we will get to our destination a lot quicker.

FAULTLESS REPUTATION

And they said, "Cornelius the centurion, a just man,
one who fears God and has a good reputation
among all the nation of the Jews, was divinely
instructed by a holy angel to summon you to
his house, and to hear words from you."

ACTS 10:22

A good reputation is worth more than gold. Cornelius was not a Jew; in fact, he was an officer in the Roman army that was oppressing the Jews. Yet he was highly honored and respected; he was highly regarded by the Jewish people. We always say that people don't have to like you but they need to respect you.

You know, when a beef cattle farmer wants to purchase a new bull for his herd, he needs to be very careful because the bull is actually half of the herd. You see a bull can make or break a farmer because he can look beautiful but if he is not fertile the cows will not conceive and the farmer will have no calves. I would always buy my bulls from a cattle breeder that had a trustworthy reputation. I would even gladly pay more money knowing that the farmer would never sell me a dud.

Today, think about your reputation. Are you happy with the way others see you or is there room for improvement? Jesus had a perfect reputation and we should copy His example.

IN A RUSH?

Now Joshua the son of Nun was full of the
spirit of wisdom, for Moses had laid his hands
on him; so the children of Israel heeded him,
and did as the LORD had commanded Moses.

DEUTERONOMY 34:9

We need to take time to prepare ourselves for the work that we have been called to. Jesus, the Son of God, Immanuel, God with us, prepared Himself for 30 years to do three years' work here on earth. So why are you and I in such a terrible rush about things? We need to be more patient.

My wife's mom and dad came to live with us after they retired. Jill's dad was a steam engineer by profession. He was very handy with tools. These men took a long time to learn the work that they had been taught.

One day he walked into the workshop and he saw me trying frantically to cut a piece of steel with a hacksaw. He said to me, "Why don't you use the whole saw blade when you are cutting and let it do the work for you instead of using the middle of the blade?"

Today, let's not be in such a rush. Let us learn from Jesus how to walk this road—it will be a lot simpler than we are trying to do it at the moment.

GENUINE PARTS

"Offer to God thanksgiving, and pay your vows to
the Most High. Call upon Me in the day of trouble;
I will deliver you, and you shall glorify Me."

PSALM 50:14-15

Why is it that whenever we get into deep trouble, we seem to call upon everyone else first, and then when no one can help us, we call upon the living God? The quick fix never lasts. It is just like purchasing a pirate part for your car. It is quick, available and cheap, but it does not last. Eventually, it will probably let you down. The genuine part will take longer and be more expensive, but it will probably last the lifetime of the car.

Jesus knows you and me better than anyone else on earth because He created us. He will get us out of trouble. He will deliver us if we call upon Him. We might not like the way He wants to do it though.

Jesus told the rich young ruler what to do to inherit eternal life (see Luke 18:18), but the young ruler would not do it. The Bible told us he became very sorrowful and walked away to a lost eternity. A preacher once told me that he thought that Jesus would be standing there with tears running down His face. He didn't say to the young ruler, "Come back and let's talk about this." No, He left him to make his own choice. Make sure you call upon the Lord and obey the Manufacturer.

RIVER OF LIFE

"Remain in Me, and I will remain in you. For a branch
cannot produce fruit if it is severed from the vine,
and you cannot be fruitful unless you remain in Me."

JOHN 15:4 NLT

Jesus is the vine and you and I are merely the branches. In the Northern Cape, running along the Orange River, are irrigation farms—many of them grow grapes. They put the grapes out in the sun and they dry into beautiful raisins, which are exported all over the world. Their vineyards are an incredible contrast to the arid desert-like conditions just a few kilometers on either side of the huge flowing river. Canals come off the river, which irrigates these beautiful grape farms.

As I rode next to one of these feeder canals, the Holy Spirit showed me that if these canals are not properly maintained—they become clogged up, broken down and damaged—then the very livelihood of these farmers would be in serious trouble.

Now, Jesus is the river of life, He is the Orange River for us and we are the canals coming off that mighty river. If we do not maintain our Christian lifestyle, spending time reading the Bible, praying and meditating, and spending time with other Christians, we will restrict the flow of the Holy Spirit into our lives. Eventually, we will dry up and die. Christianity is a lifestyle. It is a constant walk with God. Today, let us maintain our spiritual canal with God.

TRUE CONFESSION

"Confess your trespasses to one another, and pray
for one another, that you may be healed. The effective,
fervent prayer of a righteous man avails much."
JAMES 5:16

There is power in the prayer of confession, in saying sorry. I once mentored a group of men and we read this Scripture passage very carefully together, with much fear and trepidation. After we had read it, one by one, the men started to walk to the front of the large group. Some of them started to confess to God for the first time in their lives. In front of their trusted brothers in Christ, they confessed any areas of sin where the devil had had them chained and shackled for years.

I want to say to you, my dear friend, that very rarely in my 40-plus years of serving the Lord, have I ever experienced the tangible presence of the love of God like I did that night. Weeping and genuine sorrow at having disappointed the Master was confessed and then the sheer elation of leaving their confessed sin at the foot of the cross. Then there was the joy and the freedom of having had the courage to do it—it was very beautiful. I saw fathers and sons weeping in each other's arms, asking forgiveness. I saw men who had been carrying burdens on their shoulders for many years, leave it at the foot of the cross.

It was so very beautiful. Something I shall never forget as long as I live. Maybe we all should do it a lot more.

MERCY AND GRACE

Have mercy upon me, O God, according
to Your lovingkindness; according to the
multitude of Your tender mercies, blot out my
transgressions. Wash me thoroughly from
my iniquity, and cleanse me from my sin.

PSALM 51:1-2

This is the prayer of King David. David was a man who loved God so much that he wrote these beautiful psalms, but he had fallen terribly short. He had fallen into sin. He had taken another man's wife and then had him killed so that he could marry her. Nathan, the prophet, came and told him exactly what had happened and David was devastated.

Romans 3:23 tells us that all have fallen short of the glory of God and have sinned—no one is without sin. Remember the woman caught in adultery? According to the law, she should have been stoned to death publicly. They brought her to Jesus, what did Jesus say? He said, "He who is without sin among you, let him throw a stone at her first" (John 8:7). They all dropped their stones and walked away. Jesus said to that woman, "Go and sin no more. Your sins are forgiven."

Jesus is the Friend of sinners. Without Him, we have no hope. You see, we were born sinners. David says in Psalm 51:5, "Behold, I was brought forth in iniquity, and in sin my mother conceived me." Oh, but we praise God for mercy and grace because Jesus has paid for it all. All we need to do today is to say thank You to the Lord and walk in sin no more.

THE GREATEST MIRACLE

When they heard these things they became silent;
and they glorified God, saying, "Then God has
also granted to the Gentiles repentance to life."

ACTS 11:18

Peter went to Jerusalem and told the disciples that he had been to the house of a Gentile, Cornelius. Jews were not permitted to go into the homes of unbelievers and Gentiles but the Lord Jesus showed him clearly that what He has made clean, no one must make otherwise (see Acts 10:15). Whoever calls, appeals or cries out to God with a sincere and repentant heart, the Lord Jesus will not turn away or disregard. It does not matter what you have done, it does not matter what you have not done, Jesus still loves you the same.

Well, you might ask, what does He require of us then? Matthew 22:37 says to simply love Him with all your heart, all your soul and with all your mind. You know, to me the greatest of all miracles that I have ever seen in my life is to see a changed life. I have been very privileged to have seen Jesus heal the sick, open blind eyes, deaf ears…But the greatest miracle of all is the life of a "whosoever" that turns around and becomes a follower of Jesus Christ. That is a miracle indeed!

Today, do not harden your heart. Call unto the Lord and He will save you.

FORGIVEN AND RESTORED

For thus says the High and Lofty One Who inhabits
eternity, whose name is Holy: "I dwell in the high
and holy place, with him who has a contrite and
humble spirit, to revive the spirit of the humble,
and to revive the heart of the contrite ones."

ISAIAH 57:15

When we make a mistake, our Lord Jesus does not write us off as the world does. If we are truly sorry and we humble ourselves, He will forgive us and restore us completely.

The word *contrite* means to feel or express remorse. When we feel we have let the team down and have blown it completely—that is when Jesus can step in and do His beautiful work of restoration. In Matthew 26:75, we read that Peter was filled with remorse when the rooster crowed for the third time and he realized what he had done. Jesus not only forgave Peter for denying Him three times but He went ahead and made him the head of the early church. What incredible love and forgiveness.

Jesus sees the potential in you and me. He sees past the mistakes we make to what He can do through us. What He wants us to do today is to repent. God will forgive and restore us if we are contrite.

Remember, He took a broken fisherman and made him head of the church and He can take you and me today and restore us completely, if we just say sorry, remain humble and keep on going.

SEND RELIEF

Then the disciples, each according
to his ability, determined to send relief
to the brethren dwelling in Judea.

ACTS 11:29

There were food shortages because of a drought that covered much of the Roman empire. So the disciples sent as much as they could to help their fellow Christians living in Judea. The disciples heard about the terrible famine and got stuck in— they rolled up their sleeves and helped.

Don't only tell people that you love Jesus but show them that you love Him. Don't be guilty of the old adage, "In order for evil to abound, all good people have to do is nothing." Remember that faith is an action word…faith has feet! We need to get up and be doers of the Word.

As Christians, we need to keep in touch with the needs of others and bring relief where we can. We must be careful that we do not become so spiritually minded that we are of no earthly use. Jesus said: "And the King will answer and say to them, 'Assuredly, I say to you, inasmuch as you did it to one of the least of these My brethren, you did it to Me'" (Matthew 25:40). What we do for others, we do for our Lord.

Try it today. Get out there and start helping people because we have a famine in our land…people are starved for love and peace and are filled with things like depression, anxiety, fear and stress. People need to be loved, go out and love them.

THE POWER OF PRAYER

Peter was therefore kept in prison, but constant
prayer was offered to God for him by the church...
Now behold, an angel of the Lord stood by him,
and a light shone in the prison; and he struck
Peter on the side and raised him up, saying,
"Arise quickly!" And his chains fell off his hands.

ACTS 12:5, 7

Our ministry at Shalom has up to 3,000 intercessors praying around the world. That is incredible and it makes me want to weep with joy. When people ask me, "What can we do to help?" I always reply, "Please pray." That is what we need—prayer—because there is power in faithful prayer.

Billy Graham, the famous evangelist, was asked what he would change if he could live his life over again. He said, "I would pray more and speak less." Why don't we do that today? Why don't we pray about the issue that is troubling us and ask the Lord Jesus to break those chains that are holding us back. Those chains of fear, sickness and poverty—pray about it. That relationship that you can't resolve—pray about it. If they don't want to speak to you—pray! God will move them.

Peter had a soldier on either side of him and four detachments guarding him and he was released because the church prayed. His chains were broken through prayer. You and I are the church. God will move mountains for us if we pray without ceasing (1 Thessalonians 5:17).

OUR HEAVENLY FATHER

"Behold, I stand at the door and knock. If anyone
hears My voice and opens the door, I will come
in to him and dine with him, and he with Me."

REVELATION 3:20

I just love it in the morning when I sit and talk to the Savior
of the world, saying, "Lord, these are my problems, these are
my needs," and I know He welcomes me to talk to Him because
He is my Father and I am His son. Why don't you do the same?

Instead of running here and there, to and fro to people that
you don't know very well, why don't you take it to your Father?
Sit down quietly and let Him put you on His lap, put your
head on His big ample chest and tell Him what your needs are.
He will take care of you.

Do your kids need to beg from others for bread? Of course
not, they know that you will give them food to eat. They only
need to ask if they want something to eat. It is the same with
your heavenly Father, He is waiting for you to speak to Him.
You don't have to earn His favor or work for His approval because He gives all things freely.

God is your Father and you are His child. He will meet all
your needs and be there to listen to all your worries and con-
cerns. Just meet with Him in prayer.

IN HIS IMAGE

The fool has said in his heart, "There is no God."

PSALM 53:1

Charles Darwin said that new species arise naturally, by a process of evolution, rather than having been created—forever immutable—by God. He believed in a changing species rather than in an unchanging God.

Contrary to Darwin's beliefs, the Bible tells us that we are made in God's image (Genesis 1:27). Isn't that amazing? When God created you and me, He created us as individuals, not in batches of hundreds or thousands, like mass-produced products on a conveyor belt.

When He created you, He broke the mold. There is only one of you in the whole world. You are the only one on earth who has your individual fingerprints and your exact eyes. Isn't that incredible? Only one of you in the whole world! That is so beautiful and profound. That is why I love Him so much! Jesus knows us intimately, just like a mother will distinctly hear the cry of her little child above all the voices of the other children on the playground and seek him out.

Today, remember that you are not alone. You have a heavenly Father who created you, knows you and loves you. He has a purpose and a plan for you. You don't exist by chance or due to random events in the universe. The Master Designer created you in His image and has a unique calling for you.

BE HUMBLE

The people gave him a great ovation, shouting,
"It's the voice of a god, not of a man!"
Instantly, an angel of the Lord struck Herod
with a sickness, because he accepted the people's
worship instead of giving the glory to God.
So he was consumed with worms and died.
ACTS 12:22–23 NLT

King Herod was delivering a speech. The people shouted and said he was speaking like a god and straightaway the Lord struck him and he died. Never ever touch God's glory. God will not tolerate that from anybody.

Robert Murray M'Cheyne was a young Scottish evangelist who started a revival that swept all over Dundee. When people tried to praise him, he would say, "Rather than having been an instrument of the Lord, all I was, was an adoring spectator."

William Duma, the Zulu preacher, was called to preach in a big church. The church was packed and William had not arrived yet. Eventually, there was a little knock on the back door where the cleaning lady came in and there was the servant of God, ready to preach.

God uses men and women who are humble. The Lord said of John the Baptist, "There has never been a man born of a woman who is greater than John the Baptist" (see Matthew 11:11). Yet, of himself John said, "He must increase, but I must decrease" (John 3:30). Always remember, "God resists the proud, but gives grace to the humble" (1 Peter 5:5).

FACE YOUR TROUBLES

"Oh, that I had wings like a dove! I would fly away
and be at rest. Indeed, I would wander far off,
and remain in the wilderness. I would hasten my
escape from the windy storm and tempest."

PSALM 55:6-8

Running away from your troubles is not the answer. It might be very tempting, but it is not the solution. We have to bravely face the enemy and then we will gain the victory. In Ephesians 6:14, the Lord tells us to put on our armor and stand firm. Remember the battle is the Lord's. When you need to make a big decision in your life, face the challenge head-on and overcome it that way. Remember that God has not given us a spirit of fear, but of power and of love and of a sound mind (2 Timothy 1:7).

Rocky Marciano, the heavyweight boxing champion of the world, was one of the smallest and lightest heavyweight boxers. He won 49 title fights and is the only heavyweight boxer to finish his career undefeated. What was his secret? Well, he never took his eye off of his opponent. He never turned his back on his opponent. He could take tremendous physical punishment but he never turned away, he always kept on coming forward.

Face your challenges and your troubles. Stand with the Lord and He will see you through. Say to yourself, "The Lord is my helper; I will not fear. What can man do to me?" (Hebrews 13:6).

A LIGHT IN THE DARKNESS

"O full of all deceit and all fraud, you son of the devil, you enemy of all righteousness, will you not cease perverting the straight ways of the Lord? And now, indeed, the hand of the Lord is upon you, and you shall be blind, not seeing the sun for a time." And immediately a dark mist fell on him, and he went around seeking someone to lead him by the hand.

ACTS 13:10-11

We must be very careful that we do not prevent people from seeking the Lord. You see, the governor was intimidated by Elymas the sorcerer. He was trying to prevent the governor from believing in Jesus. Paul, that bold apostle, spoke up and immediately that man went blind.

You see darkness cannot live with light. You walk into a dark room, you strike a match and the blackness recedes immediately. With Jesus Christ living within us, we have victory over the darkness of sin and the devil.

I love the old song by Chuck Girard:

It's the name above all names.
And we will declare it, we will declare it.
It's the name above all names.
And we will shout it to a dying world.

Let's go out today and shout the name of Jesus. The darkness will recede and the light of God will come into your life.

NO MORE TEARS

You number my wanderings; put my tears
into Your bottle; are they not in Your book?

PSALM 56:8

Jesus knows what you are going through. He has been with you through every painful experience. He has put all your tears into His bottle and they are written into His book.

Our God is a God of great compassion. Jesus wept when He walked on this earth. He really does understand our pain and our suffering. I don't know what it is that you are going through at this very moment but He knows, so talk to Him about it. You see, He wept when He saw how distraught Mary and Martha were at the death of their brother, Lazarus (see John 11:35). He felt their pain and grief.

I was quite sickly when I was a little boy. I remember how my mom would sit by my bedside and rub my chest with ointment. If I had a fever, she would put a damp cloth on my forehead. She spoke kind words to me and sat by my side. She understood what I was going through because she was a very sickly woman herself.

Today, let us weep with those who are weeping and let us have compassion on those who are suffering. And don't forget to tell them that the best is yet to come. Jesus is going to wipe away all those tears and He is going to fill us with peace and joy and love when we are united with Him in heaven (see Revelation 21:4).

WAIT ON THE LORD

You will keep him in perfect peace,
whose mind is stayed on You, because
he trusts in You. Trust in the LORD forever,
for in YAH, the LORD, is everlasting strength.

ISAIAH 26:3-4

We need to wait for the Lord. Sometimes we do not even give Jesus an opportunity to work on our behalf. We pray and ask Him to help us and then before He can move, we attempt to do it ourselves.

King Saul was impatient when he made the sacrifice before the battle instead of waiting for Samuel. When Samuel arrived shortly thereafter, he said to Saul, "What have you done?" That impulsive and foolish act cost Saul his kingship. If God has told us to wait, we need to wait on Him.

Years ago there was a drought just after we planted our maize crop. The germinating seeds couldn't get through the hard crust of soil. Many farmers replowed and started again at an extra cost of fertilizer, fuel and lost time. I felt that God was telling me to wait. So I took a cultivator and cracked the hard crust of soil so that the little seeds could germinate. Straight after that the rain came. We had a beautiful harvest that year. We were about three to four weeks ahead of the men that had plowed their crop into the ground.

If the Lord has told you to do something, learn to wait upon Him. He will not be late, He will not be early—He will be spot on time!

SHINE LIKE A LIGHT

"For so the Lord has commanded us: 'I have set
you as a light to the Gentiles, that you should
be for salvation to the ends of the earth.'"

ACTS 13:47

We have a responsibility to show people who are living in darkness that Jesus is the Light of the world (see John 8:12). People are so lost, lonely and devastated at the moment.

I have a picture in my mind of a little boy who has been separated from his mommy in a shopping mall. He is standing alone. Everybody is busy with their own things and this little chap, his eyes full of tears, is wailing. Nobody can hear him because of the loud music. His nose is running, he is hanging onto his little teddy bear and he is beside himself. It makes me sad just to draw that picture for you, but that is what is happening in the world today.

The world is chaotic and senseless. People are groping in the darkness like never before. We have to give them the Light and show them the Way. We have to point them to Jesus. We have to get that little boy back to the safety and love of his mommy's arms.

No matter who you are, you must be bold and brave and tell others that Jesus is the Way. Everyone needs to hear—the educated and uneducated, the rich and the poor—that Jesus is the Light of the world. So go out today and shine like a light in this dark world.

AUGUST 12

A NEW CREATION

"Therefore, if anyone is in Christ, he is a
new creation; old things have passed away;
behold, all things have become new."

2 CORINTHIANS 5:17

When we are born again, we are made fresh and new. We are an entirely new creation. Without a doubt, the greatest of all miracles is new life! I've seen many miracles in my life: I've seen God open blind eyes; I have seen deaf ears unstopped; I have seen lame people walk; I have seen addictions to drugs and alcohol broken in an instant. I have even seen weather patterns change through prayers of faith and I've seen barren wombs conceive and beautiful babies born. But without a doubt, the greatest miracle and the one that still brings me to tears of joy is when one sinner repents and is born again.

If you are praying for a loved one to come to repentance, don't stop praying. When a person is born again, they get a fresh start. The old life is gone. You know what brings me more joy than anything else is to receive a letter from a little girl with big handwriting, thanking Jesus for giving her a brand-new daddy, or when I get a letter from a wife saying, "He's bringing home a paycheck at the end of the month now, and we have food to eat."

When I see a turnaround like that, there is no doubt in my mind that we serve a mighty miracle-working God. Continue to pray for your loved ones and Jesus will turn them around.

IN HIS STRENGTH

Some trust in chariots, and some in horses; but we
will remember the name of the LORD our God.
PSALM 20:7

The system of this world is all about *you* and how *you* can do anything. *You've* got it in you, *you've* got what it takes, *you* can make anything you want happen. It's all about us.

But this is wrong because it makes us think we are the greatest. Instead of placing our confidence in ourselves, it should be in God. Paul says, "I can do all things through Christ Jesus who strengthens me" (Philippians 4:13). The emphasis of that Scripture verse is not on the 'I' but rather on *Christ*.

Every single time that I am about to embark on a national Christian event I become so aware of just how weak I am. I find myself spending more and more time in isolation with the Lord Jesus because I know for a fact that if He is not going to do it, it's not going to happen.

And that's when 2 Corinthians 12:9 becomes a huge neon sign in my life—it's all about grace. The Lord says: "My grace is sufficient for you, for My strength is made perfect in weakness." When I'm weak, then I'm strong. The word *grace* is such a beautiful word. It means undeserved loving-kindness or unmerited favor.

When I am weak, then I know that Jesus is strong within me. It's not about you making it happen, but let Christ work through you.

BECAUSE HE LOVES YOU

"Behold, happy is the man whom
God corrects; therefore do not despise
the chastening of the Almighty."

JOB 5:17

Why does God chastise us if He loves us? Well, He does not want us to hurt ourselves through disobedience. Just like the mother who tells her child to wait at the stop street while the cars pass by, but the child is disobedient and runs across the road and a passing car nearly runs him over. What does the frantic mother do? She gives the disobedient child a really good spanking because of the sheer relief that her son nearly died but has been miraculously spared. It's for the love of her child that she openly chastises him.

Sometimes God does not answer our prayers in the way we asked because He knows that it would not be good for us. A young pastor once said to me, "All my life I used to pray. I asked God to give me a farm of my own but He never answered my prayers. But now I realize why I never received that farm. If God had given me that farm, I would have been so involved with the farm that I would have forgotten all about Him."

If you feel that God is correcting you, know that He has a better plan for you, "No chastening seems to be joyful for the present, but painful; nevertheless, afterward it yields the peaceable fruit of righteousness to those who have been trained by it" (Hebrews 12:11).

UNTO GOD

Even with these words, Paul and Barnabas
could scarcely restrain the people from sacrificing
to them...They stoned Paul and dragged
him out of town, thinking he was dead.

ACTS 14:18-19 NLT

One minute they worshiped Paul, saying he was a god. The very next minute they stoned him and left him for dead. You cannot look to man for your accolades or your rewards because in the eyes of the world, one day you are a winner and the next, a loser. It's like the rugby player who is the favorite of the match. Until he misses a vital penalty kick before the final whistle is blown. Then he becomes the villain of the crowd and is jeered at.

The same thing happened to our Lord Jesus when He rode into Jerusalem on a donkey. He was worshiped by the people. They lay down palm branches and even their very own clothes so that the donkey could walk upon them, but a few days later the same crowd called out, "Crucify Him" (Matthew 27:22 NLT).

Whatever we do in this life, we must do it as unto Jesus and look to Him alone for our reward, otherwise, we will be sorely disappointed. If we look to the world for recognition we will be on top of the world one minute and down in the dumps the next. When you go out today do everything as unto God and He will reward you.

HAVE FAITH IN GOD

And he believed in the LORD, and He
accounted it to him for righteousness.

GENESIS 15:6

Abraham was known as the friend of God. I don't think anybody would want a more wonderful title than that. He believed in the Lord and the Lord accounted it to him for righteousness. He wasn't known as the friend of God because he was a good man. No! Do you know that he passed off his wife, Sarah, as his sister to save his own neck, twice? That was not a good thing to do. But Abraham believed God. God told Abraham, "I want you to leave your home and take your family and your animals, take everyone and go to an unknown destiny" (see Genesis 12). Abraham never hesitated.

Abraham also waited faithfully for many years until God gave him a beautiful baby boy by the name of Isaac. And that's not the end of the story. When Isaac was a fine young, strong teenager, God tested Abraham yet again. He said to Abraham, "I want him back. You need to offer him up as a sacrifice to Me." Abraham obeyed immediately and passed the test (see Genesis 22). Romans 4:20 says of Abraham, "He did not waver at the promise of God through unbelief, but was strengthened in faith, giving glory to God."

Do we want to be known as friends of God? We've got to start walking the talk. Faith is a verb. It's a doing word. When God tells us to do something, we need to do it.

KEEP YOUR VOWS

"So I will sing praise to Your name forever,
that I may daily perform my vows."
PSALM 61:8

A vow is a solemn promise. It is unconditional. God loved Job so much because even when he lost everything he could still proclaim, "Though He slay me, yet will I trust Him" (Job 13:15).

We know what happened in the end because Job kept his vow. If we look at Job 42:12-13, "Now the LORD blessed the latter days of Job more than his beginning; for he had fourteen thousand sheep, six thousand camels, one thousand yoke of oxen, and one thousand female donkeys. He also had seven sons and three daughters." And those daughters were the most beautiful in the land. Verses 16-17 say, "After this Job lived one hundred and forty years, and saw his children and grandchildren for four generations. So Job died, old and full of days." Keep your vows to God because He will always keep His promises to us.

Many years ago, we were caught in a severe drought. The crop was dying in front of our very eyes! And I had a loan to pay back to the bank. I could actually see the farm slipping through my fingers. One day I made a solemn vow to Jesus. I said, "Lord, if You pull me through this drought, I will preach Your Holy Word till the day I die." Yes, He pulled me through the drought and yes, I'm still preaching the Gospel. God never breaks His promises and neither should we.

KEEP IN TOUCH

Greet one another with a holy kiss.
The churches of Christ greet you.
ROMANS 16:16

We need to keep in touch with one another. In Romans 16, Paul sends greetings to different churches and different people. The New Testament contains letters from people keeping in touch with others who loved the Lord and needed to learn more about Him.

As Christians, we need to keep in touch with one another. No man is an island. There are no lone rangers in the kingdom of God. We need to speak to each other. Make that phone call, send that text message, God created us to be together. He means for us to be together as a family.

Visitation is so important in the kingdom of God. I was asked to go and visit a dear old lady on her 90th birthday. She didn't know I was coming; I just popped in, gave her a little book, wished her a happy birthday and prayed with her. Her daughter contacted me later and said, "My mom's whole day was made by your visit." It took me five minutes. That's all.

Dwight L. Moody built a massive church in Chicago and he would personally visit the many members of his congregation. He would see if they were okay, if they had enough food and coal for the winter. That's how he visited hundreds of people.

Keep in touch with fellow believers, reach out to someone today.

WHAT ARE YOUR EXPECTATIONS?

"My soul, wait silently for God alone,
for my expectation is from Him."
PSALM 62:5

Our expectation comes from God alone. It's not fair for us to put that burden of expectation on anyone else. It's not fair to do it to your spouse or your parents. It is not fair to expect that child of yours to excel and put pressure on them. Put your expectation in Jesus alone!

When we have expectations, we believe that something will happen. When we spend quality time with our Lord Jesus, then we get to know His heart and our expectations will be accurate. But if we do not wait on the Lord, silently and alone in His presence, our expectations will run wild. We will start to ask and expect amiss. Remember, Jesus is not our ATM. You don't put your card in and expect Him to deliver. It is when we walk according to His ways that we can be confident that He will do what He promised.

You might know my little book *Faith Like Potatoes* and the story of how I planted the crop despite El Nino and everyone saying I shouldn't. During that time my expectation was not in the potatoes or the weather. No! It was in God and for His glory alone. God told me to plant those potatoes and, of course, He never once failed my expectation.

Through that experience, my faith grew and we received a crop of potatoes. If you put your expectation in Jesus, He will not fail you.

UP THE MOUNTAIN

"I will lift up my eyes to the hills—from whence
comes my help? My help comes from
the LORD, who made heaven and earth."

PSALM 121:1-2

I am a mountain man. I love the mountains. My wife, Jill, loves the sea and I always say to her tongue-in-cheek that Jesus never went down to the sea to pray, but up to the mountains! But the truth is that it doesn't matter where you go, it's not the surroundings that are important, it is your heart. For it is the Lord Jesus Christ and your intimate relationship with Him alone that really counts.

But you do need to get away on your own occasionally if you really want to hear a clear word from Him. Jesus did it, often the disciples were looking for Him, "Lord, where have You been? The crowds are waiting for You." He was up the mountain. He was waiting to hear from His heavenly Father.

Wherever you are, you can still hear from God. You might be in a hospital, a jail, a busy station or a dorm. Wherever you are you can still pray. Susanna Wesley, mother of John and Charles, had about a dozen children. She would pull her apron over her head to pray and her children knew that she should not be disturbed.

You don't have to go up the mountain literally, but you do have to spend time in the quiet place with the Lord every day. Make time to speak to Him today.

VALLEY GROWTH

Many are the afflictions of the righteous,
but the LORD delivers him out of them all.

PSALM 34:19

I've never met a man worth his salt who has not been through fiery trials and persecutions. It's painful at the time and those old men will tell you those aren't wrinkles, those are war maps—it's the road they've had to walk. But that is where growth takes place. Nobody in the New Testament suffered more than the Apostle Paul and he said in Romans 5:3-4, "We also glory in tribulations, knowing that tribulation produces perseverance; and perseverance, character; and character, hope."

Think of the butterfly in her cocoon. It is only through struggling to get out of the cocoon that her wings get strong enough to carry her and fly. If she was just gently taken out of her cocoon with no struggle, her wings would not be strong enough to fly.

Growth takes place in the valleys, in the dark and difficult times. You can ask any farmer; the crops are grown in the valleys in times of hardship. So do not panic. If you're going through a hard time at present, rather embrace it. Ask the Lord Jesus to assist you, to give you strength and to teach you through the tough time. You will experience spiritual growth if you persevere and trust the Lord during the struggles.

Do not despair if you are experiencing afflictions today, the Lord will deliver you out of them all.

THE MACEDONIAN MAN

And a vision appeared to Paul in the night.
A man of Macedonia stood and pleaded with him,
saying, "Come over to Macedonia and help us."
ACTS 16:9

In Acts 9, Paul had planned to preach in the province of Asia but the Spirit had told him not to. Then Paul has a vision of a man pleading with him to come to Macedonia and help them. In verse 10, we read that they immediately prepared to go.

In Acts 16, we see how much happened in Macedonia because of Paul's heeding the call of the Macedonian man. Lydia's conversion, the deliverance of a fortune-telling slave girl, Paul and Silas' imprisonment in Philippi, the conversion of the jailer and his household are some of the highlights of this trip.

In 2018, we heard our own Macedonian call when we are asked to hold a prayer meeting in Mitchells Plain in Cape Town. God identified Ashley, a young man of peace, a social worker and a man of God. He worked with drug addicts, alcoholics, prostitutes and broken people—and he was our Macedonian man.

We went to a city that was literally dying of thirst and we saw God perform a great miracle, one that I personally will never forget. We saw revival. We saw the glory of God manifest. Out of the poverty, pain and shame, we saw the flower of Cape Town emerge. And then in the middle of the meeting it started to rain!

Heed the call and go where God sends you!

GOD'S FAVOR

Then Pharaoh took his signet ring off his hand and put
it on Joseph's hand; and he clothed him in garments
of fine linen and put a gold chain around his neck.

GENESIS 41:42

God's favor! When we do it God's way, then He will do the rest. Today, do the right thing. Pay your accounts when they are due and be no man's debtor. Work with your own money and not with someone else's money. Don't keep anybody waiting. If you owe somebody something, pay them when it's due or preferably before it's due. Why? So that you can receive God's favor. Don't use what is not yours.

Joseph fled from Potiphar's wife when she tried to seduce him because he knew that she did not belong to him. She was the wife of another man. Don't play the fool. Don't think you can have an affair and get away with it. Why? Because God knows everything. Joseph did what God expected of him and God blessed him. He became second-in-command only to Pharaoh in the greatest nation on earth at the time.

Romans 6:23 says, "The wages of sin is death, but the gift of God is eternal life…" Joseph knew that obedience to God would yield far better results than disobedience. He obeyed God and did the right thing. As a result he enjoyed God's favor. Today, go out and do the right thing and God will honor you.

THE POWER OF WORDS

Who sharpen their tongue like a sword, and bend
their bows to shoot their arrows—bitter words...
PSALM 64:3

What you say is what you get and when you speak bitter, negative, untrue words, it makes you unwell. It makes you sick. Saint Augustine said of his mother, whom he loved so much, that she would never repeat what another said unless it was true and helpful—isn't that beautiful? Jesus, our Lord, spoke life. He did not speak death and that is why wherever He went, crowds of people thronged to Him like bees around a honey pot. As Proverbs 16:24 says, "Pleasant words are like a honeycomb, sweetness to the soul and health to the bones."

Many years ago, in 2005, we had one of our early Mighty Men Conferences on the farm. During a time of confession, men were coming up and confessing their sins. A policeman came up and said, "I've never told my son that I loved him and that I believe in him." At that moment, a young teenage boy came running up the aisle to his dad and the two hugged each other, with tears flowing. That young man went back home, he went back to his school and he made the first team rugby squad. He then went on to play provincial rugby because his dad spoke words of love and life over him.

Like never before folks need words of affirmation, words of encouragement. Go out and speak life and not death.

A MIRACLE-WORKING GOD

Then he called for a light, ran in, and fell down
trembling before Paul and Silas. And he brought
them out and said, "Sirs, what must I do to be saved?"
So they said, "Believe on the Lord Jesus Christ,
and you will be saved, you and your household."

ACTS 16:29-31

Paul and Silas were in chains in prison, praying and singing hymns at midnight. All the other prisoners were listening and then suddenly, a miracle happened—an earthquake. It shook the prison, opened the doors and released them from their chains. That was a God-incident so miraculous that the jailer was about to commit suicide, thinking that all the prisoners had escaped, but they were all there and accounted for. Trembling before Paul and Silas, he asked, "What must I do to be saved?"

Maybe you are asking that question: *What must I do to alleviate this crisis I am going through? This bankruptcy, this divorce, this sickness, this depression, this addiction—what must I do?* Well, you must do exactly what the disciples told the jailer to do. Believe in the Lord Jesus Christ and you will be saved.

What miracle are you looking for in your life today? Oh, I've seen so many miracles in my life. I really have and no one will ever tell me that God does not work miracles. Like Job, I can say wholeheartedly, "I know that my Redeemer lives, and He shall stand at last on the earth" (Job 19:25). Believe in the Lord Jesus Christ today.

SING TO THE LORD

Make a joyful shout to the LORD, all you lands!
Serve the LORD with gladness; come before His
presence with singing. Know that the LORD, He is God;
it is He who has made us, and not we ourselves;
we are His people and the sheep of His pasture.
PSALM 100:1-3

We need to serve the Lord with gladness. We have a choice to make: We can serve our blessed Lord Jesus with gladness and singing, or we can sit in the corner and sulk and be sad and negative about our lot in life. Thanksgiving and praise are like lights in the darkness because wherever they shine, darkness and despair are chased away. Jesus said, "I am the light of the world. He who follows Me shall not walk in darkness, but have the light of life" (John 8:12).

We were called to parliament in Cape Town a few years ago to pray for the desperate situation in the area. There was a severe drought and people were very worried. When I looked out at the crowd of people, I felt the Holy Spirit impress upon me to start singing in parliament, and all of a sudden everybody was up on their feet and they were dancing, singing and praising Jesus. A short while later, needless to say, the Rainmaker, the Lord Jesus did His miracle.

Go out today and sing praises to your Lord Jesus Christ and shine a light in the darkness of this world.

TURNED UPSIDE DOWN

*"These who have turned the world
upside down have come here too."*
ACTS 17:6

Wouldn't it be great to be described as, "These who have turned the world upside down"? The disciples were on fire for the Gospel. When they spread the Good News, they turned the world upside down.

Revelation 3:16 says: "So then, because you are lukewarm, and neither cold nor hot, I will vomit you out of My mouth." Those are very strong words spoken by the Master Himself. We mustn't be lukewarm Christians. Many years ago, I preached down in the Eastern Cape at a Christian conference. At halftime, an old farmer said to me, "Young man, you don't have to try so hard." I said, "Sir, you ain't seen nothing yet. Wait for the second half!" You know, if there's no passion, no excitement in your witness for the Lord, why should the world turn around and look to Jesus?

People are struggling with incredible pressure: the challenges of old age, the pain of losing a loved one and various financial, social and global challenges. Paul and Silas loved people and spoke about the love of Jesus Christ. That's what turns the world upside down—the Gospel! The good news about Jesus Christ is for free. You don't have to buy it, you don't have to earn it, you just have to receive it and believe it!

Tell people about your Good Friend, the Lord Jesus Christ, and you'll see a change come about.

FEELING DOWN?

Let God arise, let His enemies be scattered;
let those also who hate Him flee before Him.
PSALM 68:1

Just because you are a follower of Jesus does not mean that you are exempt from feeling down, depressed and despondent. You might be thinking to yourself, *I shouldn't feel like this because I am a child of God.* But the truth is that you are in a battle for your mind. The devil will try to tell you that you are the only one feeling depressed and that there is something wrong with you. But he is the enemy and is trying to defeat you.

Do you know that some of Jesus' greatest generals also suffered from bouts of depression? David was a man after God's own heart and yet he said: "Oh, that I had wings like a dove! I would fly away..." (Psalm 55:6). What about that great general, Elijah? He prayed that he might die. He said, "It is enough! Now, LORD, take my life." (1 Kings 19:4). And he said that just after the greatest victory he had ever had.

We don't live by our feelings; we live by faith in God! In Hebrews 13:5, the Lord says: "I will never leave you nor forsake you." We need to cling to that promise and not be defeated. Like the psalmist let us say, "Why am I discouraged? Why is my heart so sad? I will put my hope in God! I will praise Him again—my Savior and my God" (Psalm 43:5 NLT).

A LITTLE PATIENCE

And the waters prevailed on the earth
one hundred and fifty days.

GENESIS 7:24

One of the marks of great men and women of God is patience. Abraham waited twenty-five years before he received his son, Isaac, from the Lord. Noah spent 150 days in the ark before the waters subsided. Paul the Apostle was sent to the Arabian Desert for three years before God used him (see Galatians 1:18). We need to have patience and wait upon the Lord!

I've been watching a program called *Extreme Mustang Makeover* about wild horses that come from the wide-open prairies of America and have never been handled by a human being. Each trainer is given one horse and one hundred days to train that wild horse, and the one who does it the best wins.

I watched a teenage girl working with one of those horses. She worked with that horse for 100 days, every single day. Those animals were wild, very capable of hurting you badly, and yet, after 100 days of patience, love and perseverance, that young lady was on that Mustang's back, riding him around like he was a domesticated horse. It brought a tear to my eye.

Galatians 6:9 says, "And let us not grow weary while doing good, for in due season we shall reap if we do not lose heart." Don't give up. Be patient with your child, your spouse, your employees. The Lord will see you through!

OBEY HIS COMMANDMENTS

"My son, keep my words, and treasure my
commands within you. Keep my commands
and live, and my law as the apple of your eye."
PROVERBS 7:1-2

The Ten Commandments were given to us by God, not for Himself—He doesn't have to keep them, they are there to help us. They are put in place for our good. They prevent us from bending the law, taking shortcuts and telling white lies. They prevent us from that moment of madness that causes a lifetime of sadness.

Proverbs 7 is about a young man who is tempted by a woman whose husband is away and she seduces him into her house, just like an ox that is being led to the slaughter. I have seen it too many times; I have been to maximum security prisons and I have seen men, hardened criminals who are as tough as nails, and next to them stands another absolutely petrified prisoner. You can see he has come from a refined home but he made a big mistake. What did he do? He put his fingers in the till and he is in for fraud. He will tell you, "I meant to pay it back," but he didn't have time and the auditors caught him.

Don't do it! God put the commandments in place to protect us from the wiles of the devil. May the Lord bless you and keep you in Jesus' precious name as you walk in the blessing of God by obeying His commandments.

AIM FOR THE HEART

Put away from you a deceitful mouth, and put
perverse lips far from you. Let your eyes
look straight ahead, and your eyelids look right
before you. Ponder the path of your feet, and let
all your ways be established. Do not turn to the
right or the left; remove your foot from evil.

PROVERBS 4:24-27

I believe the Lord is telling us not to waste time on worthless, useless arguments. Some people like arguing just for the sake of it. They have no intention of changing at all. No one deserves to hear the Gospel twice until the world has heard it once. If someone continually argues with you about the things of the Lord, pray for them and then move on, otherwise you are wasting precious time.

I will go so far as to say that it is very difficult to win a person over to Jesus Christ through an argument. You have probably got more chance by losing the argument than by winning it because people become adamant and stubborn. They dig their heels in and they will not listen to reason.

When we are speaking about Jesus Christ, we need to aim for the heart. It is not clever words and it's not intellect, it is love that will win a soul over to Christ. Today, go out and love people and they will come to you and ask what they must do to meet the Man from Galilee. Preach the Gospel through love and, if necessary, use words.

HOLDING GROUND

Stand therefore, having girded your waist
with truth, having put on the breastplate
of righteousness , and having shod your feet
with the preparation of the gospel of peace...
EPHESIANS 6:14-15

William Booth, the founder of the Salvation Army, built the organization based on an army. They do not have fighting soldiers, but rather praying soldiers. Every time he left to go to another country, he would say, "Hold the fort!"

We need to stand. Remember, the battle is the Lord's; it is not our battle. We need to stand even though it is a very difficult thing to do because we always want to be busy doing something. We are programmed that way, aren't we? Instead of *doing*, we need to start *being*.

Now, Mary and Martha are a very good example. They both loved Jesus very much but if you look at Luke 10:41-42, "Jesus said to her, 'Martha, Martha, you are worried and troubled about many things. But one thing is needed, and Mary has chosen that good part, which will not be taken away from her.'"

Mary was sitting at the feet of Jesus and listening to His divine words while Martha was running to and fro trying to get things ready for the meal. The Lord says, "No, Martha, come and sit. I want to talk with you." The Lord created us to have fellowship with Him.

DON'T BE UNFAITHFUL

"He who calls you is faithful, who also will do it."

1 THESSALONIANS 5:24

God is faithful—it's in His character. That is who He is—a faithful God. And therefore, faithfulness in His people is very important to Him. If we go to Matthew 25:21, Jesus shares a parable and says, "His lord said to him, 'Well done, good and faithful servant; you were faithful over a few things, I will make you ruler over many things. Enter into the joy of your lord.'"

We need to be faithful to God and we need to trust the Faithful One. Early one morning, I was riding my mountain bike past an airstrip. It was absolutely dark and very misty. An airplane started up its engines and the pilots took off into a sheet of darkness. I thought, *Lord, these men are trusting that little box of instruments on the panel to keep them safe.* They had faith in that instrument panel and it took them out safely. Faith is important but faithfulness is also very important.

If you look at the definition of the word *faithfulness*, it means to be loyal and steadfast. It ranks very high in God's agenda when it comes to a man of God. If we look at 1 Corinthians 13, the last verse says, "…now abide faith, hope, love, these three; but the greatest of these is love." So the Lord really wants us to be faithful because He is faithful to us.

Do not be unfaithful today. Be faithful because God is faithful to us.

PLEASING TO HIM

"Who is able to stand before this holy LORD God?"
1 SAMUEL 6:20

In 1 Samuel 6, "fifty thousand and seventy men" were struck down because they were looking into the heart of the Ark of the Covenant. We cannot play with God; we need to do the things that are pleasing to the Lord. We must watch out for the fear of man, that is what keeps us from the fear of God. What a revolution would take place if we just did what God wanted!

What are we clinging to most in our lives at the moment? Is it our money, our reputation or our position in society? In Mark 10, there was a rich young man who came to Jesus. He said, "Good Teacher, what shall I do that I may inherit eternal life?" (Mark 10:17). And the Lord said, "One thing you lack: Go your way, sell whatever you have and give to the poor, and you will have treasure in heaven; and come, take up the cross, and follow Me" (Mark 10:21).

The Lord didn't bargain with him and say, "Listen I tell you what, just give half of your money to the poor, and come and follow Me." No, He said, "Give it all up," because that was the thing that was holding him back from serving God.

What is the thing that is holding you back from serving the Lord with all of your heart today? We need to live an undiluted life for Jesus.

FULL OF CHEER

A cheerful heart is good medicine,
but a broken spirit saps a person's strength.
PROVERBS 17:22 NLT

You know, laughter is like medicine. We need to start laughing, to start being joyful. We really need to concentrate on what Jesus has done for us. You see, joy is the keynote because God, through His Son, Jesus, has saved us.

When I am on a preaching campaign, the highlight of every meeting we have (and this is the honest truth) is not people getting out of wheelchairs and walking, or blind eyes opening and deaf ears being unstopped. It is when we make the altar call and people come forward! Old people, young people, men and women, husbands and wives, and they kneel at the altar to repent and ask Jesus to come into their hearts.

We see the tears of gratitude and thankfulness. We see those spiritual chains of addiction and oppression falling off their shoulders as they get up weeping with joy. That to me is the greatest miracle that I've ever seen.

These days there is so much pain, suffering and confusion. It is time to realize that the Lord is coming back soon and that's enough to be joyful about, isn't it?

THE HOLY ONE

Now in the synagogue there was a man who had
a spirit of an unclean demon. And he cried out with
a loud voice, saying, "Let us alone! What have we
to do with You, Jesus of Nazareth? Did You come to
destroy us? I know who You are—the Holy One of God!"
LUKE 4:33-34

Jesus is known by many titles. The one I love the most is the Friend of sinners. Jesus came for the sick, He did not come for the righteous. Jesus says, "Those who are well have no need of a physician, but those who are sick. I did not come to call the righteous, but sinners, to repentance" (Mark 2:17). That is why I love Him so much…because He came to save an unrighteous man like me!

Maybe you're reading this and thinking, *Is there any hope for a sinner like me?* Well, I want to tell you with joy in my heart that Jesus specializes in taking nobodies and making them into somebodies.

I remember a preacher coming from overseas many years ago. I was a new Christian and he said, "You will never turn a donkey into a racehorse." I said, "No, you have that wrong! I am the donkey and Jesus has made me into a racehorse!" That is exactly what Jesus does.

God takes sinners and turns them into saints. So, be encouraged today. Jesus loves you! All He wants you to do is to repent and get back in the race.

OUR HELPER

What then shall we say to these things?
If God is for us, who can be against us?
ROMANS 8:31

The Holy Spirit is available to help us with our battles here on earth at this very time. He is actually called "The Helper" because Jesus has sent Him to help us (see John 16:7). He is our Guide, our Counselor, our Protector, and even our Advocate—He speaks up for us. But we must call upon Him.

David, that little shepherd boy, was truly a mighty warrior of God. He called upon the Lord and then he subdued and conquered the whole of the Middle East—a mere shepherd boy! Why? Because he knew if God was for him there was no man who could stand against him. If you look at 1 Chronicles 18, every single battle that David fought, he won. Now, who are we going to trust? Are we going to trust ourselves or are we going to call upon the Holy Spirit, our Helper, to help us?

I remember years ago when I had just arrived from Zambia, my tractor broke down right in the middle of the planting season. I was planting a critical crop of seed maize. Timing was of the essence. My next-door neighbor, Irwin, heard what had happened. The next thing I saw was this whole fleet of red tractors coming up the road to help me plant that crop. You see, he was my friend and he helped me—I knew the Lord had sent him.

Call on the Helper today. Don't do it your way or by yourself, He will help you!

THINK BEFORE YOU JUDGE

"Do you think that David really honors your
father because he has sent comforters to you?
Did his servants not come to you to search
and to overthrow and to spy out the land?"

1 CHRONICLES 19:3

In 1 Chronicles 19, the king of Ammon died and his son, Hanun, took his place. David loved the people of Ammon because they showed kindness to him and so he sent his messengers to comfort Hanun but the young king got very poor counsel from his leaders. You see, David's messengers went to show David's commiseration because of the king's death and what happened as a result? Well, they misunderstood them and thought they were coming to spy on them.

The messengers were treated disgracefully because the young king had misunderstood what David was trying to do. They took David's messengers and shaved half of their hair off, cut their garments so their buttocks were exposed and sent them away in humiliation. Now, obviously, that really angered King David and as a result, it cost the whole nation of Ammon severely because they were totally defeated. David turned on them and conquered them.

I want to say to you, be careful that you don't judge people unintentionally because it can cost you dearly. Today, always think the best of people and their intentions, and you will find that the day will go so much easier for you.

THE SAME POWER

"And the glory which You gave Me I have given them, that they may be one just as We are one."
JOHN 17:22

The Lord Jesus Christ has given us (through the Holy Spirit) the same power that His Father gave Him when He walked on this earth. If ever people needed Jesus, it's today. A lot of people are just down. We really need to encourage them. We need to portray the presence of the Lord Jesus Christ wherever we go today. Romans 8:11 says, "But if the Spirit of Him who raised Jesus from the dead dwells in you, He who raised Christ from the dead will also give life to your mortal bodies through His Spirit who dwells in you."

We have no excuses. If Jesus Christ is our Lord and Savior, we need to go out there and encourage people in every sphere of life. When we go into the presence of people, they should see Jesus in us. They should see peace, confidence and joy. Let us show the love of Jesus. Now, why would we do that? Because it is what He did for us.

People need love; they are desperate for love. That is all that Mother Teresa did. She went into the streets where people were dying, lying in the gutter, and she would lay her hands upon them. And they would say, "But why are you doing this?" and she would say because this is what Jesus told her to do.

Go out today, love people, and the power of God will go before you.

KEEP THE VISION

Then the LORD answered me and said:
"Write the vision and make it plain on tablets,
that he may run who reads it. For the vision is
yet for an appointed time; but at the end it
will speak, and it will not lie. Though it tarries,
wait for it; because it will surely come, it will not tarry."

HABAKKUK 2:2-3

There might be a young man who has a vision of playing rugby for his country. What must he do then? Well, he had better get up in the morning and start training before he goes to school or university. You see, if you have got nothing to get up for, then you start to give up.

We really need to keep that vision sharp today, otherwise, we have nothing to study for, nothing to train for and, in fact, nothing to live for. Now, there are people in the world right now who are going to a lost eternity because they have never met the Man from Galilee. They have never heard the Word of Jesus. And we are the letter that the Lord is giving to tell the world that He is the Way, the Truth and the Life (see John 14:6).

Remember, there is more than one way to preach the Gospel. If you are a sportsman, you have an instant congregation. You can play your heart out and then tell people about Jesus because you have got a platform. A businessman can invest money into the Kingdom because we need money to get the job done. Don't wander away. Keep the vision.

IN THE SPIRIT

Satan rose up against Israel and caused David
to take a census of the people of Israel...
But Joab replied, "Are they not all your servants?
Why must you cause Israel to sin?"
1 CHRONICLES 21:1, 3 NLT

David became the greatest warrior in the history of Israel, but after God had given him all those victories, he decided to stop trusting in God and to trust in his own strength. He started in the Spirit and finished in the flesh, that was why God was so angry with him.

We had a healing meeting many years ago. When we made the call for people who were sick to come forward, a deaf man stood up. There was a large crowd waiting in anticipation as the man took out his hearing aids. I anointed him with oil and prayed the prayer of faith. He was healed!

I remember taking those hearing aids home and throwing them in the boiler. The next morning I got a phone call saying that the man wanted his hearing aids back. So I asked him, "Why do you want them back? God has healed you." In the end, he broke down and admitted that he wanted to keep them just in case.

Why did you start in the Spirit only to now try to finish in your own strength? Let's look to Jesus today. He is our healer, He is our deliverer and He is everything we need.

WALK IN THE LIGHT

"For you were once darkness, but now you
are light in the Lord. Walk as children
of light (for the fruit of the Spirit is in
all goodness, righteousness, and truth)."
EPHESIANS 5:8-9

Our eyes are darkened when our hearts are not pure. Once we shut the door to God's truth in our hearts, we cannot see where we are going. If we walk in the light of God, then we ought to shine and resemble God, and reflect His light in the darkness. We must walk with Him daily if we are going to walk in His light. People are drawn to those who walk in the light of God, just like moths are drawn to the light of a lamp in the middle of the night.

We need our "Yes" to be yes and we need to let our "No" be no. James 1:6 says, "But let him ask in faith, with no doubting, for he who doubts is like a wave of the sea driven and tossed by the wind." We need to be definite and then we will shine with the light of God and we will not walk in the darkness.

Today, go out and shine because people are in darkness everywhere. People are undecided; they don't know how to make decisions. They are going with the flow and they are getting themselves into trouble. We need to walk according to the Word of God.

HANDING OVER

So when David was old and full of days,
he made his son Solomon king over Israel.
1 CHRONICLES 23:1

David handed over the reins to his son, Solomon. In John 21:16, Jesus Christ did the same when He said to Simon Peter, "Tend My sheep." Jesus handed over the responsibility to Peter. Today, we have to hand over the reins to our young people—our children. What is so sad to me is someone who will just not release the reins.

You see, David wanted to build the greatest temple in the world but the Lord said, "You are not going to do that. Your son is going to do that" (see 1 Chronicles 28). So David equipped Solomon: He put in the money and got the wood, the timber, the artisans…he got it all set up for Solomon and he let Solomon do the job. I want to say to you today, we need to hand over the reins.

An old friend came to see me once. He was a very successful farmer and he came to see me with his son. It was so nice to meet his son. We started talking about our children. He told me about his sons and his daughter, and his grandchildren. We just sat there and we were so thankful to God for what He has done through our children.

Hand over today and enjoy it!

DECISION-MAKING

Now it came to pass in those days that He went
out to the mountain to pray, and continued all
night in prayer to God. And when it was day,
He called His disciples to Himself; and from them
He chose twelve whom He also named apostles.

LUKE 6:12-13

We need to spend more time in prayer before we make major decisions. Jesus spent all night in prayer before He chose the twelve disciples. Never be pressed into making a decision or a choice. That business deal that you have been offered…if the man is pressing you, maybe you need to decline. Why is there such a rush? Whether you are going to leave or whether you are going to stay…take your time and hear from God.

In 2008, we had the biggest tent in the world on Shalom farm. It seated 30,000 men inside and there was an overflow of men on the outside. That was a state-of-the-art tent that took up four rugby fields. A qualified team of riggers had to put it up and it took more than fifteen 30-ton trucks to bring it to the farm.

After the event, we were contacted by some businessmen who offered to buy it for us. Initially, I was overwhelmed by their kind offer but I asked if I could pray about it. Then I came back and said, "God says I can't take it." You see, it cost about a million rand to erect it and I would need a fleet of trucks to move it from one place to another. Of course, the next year we had a crowd that the tent could never have contained. Pray first and then make a decision!

DO TO OTHERS

"And just as you want men to do to you,
you also do to them likewise."
LUKE 6:31

Never ask a man to do a job that you are not prepared to do yourself...or you can't do. Always lead from the front. Hypocrisy is the thing that keeps so many from following Jesus. Another word for hypocrisy is *pretense*. You pretend that you can do the job and you are shouting at the other man but really you can't do it yourself.

We need to be honest and treat folk as we would have them treat us. Always put yourself in their shoes and then ask yourself a question: "If I was in that situation, how would I like people to treat me?"

Don't tell people how to do the job, rather show them how to do it. Like a farmer who sees the tractor driver is plowing in the wrong gear. Instead of shouting at the man, get on the tractor and show him how to plow. That is how he learns and that is how he has respect for you.

We often have riding instructors come out from the USA to show us the finer points in training horses and they are excellent. They treat an old lady and an old man with respect, always esteeming others better than themselves.

Treat people the way you would like them to treat you.

LIKE FLINT

"For the Lord GOD will help Me; therefore I will
not be disgraced; therefore I have set My face like
a flint, and I know that I will not be ashamed."

ISAIAH 50:7

You and I need to set our faces like a flint regarding the vision that God has given us. We need to remain focused. Jesus set His face to Jerusalem and He knew what was waiting for Him there—the cross, the crucifixion, but He did not turn away from the vision. Paul went to Rome where he knew they wanted to kill him but he did not change—he set his face like a flint towards his calling.

Many years ago, a friend of mine picked me up at the airport. As we were driving, he asked me, "Did you see the newspapers this morning? They are accusing a mighty man in the Western Cape of shooting dogs and terrorizing children."

Now, of course, it was a lie but the thing that really upset me was that there was a picture of me on the front cover. It was misleading. I said, "Shall I sue the newspapers?" And he said something in Latin that I have never forgotten: "*Aquila non capit muscas.*" It means, "The eagle does not catch flies." An eagle chases the big game. It is the little house birds that eat the flies.

Go out today and set your face like a flint, complete the task God has given you!

BE EXAMPLES

"And why do you look at the speck in your brother's
eye, but do not perceive the plank in your own eye?
Or how can you say to your brother, 'Brother, let
me remove the speck that is in your eye,' when you
yourself do not see the plank that is in your own eye?"

LUKE 6:41-42

Yes, we have got to get the plank out before we can see the speck. Remember, charity (which is another word for love) begins at home. We must earn the right to speak into someone's life. Can you and I honestly say with Paul the Apostle, "Imitate me, just as I also imitate Christ" (1 Corinthians 11:1)?

Now, your children will never do what you tell them to do. But what they will do is imitate you and that is quite scary. The best form of influence is by example.

Don't tell your son that he must love his wife. Show him how he must love his wife by the way you love his mother. Mothers, don't tell your daughter that she must take care of her husband; show her by the way you take care of her dad.

We really need to lead by example. We need to take that plank out of our own eye so that we can see clearly to take the speck out of our brother's eye.

Go out and imitate Christ just as Paul imitated Him.

GOOD FRUIT

"Even so, every good tree bears good fruit,
but a bad tree bears bad fruit. A good tree cannot
bear bad fruit, nor can a bad tree bear good fruit."
MATTHEW 7:17-18

Jesus said that a good tree cannot bear bad fruit, nor can a bad tree bear good fruit. He went on to say, "...by their fruits you will know them" (v. 20). So we have to stop telling people all the time that we love them and start showing them that we love them.

I remember looking at a cartoon in a magazine many years ago. There was a drawing of a little boy holding a begging bowl and asking the minister who was preaching to him with a big black Bible and a big fat stomach, "Sir, will there be food in heaven?" You and I have got to put our money where our mouth is sometimes, don't we?

It is not about the quantity by the way; it is about the quality of the fruit. A few years ago a very dear friend of mine drove 600 km to see me. He got out of the car and he said, "I want to pray over you." He anointed me with oil and prayed over me just before a major meeting we were having on the farm. Then he got back in the car and drove 600 km back home. Now that is fruit I will never forget.

It's not the quantity, it is the quality and it's the heart! Go and bear fruit today. May Jesus bless you as you produce good fruit.

QUIET TIME

*"Not everyone who says to Me, 'Lord, Lord,'
shall enter the kingdom of heaven, but he
who does the will of My Father in heaven."*
MATTHEW 7:21

A man of God came to visit me a couple of weeks ago and he said something I will never forget: "Delayed obedience is disobedience." That is right, Jesus likens this attitude to the man who built his house on the sand as opposed to the man who was obedient and built his house on the rock (see Luke 6:48).

Once during a television interview, the host asked if he could tell me something that was bothering him. He asked, "Why is it that there are so many men and women who have been called by God and are doing mighty works, who just do not finish their walk with God?" I said to the young man, "Quiet time." You see, it is impossible to speak with Jesus every day if we are living a double lifestyle. The Holy Spirit, sometimes referred to as the Hound of Heaven, will track you down. You will not fool Him. You will not be able to live an immoral life and continue having a daily quiet time with Jesus.

Where are we building our house today? Is it on the Rock or is it in the sand? Please don't compromise your time with Jesus each day because I can tell you from experience, He is the only One who will keep you safe. When the storms of life come, and I can tell you they will come, He will be your Rock. And if you are building your house upon the Rock, it will stand.

IN THE DARK

Then Jesus spoke to them again, saying, "I am
the light of the world. He who follows Me shall
not walk in darkness, but have the light of life."

JOHN 8:12

The other morning I woke up early, told my wife that I love her and said, "I am going to make you a nice cup of tea." But then I realized that the lights were out. There was a power failure and I had to grope around in the dark.

Living in the dark slows you down. When you can't see where you are going you make bad mistakes and you can't find what you are looking for. You become impatient with yourself and you make a poor fire and then you need to start again.

We need to start to walk in the light of God. You know, when you can see where you are going, you can do the job in half the time and it is a pleasant thing to do because everything is there for you and it all works out beautifully. You don't have to wait for half an hour while the stove gets hot so that you can boil the water.

Today, put your hand in the hand of God and He will lead you through the darkness. It is not the time to take the wrong road. We have to invest in the right things and we have to do the right things. Follow Jesus and you will always be in the light.

ASK FOR WISDOM

"Now give me wisdom and knowledge,
that I may go out and come in before this people;
for who can judge this great people of Yours?"
2 CHRONICLES 1:10

Solomon asked God to give him wisdom and knowledge. In Job 28:28, Job said, "Behold, the fear of the Lord, that is wisdom, and to depart from evil is understanding." Wisdom and knowledge is a gift from God and you can ask for it simply, just like Solomon did. Jesus said in Matthew 7:7, "Ask, and it will be given to you; seek, and you will find; knock, and it will be opened to you."

My late dad's brother struggled with asthma his whole life. He did not have much of an education and he was always in hospital. When he eventually left school, he became a shepherd in Scotland. He was extremely sought after by the wealthy farming community. Do you know why? Because he had a team of sheepdogs that he had trained himself and that were incredible. I have never seen a man work with a flock of sheep like that. I am talking about tending to hundreds and hundreds of sheep, all by himself with his dogs. Other farmers had to employ many men to do the same job.

Wisdom and knowledge don't come from university alone. They come from the school of life—from experience. Ask Jesus for wisdom to live this life in a way that pleases Him.

PREPARED FOR BATTLE

"Put on the whole armor of God, that you may
be able to stand against the wiles of the devil."
EPHESIANS 6:11

We are in a war. We are in a full-scale war like never before in the history of the earth. We need to be prepared each day. The devil and all his demons are afraid of the soldiers of the cross. Do not be slack by failing to put your armor on each morning. Good soldiers of the cross do not keep bad company. Don't spend time fraternizing with the enemy. Remember, before you speak to people about God, be sure that you have first spoken to God about those people. That is what an intercessor told me many years ago.

I am a beekeeper. I love my bees—I do not fear them but I do respect them. There are certain times of the day when I work with my bees and there are other times when I won't. When I put on that bee suit, I make sure that there are no openings that the bees can penetrate and sting me. Do not give the devil a foothold in your life, my dear friend. Don't be lazy, don't compromise and never turn your back on the enemy.

When we are properly kitted out, every morning before we go out, the devil knows it and he backs off. He is afraid of us because he knows we are fully armored. Go out today and tell people about Jesus Christ, but be sure that you have prepared yourself first.

DON'T BE DISTRACTED

David said to Abishai and to all his servants,
"My own son is trying to kill me. Doesn't this
relative of Saul have even more reason to do
so? Leave him alone and let him curse, for the
LORD has told him to do it. And perhaps the
LORD will see that I am being wronged and
will bless me because of these curses today."

2 SAMUEL 16:11-12 NLT

Shimei went along the hillside opposite King David and cursed him as he went, throwing stones at him and even kicking up dust. Now, you can imagine David's men saying, "King David, sort him out, deal with him, he is just a little runt!" But David said, "No, leave him." Why? Proverbs 20:22 says, "Do not say, 'I will recompense evil'; wait for the LORD, and He will save you."

When the soldiers were throwing dice and fighting over Jesus' clothes while He was dying on the cross, He didn't get distracted from what the Father had planned. No, instead He said, "Father, forgive them, for they do not know what they do" (Luke 23:34).

Maybe you are sitting there today and saying, "It is not fair. These people are not being dealt with. I have been unjustly criticized." Leave it. You and I, like King David, must not be distracted; we must not be taken off our course by accusations that have no truth in them, by people who are throwing stones at us. We must rise to the occasion and keep on with the mission that God has called us to.

A COMPARABLE HELPER

...and Joanna the wife of Chuza,
Herod's steward, and Susanna, and many
others who provided for Him from their substance.
LUKE 8:3

Jesus had many women who traveled with Him and they took care of Him and the disciples. You don't hear much about them but I want to tell you, they wouldn't have made it without those women. They supplied the needs of the disciples and the Master from their very own finances and personal substance. I just want to praise God this morning for the women-folk.

When I travel overseas, Jill always packs my suitcase. She puts stuff in and I take it out! I always tell her, "I won't need that," and, "I won't need this," and she says, "Take it, just in case." And every single time I need that extra shirt because the other one got messed up, I say, "Thank You, Lord, for a good wife."

You know, a woman can make or break a man by the way she takes care of him. We really need to appreciate our women-folk. Once the honeymoon is over, when the hard-working man comes home at night he wants to come home to a place that is full of love and care, where the children are nicely bathed and in their pajamas, and there is a hot meal on the table…that makes a man keep going.

I just want to thank Jesus today for creating our help-meets, our soulmates, who give us godly counsel all the time.

GODLY INTEGRITY

"...we should live soberly, righteously,
and godly in the present age."

TITUS 2:12

Luke 17:17-18 says: "So Jesus answered and said, 'Were there not ten cleansed? But where are the nine? Were there not any found who returned to give glory to God except this foreigner?'" There were ten lepers that Jesus healed. Only one came back to say thank you and he wasn't even a Jew—he was a Samaritan.

So often, unfortunately, many unbelievers can put us Christians to shame when it comes to good manners, integrity and just plain honesty. We need to let our walking do the talking. We need godly integrity.

Many years ago, I had the privilege of visiting Regent University. And I heard an interesting story. A young student applied for a bursary to attend this very prestigious house of learning and he was told by post that he had been accepted. Needless to say, he was ecstatic. Well, he packed up all his gear and arrived at the massive campus to register but the lady at reception said, "Unfortunately, you have been turned down."

"Why?" the young man asked. "Because you didn't say thank you." We have really got to watch our manners. We have got to watch the way we act. There are many people who don't even know Jesus, who can put us to shame when it comes to good, basic manners. Go out today and let your walking do the talking.

TEMPLE OF GOD

"But will God indeed dwell with men on the earth? Behold, heaven and the heaven of heavens cannot contain You. How much less this temple which I have built!"

2 CHRONICLES 6:18

Solomon spoke the above words after he had built the most incredible, majestic, mighty and glorious structure that has been built on the face of the earth. And yet he said, "Can God dwell in a man-made place? There is nothing on earth, Lord, that can contain You!" What a God you and I serve!

How often do we forget that? John 1:1 says, "In the beginning was the Word, and the Word was with God, and the Word was God." God said one word and everything that you can conceive and see was made in an instant. Oh yes! And by the way, that Word is Jesus—majestic and glorious!

We need to respect Him so much more, don't we? He is indeed the Savior of the world and if it weren't for God's only Son, we would be on our way to a lost eternity. John 3:16 says, "For God (that same God who Solomon is talking about) so loved the world that He gave His only begotten Son, that whoever believes in Him should not perish but have everlasting life."

And that is why we, as believers, so often weep with joy and with reverence when we hear the name of our Beloved mentioned. No, He can never be housed in a building but He can be housed in our hearts!

SEPTEMBER 26

MY BROTHER'S KEEPER

Then the LORD said to Cain,
"Where is Abel your brother?" He said,
"I do not know. Am I my brother's keeper?"
GENESIS 4:9

Are you your brother's keeper? This is actually a serious question and the answer is a resounding, "Yes, I actually am!" You and I have a responsibility to take care of one another. And it is so easy to give to those who appreciate what you are doing for them and who also can respond in like manner. But it is not so easy when you do it for those who don't even know that you did it, or for those who don't appreciate it.

One of my intercessors and a dear son in the Lord sent me a short clip the other day and it touched my heart deeply. It is just a lighthearted clip but it speaks volumes.

It shows a man who has broken down on the side of the road. The car's bonnet is lifted and there is smoke coming out of the engine. All of a sudden, some good Samaritan stops to see if he can help. When he walks up to the car, he sees the man barbecuing some meat under the bonnet. He offers to share with the good Samaritan.

I just want to say to you today, you can't out-bless the Lord Jesus Christ. The more you give to Him, the more He gives back to you. Today, go out and bless somebody and in doing so, the Lord has told us that we will be blessing Him. It is a far greater pleasure and a gift to give than to receive.

DO NOT SLUMBER

But Jesus went to the Mount of Olives.
Now early in the morning He came again
into the temple, and all the people came
to Him; and He sat down and taught them.
JOHN 8:1-2

We have to get up and get going in the morning! I don't think that our beloved Jesus ever slept in or overslept…or didn't get up in the morning. I don't think there is one place that you will find in the whole Bible where the Lord had to be woken up, apart from the time He was sleeping in the ship, but that was for a different reason. He was an early riser.

One of my trustees gets up at 1:30 AM every morning. That is when he does his work and has his quiet time. He has done it his whole life. You might say, "Well, Angus, I am a pensioner now." Well, this man is 87 years young! We have got to get up in the morning.

You know, Jesus always conferred with His Father before He conferred with the people and that is why you and I need to spend time early in the morning with the Lord. Otherwise, poverty, as it says in Proverbs 6:10, will come upon you. Have you noticed how many things seem to go so much smoother when you get up in the morning and you do them straightaway?

Get up in the morning. Discipline yourself and your day will go so much smoother. Speak to Jesus first!

EYE FOR AN EYE

"Do not be overcome by evil,
but overcome evil with good."
ROMANS 12:21

Don't allow evil to drown you because it will rob you of your joy. It will actually make you sick—rather overcome evil with good. Let us show kindness to all men and trust God for the results. Remember, revenge belongs to God and He will set the record straight. That is why we are called to pray for our enemies and for those who oppress us.

In Old Testament days they would say, "An eye for an eye and a tooth for a tooth." But Jesus says in Matthew 5:38-39, "You have heard that it was said, 'An eye for an eye and a tooth for a tooth.' But I tell you not to resist an evil person. But whoever slaps you on your right cheek, turn the other to him also."

Wow! That is a powerful statement, but why should we do this? Because that is where you get the victory. Today, give those difficult relationships and those situations to the Lord Jesus Christ and He will carry your burdens for you.

Nothing on this earth is more powerful than unconditional love. Now, if you and I forgive, then it stops. But if we say, "No, I want to have my own revenge,"…an eye for an eye and a tooth for a tooth…half the world would be walking around toothless and blind. We need to forgive and remember that it takes two to tango. Get ready today for your miracle. It might be at work, it might be in school and it might even be in your own home. Jesus will do it for us.

HOMECOMING

"Moreover, concerning a foreigner, who is not of Your people Israel, but has come from a far country for the sake of Your great name and Your mighty hand and Your outstretched arm, when they come and pray in this temple; then hear from heaven Your dwelling place, and do according to all for which the foreigner calls to You, that all peoples of the earth may know Your name and fear You, as do Your people Israel..."

2 CHRONICLES 6:32-33

What a beautiful promise! And so is the promise we receive in Romans 10:13, which says, "For 'whoever calls on the name of the LORD shall be saved.'"

Maybe this devotion is for you, my dear friend, who has been in the far country and you are not sure whether Jesus will welcome you back again. I have good news for you! He is waiting for you with outstretched arms just like the father did for his prodigal son.

The Lord says in Revelation 3:20, "Behold, I stand at the door and knock. If anyone hears My voice and opens the door, I will come in to him and dine with him, and he with Me." He is waiting for you. It doesn't matter what you have done, who you are, or what nation you come from. If you sincerely repent and call upon the name of the Lord Jesus Christ, you shall be saved.

Let Jesus wipe away your tears today. Apologize to Him, come home, and start a new relationship with your heavenly Father.

TESTIFY

And he went his way and proclaimed
throughout the whole city what
great things Jesus had done for him.

LUKE 8:39

The power of personal testimony! You know that is what brought Jill and me to Christ. It wasn't a great preacher; it was ordinary people, getting up into the pulpit and sharing about what Jesus had done to change their lives. You see, you can't argue with a testimony—either you believe it or you reject it because you weren't there. There is something so innocent, so pure about an honest, simple testimony.

The day after Jill and I gave our lives to Christ, my neighbor and I were on our way to a cattle sale. He was a big tough guy. We were driving down the road and the Holy Spirit tapped me on the shoulder and said, "Testify. Tell him what has happened to you!" I stuttered and nervously said, "Something happened to me yesterday. Jesus touched my life and He has given me freedom." I looked at him. He went a bit grey and said, "Angus, I am pleased for you."

A few years later, I was sitting in my farm office when this same man came to me and said, "Angus, I need help." I went to his house and on our knees in the lounge, in front of his family, we prayed the Sinner's Prayer together. Go out today and tell someone what Jesus has done for you.

THE WORD

"So shall My word be that goes forth
from My mouth; it shall not return to Me void,
but it shall accomplish what I please, and it
shall prosper in the thing for which I sent it."

ISAIAH 55:11

There is power in the spoken Word of God. You see, Jesus is the Word: "In the beginning was the Word, and the Word was with God, and the Word was God" (John 1:1).

Years ago, I got an invitation from an old gentleman who asked if he could meet me. I was going to a conference and I said I would stop by on my way there. As I walked into his house, I strongly felt the presence of God. I asked him, "Can you please pray for me? I want the anointing of God on my life. I want your mantle." He said, "Yes, Angus."

He went into his bedroom and got a bottle of oil. I got on my knees in the lounge and he anointed me with oil. But do you know what amazed me most about that old gentleman? He spoke pure, undiluted Scripture from memory!

I went on my way to that men's conference and I have never seen the power of God move like it did that weekend. Men on their knees, broken, weeping, restored, healed, set free. Go out today and use the Word of God for everything. Read it! Memorize it and most of all believe it—Jesus is the Word!

THE LITTLE CHILDREN

Then little children were brought to Him that He might put His hands on them and pray, but the disciples rebuked them. But Jesus said, "Let the little children come to Me, and do not forbid them; for of such is the kingdom of heaven."

MATTHEW 19:13-14

Don't discourage your children from entering into God's kingdom. You might say, "No, Angus, I would never do that!" But why does mom have to take them to church alone? Why do you sit in the car park reading the newspaper until the service is over? Don't you know that your child will do exactly what you do when they are older, because you are their absolute hero? Don't prevent them from coming to Jesus. You have to lead from the front. You need to read Bible stories to them before they go to sleep—that is not mom's job alone.

You know, we have a prayer meeting every Monday afternoon in the chapel on the farm. We have several little children, between the ages of five and fourteen, who come up on their bicycles with all the adults. They get involved in praying. These little guys are praying one after the other. They are reading Bible verses—it is so beautiful. It brings tears to my eyes.

Please don't, in any way, stand in the way when your little boy or girl wants to go to church. Go with them. Lead from the front.

GOOD SEED PAYS

Let us not grow weary while doing good, for in
due season we shall reap if we do not lose heart.

GALATIANS 6:9

There is a big seed company very near Shalom farm that had a
slogan many years ago that read: "Good seed does not cost,
it pays."

I had the privilege of speaking at a Mighty Men Conference
in South Africa a few years ago where the organizers said to me,
"You have two very special guests who want to meet you. They
have come all the way from France to be here this weekend."
The one was a taxi driver in France and he had come over with
his brother. Now, this taxi driver once dropped of some passen-
gers and they had left a book in the back of the taxi, which he
started to read. It was one of my books.

Now, I want to tell you, I have written many books over
many years, and sometimes I get weary and I say, "Lord, is
anybody going to read these books?" Of course, the devil says,
"No, no one is going to read those books of yours." Yet I have
persevered and what has happened? In due season, I am reap-
ing. I met these two wonderful men of God and it was because
of a sccd sown, a book left in the back of a taxi in France.

Folks, don't give up today. Keep on doing what you are doing for the Lord and the Lord will reward you. In due season
we will reap if we do not give up doing good. Remember, good
seed doesn't cost, it pays.

PASSING THROUGH

Jesus replied, "Foxes have dens to live in,
and birds have nests, but the Son of Man
has no place even to lay his head."
MATTHEW 8:20 NLT

You and I really need to cut our coat according to our cloth. What does that mean? It simply means to live according to your financial limitations. Remember, this home is not our eternal home—we are just passing through. Heaven is our home. You know, some of us are so bogged down with the things of this world that if Jesus were to return tomorrow, we wouldn't be able to go home with Him because we owe too much!

When Jesus sent the disciples out to preach and to heal the sick, He told them clearly in Luke 9:3, "Take nothing for the journey, neither staffs nor bag nor bread nor money; and do not have two tunics apiece." In other words, we need to travel light. Now, I am not suggesting that we must become irresponsible; we have to make provision for our families and our loved ones. But we should not let worldly possessions bog us down.

Just look at the reindeer herders in the frozen North. They travel with their animals and they live in tents. You will see them one day and the next day they've moved on, following the seasons with their animals.

You and I need to get ready for the coming of the Lord. Keep watching the clouds because one of these glorious mornings, we will see Him coming in the clouds.

CALL UPON HIM

"However I did not believe their words until I
came and saw with my own eyes; and indeed
the half of the greatness of your wisdom was not
told me. You exceed the fame of which I heard."

2 CHRONICLES 9:6

The Queen of Sheba had probably traveled for a few months from Ethiopia to Israel to meet King Solomon. She met the wisest, richest man on earth and she came to hear from him. When she arrived, she could not believe what she saw. The wealth, the organization, the wisdom that she had heard about was only half of what she actually saw for herself.

Why is it that you and I run to and fro to seek man's counsel when Jesus our Lord is sitting quietly, waiting for us to come to Him? He wants to help us and He wants to guide us. Matthew 11:28-29 says, "Come to Me, all you who labor and are heavy laden, and I will give you rest. Take My yoke upon you and learn from Me, for I am gentle and lowly in heart, and you will find rest for your souls."

You and I have all the counsel, the power and protection at our disposal. All we have to do is to ask Him for it. That is exactly what King Solomon did and God granted it to him. Please, today, don't run all over the place. The Lord says, "Call to Me, and I will answer you, and show you great and mighty things, which you do not know" (Jeremiah 33:3). Call upon Him today and He will answer you.

JESUS CHRIST

He asked His disciples, saying to them,
"Who do men say that I am?" Peter answered
and said to Him, "You are the Christ."
MARK 8:27, 29

When I gave my life to Jesus Christ, I did not give my life to an ideology or a certain denomination. No, I gave my life to a Person, to Jesus Christ—my Best Friend! Today we need to let our faith in the Lord Jesus Christ do the talking. Don't just tell folks that Jesus is your Friend, show them that He is your Friend by your actions.

I remember years ago a man came to visit me. He was a school teacher who was traveling around South Africa with a group of his students and he said to them, "I am going to prove to you that Jesus Christ is alive. We are not going to take one cent with us. The Lord is going to provide for us."

He arrived in Greytown and sat in that little house of ours one night prophesying over us. Now, Jill and I had just given our lives to the Lord. I hadn't even started preaching but he started telling me about things that would happen. Every single one of those things that he prophesied has taken place. There is more evidence today in my life that Jesus is alive than the day I met Him and gave my life to Him.

Today remember that He is the Christ; the Son of God, He is the soon-coming King. He loves you and He died for you.

HEMMED IN

"How often I wanted to gather your children
together, as a hen gathers her chicks under
her wings, but you were not willing!"
MATTHEW 23:37

When a young mother has bathed her beautiful baby, she wraps it up tightly—so snug and so secure. You and I need to be hemmed in by the Lord Jesus Christ today. To be "hemmed in" means to be surrounded closely on all sides. That makes us feel secure and safe.

People are so distressed today. Nothing seems safe, secure or certain anymore. In Israel there is a little church on the Mount of Olives that overlooks the Kidron Valley. Jesus sat there and that is where He said, "I would just love to gather you together but you are not willing." Let the Lord hem you in. Let Him look after you like a mother hen looks after her little chicks. Don't push Him away.

You know, one night we were driving home. It was a rough road; it had been raining and there were potholes everywhere. There was a huge 30-ton truck in front of us. We decided to tuck in behind him. He had massive red brake lights and every time he came to a pothole, he would tap his brakes and we'd know there was a pothole coming. We just settled in behind him and he took us safely to our destination.

Why don't you and I allow Jesus to guide us? He wants to. Let's just allow Him to look after us and wrap us up, nice and tight, and take us to our destination.

RED HOT

"For whoever is ashamed of Me and My words, of him the Son of Man will be ashamed when He comes in His own glory, and in His Father's, and of the holy angels."
LUKE 9:26

We have to stand up and be counted in these days—it is not optional. The hardest place to be a Christian is in your own hometown or environment. It is much easier to be a Christian out there in the world where nobody knows you.

At my age, people have already made up their minds what they think about Christians and we have made our stance. But for the younger generation, it is a struggle in an unforgiving and sometimes ruthless society, especially at school or at university. The easiest thing to do to make your stand for Christ is to make it crystal clear the first day you go to school or university—right from the start.

The worst thing for that young person to do is to be lukewarm, and to blow hot and cold. No one will like you for that. Jesus Himself said, "I know all the things you do, that you are neither hot nor cold. I wish that you were one or the other! But since you are like lukewarm water, neither hot nor cold, I will spit you out of my mouth" (Revelation 3:15-16 NLT).

Let us be red hot for the Lord Jesus Christ. Never be ashamed to take a stand for Jesus and share the Gospel. As Paul says, "I am not ashamed of the gospel of Christ, for it is the power of God to salvation for everyone who believes" (Romans 1:16).

DOING OUR BIT

Then Peter answered and said to Jesus,
"Lord, it is good for us to be here; if You wish,
let us make here three tabernacles:
one for You, one for Moses, and one for Elijah."
MATTHEW 17:4

Peter, James, and John had seen the transfiguration of the Lord Jesus Christ and had experienced the presence of Almighty God on the mountaintop. Peter wanted them to stay there but Jesus said, "No, we cannot stay there. We cannot stay in that nice, secure and peaceful place. We have to go down into the valley where the people are. We have to roll up our sleeves and get to work…to help the poor, the needy, the widow and the orphan, those who use and even abuse you."

Why can't we just stay secluded and safe from all the ugliness that goes on in this tired old world? Well, because Jesus loves the prostitute, the drug addict, the thief…not that He loves what they are doing but He loves them and He wants us to help them.

The very first thing that happened when Jesus came down from the Mount of Transfiguration was that He was confronted by a multitude of people. A desperate father came to Him and said, "Please help, my little son is an epileptic," and Jesus cured the boy that very hour. We need to get involved.

Remember, first the mountain and then the ministry. We have to get the balance right. First, spend time with the Lord and then go down into the valley and help the people.

GOOD COUNSEL

"My little finger shall be thicker than my father's waist!"
2 CHRONICLES 10:10

These words were spoken by the foolish young King Rehoboam. He had taken over from his father, who was none other than the wisest man who had ever lived, King Solomon himself. The people came to him and said, "Lighten our burden and we will serve you." The elders advised him to listen to the people but the young king listened to his friends instead, who said, "Make it harder for them." As a result, he lost his kingdom.

Do not disregard priceless advice which is often given freely and in love. Many years ago, some young farmers decided to grow a crop that had never been grown in this area before. We live in a very misty area, which means it is always damp and rainy in the summertime. The older farmers in the area said that the particular crop would not grow here but the young farmers did not take notice. They planted that crop.

Initially, the fields looked beautiful but when it came time to harvest, the crop fell over. It lay on the ground and became moldy. We need to listen to the counsel of men and women who have been there before. Jesus said in Matthew 11:29, "…learn from Me, for I am gentle and lowly in heart, and you will find rest for your souls."

Go out today and listen to the counsel of experienced godly people who have been there before. They will save you a lot of pain and a lot of tears.

GRACE AND MERCY

For by grace you have been saved through faith,
and that not of yourselves; it is the gift of God,
not of works, lest anyone should boast.

EPHESIANS 2:8-9

Mercy is something to be grateful for. It is an opportunity to say sorry, to make amends, and that is why, as an evangelist, the altar call is so critical. It is where the battle is at its fiercest. The devil says, "Don't move. Don't make a fool of yourself. Don't go up there and say sorry to Jesus." The Lord says, "Repent and be saved."

If you look at those old videos of Billy Graham, thousands of people came forward and bowed the knee at the altar to ask for forgiveness. It warms my heart. I have seen it time and time again, and it never ceases to amaze me. I have seen husbands and wives, young men and their dads, mothers and daughters, old people with walking sticks, coming forward, tears streaming down their faces, asking for forgiveness. God wants to say to you today, you too can say sorry.

Philip Yancey once wrote, "Grace means there is nothing we can do to make God love us more…and grace means there is nothing we can do to make God love us less." He just loves you. He will take that burden that is crushing you, He will give you that forgiveness you are looking for and He will give you new life.

HE CAME TO SAVE

"For the Son of Man did not come to
destroy men's lives but to save them."
LUKE 9:56

Jesus is not here to condemn people. He is here to save us, to save the lost. Now James and John got it the wrong way around. They became very angry because they had come to a village and wanted to prepare a place for the Master to sleep that night but they were chased out of the village. They were so angry that they said, "Lord, do You want us to command fire to come down from heaven and consume them, just as Elijah did?" (Luke 9:54). But the Lord rebuked them and said, "No, I came to save them." You and I need to be patient. We need to remember from whence we came.

I often wonder what people must have thought when Jill, our children and myself, walked into that little church 40-odd years ago for the first time on that Sunday morning. They must have looked around and said, "Look what the cat dragged in!" But the Lord never ever writes people off. He came to save us. Never write anybody off; always keep the door wide open.

Jesus came to offer us the Gospel, freely, not by threat nor through fear. In Matthew 11:28, He says, "Come to Me, all you who labor and are heavy laden, and I will give you rest." Today, ask the Lord to show you someone who needs help. Go to them by faith and share the Good News in the Name of the Lord Jesus Christ.

HUMILITY

"God resists the proud,
but gives grace to the humble."
1 PETER 5:5

Always remember, pride comes before a fall. Our Lord Jesus Christ was the most humble Man to have ever walked on the face of this earth. Now remember, to be humble does not mean to be weak. It is controlled strength…that is what a humble man is.

Moses was not a weak man and yet the Bible tells us clearly in Numbers 12:3 that he was the most humble of any man on the face of the earth at that time. There was nothing soft about a man who could lead an entire nation through the desert for 40 years, who could stretch out his rod by faith and see a sea separated so that God's people could walk through it.

We need to be more gentle in these stressful times that we are living in. We need to love one another. The lowliest Christian is the loveliest Christian. Augustine said, "It was pride that changed angels into devils; it is humility that makes men as angels."

Young men should treat young ladies with great respect and gentleness. Don't be afraid to stand up and give an old lady your seat. That is not being a sissy, that is being a humble man of God. These are the things that make you humble before God. It is not so much what we say but who we are that impacts people. So, walk in the power of God and the humility of Jesus!

DON'T WORRY

Then He said to His disciples,
"Therefore I say to you, do not worry
about your life, what you will eat;
nor about the body, what you will put on."
LUKE 12:22

Jesus is telling you to stop worrying. It doesn't help you at all—it just makes you sick. It makes you confused; it makes you go the wrong way and make bad decisions. Do not worry about tomorrow…the Lord says today has enough problems of its own (see Matthew 6:34).

Why are you worrying about tomorrow? We need to take it one day at a time. Matthew 6:33 says, "Seek first the kingdom of God and His righteousness, and all these things shall be added to you." Do your best and then leave the rest to Jesus.

If you are a young student worried about your exams, study hard, do your best and leave the rest to God. You will be surprised at how those answers will come to you when you are writing your exam. Maybe you are a businessman and you don't know what you are going to do. Just do what you can today… the Lord will take care of the rest. Maybe you have a medical problem and you don't know what you should do about it. Ask God, leave it to Him and carry on living.

Let us start to trust God and stop worrying. Instead, keep your eyes fixed on Jesus, the Author and the Perfecter of your faith.

PLOW STRAIGHT

Jesus said to him, "No one, having put his hand to the plow, and looking back, is fit for the kingdom of God."

LUKE 9:62

There is no turning back for us. Why do we want to go back to Egypt? Is it to eat melons and cucumbers? Is it to have a place to bury our dead? That is what the people of Israel wanted to do when it got tough in the desert. They wanted Moses to take them back to the old places. We cannot possibly plow a straight line if we keep on looking back. You know, the Bible tells us in John 8:36, "Therefore if the Son makes you free, you shall be free indeed." So, why do you want to go back? We need to press forward…We really need to keep our eyes fixed on heaven, on eternity.

Years ago, I heard a story of a plump Muscovy duck with small little wings. He had never flown in all his life…he just ran up and down the chicken run in all the mud, flapping his little wings. He had as much food as he wanted to eat and was quite happy. One day, he looked up and heard the cry of a flock of spur-winged geese flying in a V-formation. They weren't fat; they were actually quite lean. But they were free. They would never return to the confines of a muddy chicken coup. They flew focused on what lay ahead.

We really need to keep our focus on the goal, on the destination! Today, keep your focus on the goal and do not look behind you.

PROPERLY PREPARED

*"For which of you, intending to build a tower,
does not sit down first and count the cost,
whether he has enough to finish it."*
LUKE 14:28

Preparation is vital in these times. There is no room in the king-dom of God for people who are just winging it. I watched a documentary once about Robert Scott, Ernest Shackleton and Roald Amundsen who each wanted to be the first man to reach the South Pole in Antarctica. You know, Scott was a passionate man but he did not prepare well…he made it to the South Pole in second place but at a tremendous cost. He lost all of his men, every single one of them died.

Shackleton was an extremely brave man. He got to within 97 km of the South Pole but he had to turn back because he was in danger of starving. He went back defeated because he did not prepare well. Roald Amundsen, on the other hand, was prepared. He learned from the Netsilik Inuit people in Canada. He put on the correct clothes and used dogs to pull the sledges. On a preliminary trip, Amundsen even put deposits of food supplies for the journey ahead. Because he was prepared, he was the first man in the world to reach the South Pole.

You and I need to prepare ourselves better. We need to pre-pare for the coming of the Lord Jesus Christ. He is not coming soon…He is on His way! We need to be prepared and we need to be ready for His coming.

ORDINARY PEOPLE

Then He said to them, "The harvest truly is great,
but the laborers are few; therefore pray the Lord of
the harvest to send out laborers into His harvest."

LUKE 10:2

The Lord Jesus is looking for workers. He is looking for a labor force to do a great work. We are talking about the greatest revival that will come amongst God's people in these last days. That is right, we have to roll up our sleeves and get to work. Jesus is not talking about theologians, about doctors of divinity or even professors of the faith. No, He is talking about ordinary workers—people like you and me. The worldwide revival that is coming is going to happen through ordinary people like us.

Recently a group of young farmers and businessmen came to see me. They had a burning desire to see their community changed and saved, and they said, "What can we do?" So, I told them, "Don't lose your identity."

If you are a farmer then live and act like a farmer, and tell people about Jesus in your own way. If you are a businessman, do exactly the same. Why do you want to change? The Lord is calling for laborers, unskilled manual workers.

It doesn't matter who you are, go out there and tell people about the soon-coming King. That is all they want to hear about. This is the time for ordinary people to go out and witness for Christ.

A NEW VISION

"The LORD is with you while you are with Him.
If you seek Him, He will be found by you;
but if you forsake Him, He will forsake you."
2 CHRONICLES 15:2

There are none so blind as those who do not want to see. Don't you want to see, don't you want to live today?

Helen Keller was born on 27 June 1880. When she was a little baby, she fell ill and was left blind and deaf…Can you think of anything worse? It must be like being put in a cell with no windows and no doors. But her teacher taught her to communicate by using her finger to spell out words on the palm of Keller's hand. Do you know that Helen Keller eventually went to university? She traveled to 35 countries around the world, speaking on behalf of the blind and the deaf.

You and I need to seek after Jesus today with our hearts and not with our heads. Helen Keller said, "The only thing worse than being blind is having sight but no vision."

Do you have a vision today? Proverbs 29:18 says, "Where there is no revelation, the people cast off restraint; but happy is he who keeps the law." Ask the Lord today to give you new vision…It will make you get up in the morning and get on with the work. It will take your eyes off of yourself and put your eyes back on Jesus and on other people.

VACANT OF SELF

"Blessed are the poor in spirit,
for theirs is the kingdom of heaven."
MATTHEW 5:3

We need to be totally dependent on Jesus today. We need to be brutally honest with ourselves and realize that we can do absolutely nothing without God. We cannot even help others. How can the blind lead the blind? It's impossible. When we die to self, we empty ourselves, then God can use us to assist others. You can't help a drowning man if you don't know how to swim.

When Jill and I first got saved, I wanted to give the farm away. I wanted to go to Bible college and become a pastor. But God said to me clearly in my heart: "Stay on the farm and make a place for others," which is what we did and are still doing.

William Duma, a Zulu herdsman on our farm, met Jesus in a special way and he emptied himself completely. He would do nothing without God's permission. One day he was invited to go to Israel along with a group of ministers. All of them jumped at the opportunity and said, "Thank you very much. We are willing to go." Not William Duma! He said, "Can I let you know tomorrow? I need to ask permission from my Lord today."

We need to empty ourselves. We need to become vacant inside so that God can fill us with His goodness so that we can be a blessing to others.

STAY SALTY

"Salt is good for seasoning. But if it loses its flavor,
how do you make it salty again? Flavorless
salt is good neither for the soil nor for the
manure pile. It is thrown away. Anyone with
ears to hear should listen and understand!"

LUKE 14:34-35 NLT

Don't lose your flavor! Wherever Jesus went, He caused either a riot or a revival but He was never in-between. You and I must remain salty. People don't have to like us but they must respect us—and they will if we remain salty.

Jesus put a fire back into Peter when he had lost all hope and had gone back to fishing. He can do the same for us today. Father God desires to put new salt back into our very souls today…giving us something to live for, to get up in the morning for and to die for if necessary. He wants us to live, not merely exist. He wants us to realize our dreams but we must be salty.

Let's make a difference in this tired and flavorless world we live in today. You know, I want to say something to you and I mean this from the bottom of my heart, if you offer me a nice bowl of porridge but don't put any salt in it, I won't eat it.

Don't offer me a cup of tea (by the way, I love tea) that is lukewarm because I won't drink it. The tea needs to be red-hot and that porridge must be salty. So remain salty while you go out and make a difference in somebody's life.

A SOFT WORD

A wrathful man stirs up strife, but he
who is slow to anger allays contention.
PROVERBS 15:18

A very dear friend of mine sent me a short story called *The Last Pamphlet.* It's the story of a little 11-year-old boy who was handing out Christian pamphlets on a cold rainy day. After he had walked around for about two hours, he was soaking wet. He still had one pamphlet left so he went and knocked on the door of a house.

He rang the bell and knocked, but there was no answer. Eventually he turned to leave, but the door opened and an old lady said, "Can I help you?" He said, "Mam, I just wanted to tell you that Jesus loves you very much. I want to give you a pamphlet that will tell you all about Him and His great love for you."

That soft, gentle greeting on that cold miserable day saved an old lady's life. You see, she was contemplating suicide but that little wet smiling face, standing at the door with a gentle soft loving word of Jesus, literally saved her life. A week later she gave her testimony in church. She was now following Jesus Christ because there was a little boy, a little angel, who had come to see her and told her about Jesus. She was no longer lonely.

Today, go out and give a sweet, gentle comment of encouragement to someone. It might even save a life!

GODLY GENERATIONS

Blessed is the man who fears the LORD,
who delights greatly in His commandments.
His descendants will be mighty on earth;
the generation of the upright will be blessed.
PSALM 112:1-2

If you are a godly man, your family, your children, your grand-children and even your great-grandchildren will be rewarded because of your lifestyle. I hear of many elderly men putting money aside for their children and their grandchildren. Now that is a wonderful thing to do but I want to tell you, the greatest gift you can leave for your children or your children's children is your example as a follower of Jesus Christ.

I have met countless people who have told me that when they were young, they watched their grandparents reading the Word and praying for their families. The greatest gift you can give to your family is to pray for them daily—pray for their salvation and pray for the peace of God to be in their hearts. Pray that they will succeed in what they are attempting to do in this life.

We need to get our priorities straight. It's one thing to leave a lot of money behind for your children and your grandchildren but if they have no direction, no vision in life, you are actually hanging a millstone around their neck. Rather pray for them that they will meet the Savior of the world and become ambas-sadors for Jesus Christ. That is the greatest legacy you can leave your family.

BACK TO THE BIBLE

So they taught in Judah, and had the Book of the
Law of the LORD with them; they went throughout
all the cities of Judah and taught the people.
And the fear of the LORD fell on all the kingdoms
of the lands that were around Judah, so that
they did not make war against Jehoshaphat.

2 CHRONICLES 17:9-10

It is the Word of God that brings peace. Romans 10:14 says, "How then shall they call on Him in whom they have not believed? And how shall they believe in Him of whom they have not heard? And how shall they hear without a preacher?" People need the Lord desperately now more than ever before.

People are perishing at the moment because of a lack of knowledge of the Word of God. You see, people don't know about the power that is available to them through Almighty God. They might be educated but they need Jesus.

I remember years ago taking the Seedsower—a big yellow 20-ton truck with one word on the side of it: JESUS—filled with Bibles, clothes and food right up to the north of Central Africa. And I tell you what, those people were very poor. Some of them hardly had any clothes on. But you know, the funny thing was, they didn't want the clothes or the food, they wanted the Bible!

You and I need to pray desperately, not only for South Africa but especially for the first-world nations, that they get back to the Bible.

THE FAITHFUL ONE

He who calls you is faithful, who also will do it.
1 THESSALONIANS 5:24

The emphasis is actually on Jesus and not on ourselves. He is the trustworthy One and no one else. He will finish the work in our lives, therefore all we need to do is put our complete faith in Him. He will keep us fit for the coming of the Lord. Jesus is completely dependable when He says something; we can be sure that He will do it. He will surely make it happen, we just need to be patient and hopeful.

A while ago, we were invited to the Northern Cape to help in a desperate situation where there was no rain, only fire and devastation. It was a pitiful sight to see; it looked completely hopeless. Those very brave farmers, shopkeepers, businessmen and schoolchildren put their faith in the Faithful One and not in their circumstances of fire, drought, heat and devastation. And do you know what happened? The Faithful One, Jesus, came through for them. Rain, gently-soaking, prayer-answering rain fell all over the Northern Cape.

I don't know what your situation is—maybe you are facing a so-called hopeless situation—but I want to tell you, don't put your trust or your effort or your faith in yourself. Put it in the Lord Jesus Christ and He will come through for you. God will honor His word. Remain focused on the Faithful One. It will change your whole outlook on life.

THE REFINER'S FIRE

And not only that, but we also glory in tribulations,
knowing that tribulation produces perseverance;
and perseverance, character; and character, hope.
ROMANS 5:3-4

Are you suffering at the moment? Are you going through a fiery trial? Well, I want to tell you, I have never met a person worth his salt who has not been through the fire. You see fire purifies, it takes out and it burns off all the rubbish in our lives. It is never wasted unless, of course, we do not learn from it. If we don't, then we need to go through that fiery trial again until we learn from it.

The Lord Jesus is the one who disciplines and chastises those He loves. Hebrews 12:11 says, "Now no chastening seems to be joyful for the present, but painful; nevertheless, afterward it yields the peaceable fruit of righteousness to those who have been trained by it."

We must not be afraid of hardship, pain, or suffering because we are not in that fire alone. Remember, Jesus is walking with you through it. He understands how painful it is because He is doing the pruning. He is holding the pruning shears in one hand and never forget that that hand has got a hole in it…put there by a rusty old nail…and as He is pruning us, He is suffering even more than we are. So today, don't be afraid about suffering. Trust Him and He will bring you through.

THROUGH THE FIRE

"...looking unto Jesus, the author and finisher of our faith, who for the joy that was set before Him endured the cross, despising the shame, and has sat down at the right hand of the throne of God."

HEBREWS 12:2

Jesus suffered before He went home to be with His Father in heaven. Maybe you, too, are in the fire today, my dear friend, and you say, "Lord, there is no way out. Lord, why are You doing this to me? Lord, why am I suffering?" Maybe it is because that dross, that rubbish, needs to be burned out of us. I am talking about pride, arrogance and self-centeredness. No more doing it my way—it doesn't work. The only way that works is God's way and God teaches us, through the fiery trials and through the suffering to appreciate things.

Farmers who experience extreme drought and devastating fire appreciate rain more than anybody else because they haven't had rain for many years. I have seen farmers—big, strong men—weeping but the Lord was there all the time. No, He didn't cause the drought but He worked with them through it, always remember that. God will never reject a broken and contrite heart (see Psalm 51:17).

Today, endure that pain remembering that it is the symbol of the Christian—the cross. It is the cross of suffering and God will bring you through; He will make you a better person because of it.

BEAUTIFUL BLESSEDNESS

Blessed is he whose transgression
is forgiven, whose sin is covered.

PSALM 32:1

What a beautiful promise from the Lord for us—reconciled to God, brought back to Jesus. You know, the Lord has a bad memory…when He forgives you, He forgets. Not like us who forgive and then when it suits us we say, "Remember that thing you did to me?" Jesus doesn't do that. That is why it is such a blessed thing to be forgiven by the Lord.

You don't have to wait for heaven to be forgiven—it can start right here on earth today. John 3:16 says, "For God so loved the world that He gave His only begotten Son, that whoever believes in Him should not perish but have everlasting life."

You see, you can't earn it, buy it or work for it—it is free so just receive God's forgiveness. Now, there is someone in the Bible who knew exactly what that meant and his name was Zacchaeus. Jesus said to him, "Zacchaeus, I am coming to your house today!" And if we look at Luke 19:8, it says, "Then Zacchaeus stood and said to the Lord, 'Look, Lord, I give half of my goods to the poor; and if I have taken anything from anyone by false accusation, I restore fourfold.'" Surely blessedness came into that man's heart that day.

My dear friend, maybe Jesus wants to come to your house today. I am talking about your very own life. Remember that Jesus died for you. All you have got to do is say, "Thank You, Lord!" Receive it and believe it.

LOVE ONE ANOTHER

He said, "More than that, blessed are those
who hear the word of God and keep it!"

LUKE 11:28

We cannot bend God's Holy Word. If you want His blessing and His power in your life then you have to obey the Lord. You have to obey the Word of God, there can be no compromise. Luke 8:21 says very clearly, "He answered and said to them, 'My mother and My brothers are these who hear the word of God and do it.'" Remember, Jesus was teaching and they came to Him and said, "Your mother and your brothers are outside." He said, "Who are my mother and my brothers but those who obey the word of God." You know, it is such a wonderful thing, folks, to be a follower of Jesus Christ. You have so many friends right around the world.

I once got an invitation to go to Israel and I went down to the Dead Sea, the lowest point on earth, to speak at the Feast of Tabernacles. It was amazing. More than 80 different nations from all over the world, all speaking different languages, came together to celebrate. But do you know something? I love those people and they love me because of the love of God in us. Remember, John 13:34 says, "A new commandment I give unto you, that you love one another; as I have loved you…"

Go out today and love others, especially those in the family of believers!

COUNTERFEIT

"The lamp of the body is the eye.
Therefore, when your eye is good, your whole
body also is full of light. But when your eye
is bad, your body also is full of darkness."
LUKE 11:34

The eye is the window of the heart, so we need to ask ourselves a question today: What are we looking at? We need to discipline ourselves. There are so many people at the moment who are suffering from depression, fear and anxiety because of what they're watching. What are you watching? When it comes to things like television, social media and smartphones, we have to remember that the quickest way to poison our souls is through what we watch.

You know, it is just like eating healthy food and keeping good strong friendships. We need to look at godly wholesome programs on our devices and on television. Some people say, "No, it is okay to watch negative, ungodly material because that is how you learn about what is safe and what is dangerous." I disagree completely. When they teach people to tell the difference between counterfeit and real money, they never let them look at the counterfeits, only at the real authentic notes. Now, while these people are examining these notes, every now and again they will slip in an artificial note to test them but straightaway the people will recognize it.

Today, keep your eyes on Jesus. He is the One who will bring you joy, hope and abundant life (see John 10:10).

FIXED ON JESUS

"Those who do wickedly against the covenant he shall corrupt with flattery; but the people who know their God shall be strong, and carry out great exploits."

DANIEL 11:32

We have to get into that quiet place away from the distraction of this troubled world. As things become more hectic, we need to draw closer to the only One who can truly save us. We have to keep in touch with God.

You know, in the Garden of Gethsemane, on the night that the Lord Jesus was betrayed, all of His disciples ran away… they ran away from the only Person who could help them and protect them (see Matthew 26:56).

We have to remain focused on God because it is He and He alone who will keep us in peace. In John 16:33, Jesus says, "These things I have spoken to you, that in Me you may have peace. In the world you will have tribulation; but be of good cheer, I have overcome the world."

Let's take our eyes off the things of this world and look to the Prince of Peace Himself, our Lord Jesus Christ. He will ultimately overcome all of our difficulties in this stormy sea that we are sailing at the moment. He will never move. There is nothing that will move Him because He is your protector and He is your Savior.

MEASURING OUR WORDS

"Therefore whatever you have spoken in
the dark will be heard in the light, and what
you have spoken in the ear in inner rooms
will be proclaimed on the housetops."

LUKE 12:3

Remember, if you haven't got anything good to say about someone, then rather don't say anything at all. You best let your words always be sweet because one day you might have to eat them. Unfortunately, this is an area I am still working on because I tend to speak before I think…and it gets me into trouble sometimes.

They say a new Christian should be locked up for the first six months because he is like a bull in a china shop! He is so full of exuberance and joy that he wants to tell everybody everything and sometimes he gets it wrong. Be careful how you speak. Remember that old saying, "Sticks and stones may break my bones but words will never harm me"? That is an absolute lie! If you get a couple of bones broken they will soon heal but when you say an ugly, damaging word, it can stay with a person forever.

Remember, a word spoken by faith can perform miracles. It can open seas! It can heal a dying person, and make a barren woman conceive! Today, measure your words and let them be encouraging because people are hurting all over the world. Phone someone and give them a kind word today. Pray for somebody who is really taking strain and you will be surprised at how good you will feel.

TIME WITH JESUS

"Are not five sparrows sold for two copper coins?
And not one of them is forgotten before God. But the
very hairs of your head are all numbered. Do not fear
therefore; you are of more value than many sparrows."

LUKE 12:6-7

You might be feeling a bit lonely and think that no one cares for you, but rest assured that Jesus cares. He even knows how many hairs are on your head. You don't have to be lonely. There is a Friend who sticks closer than a brother (see Proverbs 18:24). Jesus cares so much for us that He even laid His own life down to protect us. John 15:13 says, "Greater love has no one than this, than to lay down one's life for his friends."

Talk to Him today; He really wants to hear from you. Tell Him of all your troubles and all your fears. He has lots of time for you. He is never in a rush and He is a very good listener, which is hard to find these days.

You know, my wife is my best friend here on earth. She knows me so well. She knows what food I like, what books I read and even what clothes I like to wear. She even knows who my heroes in the Bible are. We can go into a crowded room and, from opposite ends of the room, we just look at each other and communicate without saying a word. It is because we spend time together.

Spend more time with Jesus today. He has so much more He wants to show you.

SPEAK LIFE

"But when they deliver you up,
do not worry about how or what you should
speak. For it will be given to you in that hour
what you should speak; for it is not you who speak,
but the Spirit of your Father who speaks in you."
MATTHEW 10:19-20

We must allow the Lord Himself to direct our words and nothing else. If the words we speak are from heaven, it is like hot bread coming out of the oven—delicious to eat. We need to speak what God tells us.

If you are talking about something that is not from God, then there is no passion, no conviction. It is just a case of going through the motions. It will fall on deaf ears and achieve nothing. People are starving for the Word of Life. They are looking for hope, direction, truth, joy and, most of all, they are looking for love.

You and I need to spend more time in the presence of God than we do preparing flowery messages that are lifeless. People want to know, "What does God say about this situation?" If we look at John 1:43-50, Jesus told Nathaniel all about himself before Nathanael had ever met Him. Jesus told Nathanael the kind of man he was and where he had come from, which instantly made Nathanael a follower of Jesus.

Today, go out and bless somebody. Just speak life over them, tell them what Jesus means to you.

ETERNAL INVESTMENT

"Store your treasures in heaven, where moths and rust cannot destroy, and thieves do not break in and steal."
MATTHEW 6:20 NLT

Where a man's heart is, that is where his treasure is, too! The wisest man who ever lived, Solomon, was also the richest man. He called making money or striving after wealth vanity. He said it is like chasing the wind (see Ecclesiastes 1:14). We need to invest in heavenly things.

Look at the parable of the rich fool (see Luke 12:13-21), where the rich man had a wonderful crop and said, "I am going to build new barns, then I am going to store up all my crop in those barns so that I can eat, drink and be merry." But the Lord said, "You fool, tonight your very life will be required of you." We need to invest in eternal things!

When John Wesley died, the only money noted in his will were the coins in his pockets and dresser. Although he wrote many books, he put most of his money straight back into the ministry. George Müller built a children's home in Bristol, England that took care of tens of thousands of children. Surprisingly though, he gave up any set salary for the last 68 years of his life, completely trusting God to provide for himself and the orphanage.

I want to say to you today, let's not waste our money and effort on things that will perish with rust and just disappear. Let's rather invest in heavenly things that will last forever.

LISTEN TO THE HOLY SPIRIT

Jesus came and touched them and said,
"Arise, and do not be afraid."
MATTHEW 17:7

It is so important to touch people with God's love. That was what Mother Teresa did, she touched people. She didn't preach, she just touched them with the love of Jesus and changed their lives.

I remember many years ago, when we had one of the Mighty Men Conferences on the farm, I was walking down the sawdust trail up to the platform to start preaching. As I was walking, there were many men around me and I felt the Holy Spirit say to me, "This man you are walking past, touch him on the shoulder and whisper in his ear that Jesus loves him." So I did it.

I carried on walking up to the pulpit to preach the message. A few weeks later I got an email from that very man. He said, "I was there that weekend. The music was wonderful. The preaching was good but nothing touched my heart as much as when you touched me on the shoulder and told me that Jesus loved me. My life is transformed, I am now following Jesus Christ." We need to be obedient to what the Holy Spirit is telling us.

What a mighty God we serve. Go out today and touch somebody with God's love—let them know that Jesus loves them.

BE READY

*"Therefore you also be ready, for the Son of Man
is coming at an hour you do not expect."*
LUKE 12:40

We need to keep short accounts with men and with God. We need to stand, that is what Ephesians 6:14 says. We are to put on the armor of God and stand because the battle is the Lord's and the Lord is coming back very soon. No man knows the day or even the hour, not even Jesus Himself (see Matthew 24:36).

But you see, a good farmer knows the seasons of the year. When the fig tree blossoms, we know that summer is coming. Mark 13:28-29 says, "Now learn this parable from the fig tree: When its branch has already become tender, and puts forth leaves, you know that summer is near. So you also, when you see these things happening, know that it is near—at the doors!" We can see the signs everywhere that the Lord is not coming soon—He is already on His way. Our champion is coming back to fetch us and He is coming in glory with all His angels!

The well-known gospel singer Keith Green, who was dramatically converted from drug addiction to singing the Gospel, once said, "If the world took six days and that home 2,000 years, hey man, this is like living in a garbage can compared to what's going on up there."

Be ready. The Lord is coming for His bride.

OUR YOUTH

Let no one despise your youth, but be an
example to the believers in word, in conduct,
in love, in spirit, in faith, in purity.

1 TIMOTHY 4:12

Don't despise the youth. Do you know that Josiah was eight years old when he became king of Israel? That is right, and he restored the House of the Lord to its original condition because it was in a mess. In fact, he reinforced it.

I know of situations where a father will not trust his child to take over the business. One man was no less than 60 years old before his father, who was nearly 90 years old, finally gave him authority to take over the business. What was the result? Well, by that time the son had totally lost his vision for the business and so it just fell apart. We need to give the young people an opportunity to show us what they can do. What is the worst thing that can happen? Well, maybe we lose a business but we will gain a son.

I remember a lovely story of a family where the young boys came back from agricultural college and told their dad that they wanted to change the whole system on the farm. The dad was reluctant at first but told them to go ahead. His sons then sold all the cattle and started to farm with fynbos, which are wildflowers. They picked, stored and shipped these wildflowers all over the world. The last I heard, they had the biggest business in town. Don't restrict your children, give them a chance. They will not disappoint you.

DO IT TODAY

Then He answered them, saying, "Which of you,
having a donkey or an ox that has fallen into a pit,
will not immediately pull him out on the Sabbath day?"
LUKE 14:5

No one likes going to church more than me and I really mean that. I love going to church but there are priorities. Now, priorities are the things we deem more important than others and that is why it is so very important to always ask yourself a simple question: What would Jesus do? And then take that option.

The main thing is to make sure that the main thing in your life remains the main thing. Make that phone call, go visit that person, write that letter, write that email! Do not procrastinate. If you leave the ox in the pit until after church on Sunday, he will be dead.

You know in Zulu we say, "*Kusasa, uma iNkosi izovuma,*" which means, "Tomorrow, if the Lord wills…" But you know something, tomorrow might never come. Today might be the most important day in your life. If you don't visit that old person they might not be there tomorrow and that will cause a lot of regret.

We really need to get our priorities in order. So what do we do? Well, we take the ox out of the pit and then we go to church. Today, sit and meditate on what the Lord wants you to do with your life.

ENJOY GOD'S CREATION

"Be still, and know that I am God; I will be exalted among the nations, I will be exalted in the earth!"
PSALM 46:10

It is time for us to take an account of our situation. Are we spending enough quiet time with God? You see, Jesus is still very much in control, irrespective of what the media might tell you. Did you see the sun come up this morning, my dear friend? Oh, it was magnificent! Now, I don't care whether you are in New Zealand, in the USA or in bonny Scotland, the sun came up this morning, didn't it? It was beautiful.

Did you hear the heavenly orchestra that was playing first thing in the morning for you? Well, on the farm we usually start off with the dove, shouting out, "Peace on earth!" Followed up by a troop of guinea fowl parading past the front of our garden and then the shrill call of a pair of eagles that are nesting in a tree. And then to hear the faint call of the Burchell's Coucal, which is an African rainbird. It sings the most beautiful music you have ever heard, especially in the ears of the farmer. "Kukukuku," it sings, "The rain is coming."

I want to encourage you today to take time out to smell the roses because they won't be there forever. Enjoy God's creation wherever you are. He loves you, He wants to talk to you but please sit down with that cup of tea or coffee and be attentive to His creation. Be still and know that He is God.

GOD'S WAY

"But seek first the kingdom of God
and His righteousness, and all these
things shall be added to you."
MATTHEW 6:33

That is a very simple and straightforward statement, yet so many times we just do not seem to get it. We get many letters asking, "Why has God done this to me? Why have I never got any money? Why are my children so rebellious? Why is God punishing me?"

We cannot blame it all on God or even on the devil. We must be honest with ourselves: Some of us are too lazy to seek the Lord's will for our lives. We seek God's council from every Tom, Dick and Harry who just happens to be around, which is dangerous. We have got to seek the Lord.

I spoke to a progressive young farmer one day who told me that he was tired of all the new programs that the reps were trying to push down his throat...the new methods of farming that are supposedly bigger, better and quicker. The problem is, a lot of those programs aren't sustainable. We have got to get back to basics; we have got to start doing things God's way.

As a farmer, I use my Agricultural Manual, which is what I call my Bible, for everything. God made it for us and He wants us to use it. We have got to start seeking God's way. Stop being greedy. We have got to start taking time to make decisions. We have to start putting back into the soil, not just taking out of the soil, and then God will start to prosper us.

GO OUT

"Then the master of the house, being angry,
said to his servant, 'Go out quickly into the streets
and lanes of the city, and bring in here the poor
and the maimed and the lame and the blind.'"

LUKE 14:21

Jesus loves all people and He invites everybody to His banquet table—the poor, the rich, the weak, the strong, the old, the young, even those who have made mistakes and those who have been written off by society. All we have to do is simply accept His invitation to come to the banquet. Romans 10:13 says, "For 'whoever calls on the name of the LORD shall be saved.'"

You know, one of my heroes is Dwight L. Moody. He was an American who lived in Chicago a long time ago. He was a shoe salesman by trade, but came from a farming background. He got gloriously saved. That is right, he went to the banquet and Jesus saved him.

He got so excited. So he went to Chicago and opened a Sunday school for poor inner-city and immigrant children. He drew children there with candy and pony rides, and adults with evening prayer. He was desperate for them to be saved and become followers of Jesus Christ.

You and I need to do the same today. Let's go out to the highways and byways, and tell people that Jesus loves them.

FINISH WELL

"For who would begin construction of
a building without first calculating the cost
to see if there is enough money to finish it?"

LUKE 14:28 NLT

Don't start if you have no intention of finishing. Remember, no one is interested in good starters, it is good finishers that folk are looking for these days. John 17:4 says, "I have glorified You on the earth. I have finished the work which You have given Me to do." Jesus finished the work that His Father sent Him to do. It was "Mission Accomplished"—He finished the job.

Now maybe you are reading this and wondering whether you should continue with your university studies because it is getting very tough. Keep on keeping on; you will finish it. Maybe it is a business that you have just started and you are saying, "I don't know if I can complete this." If God has called you to do it, He will give you the strength and the courage to finish. Maybe you are struggling in your church as a pastor and you just think, "Is it going to work or not?" Keep on preaching the Gospel. Perhaps you are struggling in your marriage and you say, "Angus, we just can't get on…" You have to, you made a covenant, a commitment. Finish the job!

Some of us don't realize just how close we are to the finish line. Maybe it is just around the next corner. Keep on running. Keep your eyes on the Lord, He will give you the strength to finish the job.

OPEN OUR EYES

So he answered, "Do not fear, for those who are
with us are more than those who are with them."

2 KINGS 6:16

Elisha prayed that the Lord would open the eyes of his servant to see all the chariots of fire and all the angels that were on the mountains around them. This servant was petrified because the Syrians had come to attack them, but the prophet asked God to open his servant's eyes so that he could see there are more that are for us than against us.

Ephesians 3:20-21 says, "Now to Him who is able to do exceedingly abundantly above all that we ask or think, according to the power that works in us, to Him be glory in the church by Christ Jesus to all generations, forever and ever. Amen." Do not limit God. If God is for you today in whatever you are looking for, then you have the majority!

When you go out to shoot a massive buffalo, you need to use a very powerful rifle and not just a child's pop gun. And yet that is exactly what many of us try to do in our everyday lives. We try to take on challenges in our own strength and we fail miserably.

Today, let's go out and face that challenge with a scud missile, not a child's pop gun. Philippians 4:13 says, "I can do all things through Christ Jesus who strengthens me." Jesus has given us everything we need to stand against the enemy.

YOUR PASSPORT

For our citizenship is in heaven, from which we
also eagerly wait for the Savior, the Lord Jesus Christ.
PHILIPPIANS 3:20

Have you got your passport in order? How many times when you want to go on a trip do you look for your passport and find that it's expired? You need to get your credentials in order. This is not our home here on earth—you and I are simply passing through. So I ask again, do you have your credentials in order?

What are our credentials? Well, we believe that Jesus Christ is the risen Son of God and not only do we believe it, we also live it. Now, remember the thief on the cross? He left it pretty late before he got his credentials in order, didn't he? However, I believe we shall see him in heaven, just as Jesus promised him. Make sure that all your family and friends have got valid passports to heaven—we don't want to leave anybody behind.

Jesus spoke more about heaven than about this earth. You and I are simply travelers in a foreign land…we're sojourners passing through so don't get too comfortable.

Can you imagine the welcome we will get when we finally arrive home in heaven? When Jesus is standing there, all the saints, myriads of angels and your own family that have gone ahead before you, Jesus will say, "Well done, good and faithful servant. Now you, too, can enter into the joy of the Lord!"

DEATH BEFORE LIFE

"Most assuredly, I say to you, unless a grain of
wheat falls into the ground and dies, it remains
alone; but if it dies, it produces much grain.
He who loves his life will lose it, and he who hates
his life in this world will keep it for eternal life."

JOHN 12:24-25

Jesus went through a lot of suffering to bring many sons to glory and so we, too, need to be prepared, through much suffering, to bring people to salvation (see Hebrews 2:10). It's a very costly thing to follow after the Lord. It means dying in order to live. Yes, if you want to live, you have got to die. If you want to have eternal life, you must be prepared to die to your own desires.

Farmers buy seed that has been treated with insecticides so no insects can damage the seed. If you put it in a special room, where the temperature is controlled, that seed can remain in the room for years and nothing will happen. It is only when you take the seed and put it into beautiful damp soil that it will germinate and grow into a beautiful crop. The seed must die for new growth to take place.

Today, spend yourself on behalf of another soul and the Lord Jesus Christ will honor you.

WINNING SOULS

"Even though I am a free man with no master,
I have become a slave to all people to bring many
to Christ...When I am with those who are weak,
I share their weakness, for I want to bring the weak
to Christ. Yes, I try to find common ground with
everyone, doing everything I can to save some."

1 CORINTHIANS 9:19, 22 NLT

If we want to get through to people with the Gospel, we need to identify with them and see them as better than ourselves. When in the changing room with a team of sportsmen, we speak sport. When we are sitting with a group of cowboys in the corral, we speak horses. We must find their heart and their trust first before we start to speak to them about their salvation.

I will never forget preaching to a group of farmers down in the Eastern Cape. The one old farmer came up to me and said, "Speak to us so that we can see you." I thought to myself, "What does he mean by that?"

What he meant was, "Speak from your heart. We want to know you and then we will trust you." In other words, get down to where it is really happening. Get your hands dirty.

When we preach to people, we don't preach down to them, rather we preach up to people. The Lord Jesus was the greatest soul-winner of all. Follow His example today. Be yourself and tell people about Jesus.

ENCOURAGEMENT

"The Sovereign LORD has given me His words
of wisdom, so that I know how to comfort the weary."
ISAIAH 50:4 NLT

Many years ago, as new believers, my wife and I had a whole group of young teenagers stay with us on the farm for a few days. I took them up to the Drakensberg mountains. Now these young men had never been into the mountains; they were city boys, and I myself wasn't a very experienced mountaineer but off we went.

We got to the base of the mighty mountains and we started our trek up the contour paths. As we went higher and higher, the path got narrower and the gorges got steeper until…just before we got to the top, there was a sheer drop on one side and on the other side was a wall of rock. The path was just wide enough for one person.

Well, towards the top the boys were getting tired, they were getting short of oxygen and things were looking a bit dreary. I said to them, "Boys, we need to keep going. Keep going…" They kept on and eventually, they got to the top. I want to tell you that they were so relieved.

We encouraged them to keep going and they made it to the top. When we got back to the farm, they came to me and said that it was the greatest time of their lives. They were pressed hard but with encouragement, they made it to the top.

Go out today and encourage somebody to keep on, we are nearly home.

FOR JESUS' SAKE

*"If you have faith as a mustard seed, you will say
to this mountain, 'Move from here to there,' and it
will move; and nothing will be impossible for you."*
MATTHEW 17:20

More than 32 years ago, the Lord Jesus called me in my prayer room, almost audibly, to go into the world and hire stadiums, sports fields and town halls to have campaigns, preach the Gospel and pray for the sick. It has been the most exciting life that I could ever have dreamed of but it hasn't come without blood, sweat and lots of tears. I remember driving into Ladysmith, KwaZulu-Natal in my farm clothes to book the first town hall. The Lord asked me three questions:

1. "Are you prepared to be a fool for me?" I said, "That is easy Lord, I am a fool anyway."
2. "Are you prepared for people to say all manner of evil against you for My sake?" I swallowed hard and said, "I think I can do that, Lord."
3. "Are you prepared to see less of your family for my sake?" I must say that the tears started to run down my cheeks because I am a farmer, I am used to coming home every single night. I said, "Lord, by Your grace."

That was the beginning of the very first campaign that we ever had. I want to say to you today, if you have the faith the size of a mustard seed, that mountain will move but you must be prepared to go through with it for Jesus' sake.

WHO DO YOU SERVE?

"No one can serve two masters; for either he
will hate the one and love the other, or else he
will be loyal to the one and despise the other.
You cannot serve God and mammon."

MATTHEW 6:24

We cannot serve two masters—it is either almighty God or its mammon, which is worldly things. We will either despise one or the other. We will either hate the one or love the other. We cannot keep sitting on the fence—it can be very uncomfortable, especially if it is a barbed wire fence!

The rich young ruler had to make a choice and he chose the way of mammon. Luke 18:23 says, "But when he heard this, he became very sorrowful, for he was very rich." You see this young man kept all the laws; he went to church, he paid his tithe, he did everything he had to do but then Jesus tested him...he had to make a choice. Unfortunately, he chose to follow after his riches.

It doesn't matter what it is, if anything is more important to you than the Lord Jesus Christ it becomes an idol and it must be dealt with today.

We must put Jesus Christ first and foremost in our lives. He is a good Master; He is gentle and He is full of love so choose today to serve Him with all your heart.

MAKING A PLAN

In those days Hezekiah was sick and near death.
"Remember now, O LORD, I pray, how I have
walked before You in truth and with a loyal heart,
and have done what was good in Your sight." And
Hezekiah wept bitterly. "I have heard your prayer,
I have seen your tears; surely I will heal you."

2 KINGS 20:1, 3, 5

If we conduct our lives according to the principles of God, we can hold the Lord to His promises. If we don't, we have nothing to say.

You know, when I've tried to make my own plans as a farmer, not one of them has worked out. Today, why not bring Jesus into your game plan? Why don't you start doing things God's way, then you will prosper. Pray with your family every morning. Pray with your staff every day before you start work. Stand up and speak up for God.

A few years back I was invited to speak at a very prominent bull sale. A very successful agricultural family was having their annual bull sale and they asked me to speak, so the pulpit was the auctioneer's block.

I spoke from my heart and I prayed with the people. That family has one of South Africa's most prosperous agricultural enterprises. A lot of people say, "Oh, but they are just lucky." No, they are not ashamed to speak up and acknowledge that Jesus Christ is the Lord of their enterprise. Do it today, just like Hezekiah, and see what God will do for you.

TRUST GOD

Behold, the eye of the LORD is on those who fear
Him, on those who hope in His mercy, to deliver their
soul from death, and to keep them alive in famine.
PSALM 33:18–19

Never put your trust in man; only trust in the Lord your God. In times of drought, we don't look at the clouds, we trust in the Lord. In times of sickness, we don't look at the arm of flesh, we keep our eyes on the Great Physician. In times of financial stress, we don't run to and fro from this bank to that bank, we keep our eyes fixed on Jesus.

In times of hardship, we will not be put down. We put the armor of God on and we stand (see Ephesians 6:14). We don't turn and run. We look the devil in the eye and we draw a line in the sand. We say, "This far devil, no further." Remember, Jesus will open the Red Sea before us. He did it for Moses and the Israelites, and He will do it for you and me.

Stand still and see the glory of God because the enemies you see today you will never see again for the Lord will fight for you (see Exodus 14:13-14).

That Red Sea is not a pond, it is an ocean. The most powerful army in the world was coming upon the Israelites but God saved them. Maybe you are there today. Put your trust in the Lord, He will deliver you. He has been doing it for me for as long as I have put my trust in Him.

CHANGING ADDRESS

The LORD cares deeply when His loved ones die.

PSALM 116:15 NLT

What a comforting Scripture that is! I once had the privilege of attending a very large funeral service. When I arrived, the church was packed with many people coming to pay their respects to a well-loved man. Many tears were flowing and yet I sensed a tremendous peace, even joy, in the service. The minister brought a very confident and powerful word from God. "Why?" you might ask. Because the man he was speaking about was a friend of Jesus, so he could honestly comfort the grieving family with words of eternal life and hope—that the man was not dead but had simply changed address!

Unfortunately, I have also attended funeral services where the people are not sure whether the deceased man or woman was a Christian. It's a very sad service to attend. It is hard for the preacher to try and comfort the family, which makes it empty and very unpleasant. But that funeral service I attended where the man was a believer was full of joy and peace and love. Yes, there were lots of tears because he was very well-loved, but everyone knew that they will one day see him again.

Today, make your peace with your Maker, Jesus Christ. Be like the criminal on the cross who said, "Lord, remember me." I believe the Lord will say, "Today, you will be with Me in paradise."

ENCOURAGE EACH OTHER

"It would be better for him if a millstone were hung
around his neck, and he were thrown into the sea,
than that he should offend one of these little ones."

LUKE 17:2

These are strong words from the Lord Jesus! A millstone weighs about five tons so the Lord wasn't playing games here. He says, "Do not cause one of these little ones (a new Christian or believer) to stumble." If we do, there are severe consequences.

If we do not have anything good and wholesome to say about someone, rather say nothing at all. There is enough negative and condemning gossip around—we do not need to add to it. We must encourage one another. The Lord wants us to build each other up.

When I was a very young man in my early twenties, I worked for a gentleman in Zambia. He had a big farming enterprise and he was a very colorful character. But do you know something? He was probably one of the greatest encouragements to me in my early farming career. I eventually left him and started farming on my own. He would often pop over to my farm in the middle of the day and tell me to get into his vehicle. We would drive around my farm and he would constructively criticize anything that I was doing wrong. He used to really build me up with constructive criticism and encouraged me to start working consistently.

Let us encourage other people in their walk with the Lord Jesus Christ. It is so vital these days.

THE PEARL

*"Again, the kingdom of heaven is like
a merchant seeking beautiful pearls, who,
when he had found one pearl of great price,
went and sold all that he had and bought it."*
MATTHEW 13:45-46

I want to say to you today that we need to seek that pearl of great price. Why should someone give up a promising career to go off to a distant land and live an obscure life? Well, simply because they have found something of greater value, something much more precious.

The big fisherman Simon Peter and his friends James, John and even Andrew found it. Matthew, the tax collector, left his desk with all his money on it and walked away because he found it. What about that short little man Zacchaeus who climbed the tree? He found it and he repaid all the money that he had stolen from his fellow man.

Today, we need to look at Revelation 3:20, where Jesus says, "Behold, I stand at the door and knock. If anyone hears My voice and opens the door, I will come in to him and dine with him, and he with Me."

Stop looking for the pearl of great price in the wrong place. Open up your heart today and say, "Jesus, I need You more now than ever before. I have realized that looking for things in the world is like chasing the wind. Today, I want to find You in a very special way." Then go out and find that pearl of great price.

ENQUIRING OF GOD

And David inquired of God, saying,
"Shall I go up against the Philistines?
Will You deliver them into my hand?"
The LORD said to him, "Go up,
for I will deliver them into your hand."

1 CHRONICLES 14:10

King David was such a great leader in Israel because he sought God's instruction before anything or anyone else. Now, we always say here at Shalom, "A good idea is not always a God idea and a need doesn't justify a call." What does that mean?

It means that when the Lord Jesus Christ walked the earth, He didn't heal all the sick and He didn't feed all the hungry. He only did what His Father in heaven instructed Him to do.

You know, often people come to me and they say, "How can a God of love allow me to suffer so much?" But when they start to share their story, it turns out that it wasn't God at all. It was their own idea and their own plan that had failed. It wasn't God who said you must marry an unbeliever. It wasn't God who told you to go into business with a man who does not serve Him.

Ask yourself one question today: "Is this what God wants me to do?" You might wonder how to enquire of God. Well, first of all, you must pray, read the Bible and seek godly counsel. And then you must have peace in your heart and confident faith in God's plan.

J-O-Y

"The joy of the LORD is your strength."
NEHEMIAH 8:10

Are you full of joy this morning? My wife, Jill, reminded me of the acronym for J-O-Y:

J—Jesus first
O—Others next
Y—Yourself last.

First the Lord Jesus Christ and then other people, and only then yourself. When you do that, you will be full of joy. We need to count our blessings and number them one by one! Folks, we really ought to be full of joy because Jesus is coming soon. We need to count our blessings.

If you love the Lord Jesus, as I am sure you do, then your name is written in the Lamb's Book of Life. Today we are one day closer to the coming of the King. Isn't that something to be joyful about? And the Lord has promised us in 1 Corinthians 10:13 that He will not allow us to be tempted above that which we can handle. He won't give you a burden you can't carry. We really need to remember, it is the joy that Jesus set before us that keeps us going.

You know, I have got a very dear friend and every time I phone him to ask him how he's doing, he says, "Angus, I am so well." You know, I just love phoning that man. I want to say to you today, go out and bless somebody. First Jesus, then others and then yourself.

OUR FOCUS

You ran well. Who hindered
you from obeying the truth?
GALATIANS 5:7

You were running superbly, so who cut you off? You were lead-ing, doing an excellent job, so who led you off the course, causing you to take your eyes off Jesus? Just a little yeast turns the whole loaf of bread.

If we look at 1 Corinthians 9:27, Paul says, "But I disci-pline my body and bring it into subjection, lest, when I have preached to others, I myself should become disqualified." We must walk the talk. We must hold the course. You and I must not deviate to the left nor to the right. Our salvation is in Jesus Christ alone! Our concentration, our hope, our peace is found in the Gospel of Jesus Christ—in Him alone!

My brother, who was a very good golfer, told me a story once about a major tournament. A golfer was on the 18th green; putting for one of the biggest trophies in the world. As he lined up the ball and was about to strike, a train went past and the driver of the train blew the horn. The golfer putted the ball and it went straight into the hole. Afterwards, the organizers came to him and said, "We want to apologize for distracting you as you were going to put the final ball." The bemused golfer looked up and said, "What distraction?" He never even heard the horn going off because he was completely focused.

We need to focus on the Lord Jesus Christ and He will see us home.

THE FIFTH COMMANDMENT

"Honor your father and your mother, that
your days may be long upon the land which
the LORD your God is giving you."

EXODUS 20:12

This is the first commandment out of the Ten Commandments with a promise added to it. Honor your mom and dad, so that your days may be long in the land and so that you might prosper. It is a very special commandment. You see, when you honor Mom and Dad, you bring dignity into the home.

When I see the way in which a young man or a young woman respects their mom or their dad, it often brings tears to my eyes. It is such an incredible privilege to have a mom and dad still alive in the home, isn't it? You know I have often said, I would give a million dollars to be able to sit down and have a cup of tea with my mom and my dad, but I will have to wait until I see them again in heaven one day.

I want to say to you today that family is so important to our heavenly Father. John 19:26 says, "When Jesus therefore saw His mother, and the disciple whom He loved standing by, He said to His mother, 'Woman, behold your son!' Then He said to the disciple, 'Behold your mother!' And from that hour that disciple took her to his own home." Now, Jesus said that when He was hanging on the cross in excruciating pain and yet He had a heart for His earthly mother and His brother. Today, love your parents and love your children.

PRAY CONSISTENTLY

Then He spoke a parable to them, that men
always ought to pray and not lose heart.

LUKE 18:1

We need to pray consistently and not lose heart. The power that is found in consistent prayer is amazing. Galatians 6:9 says that if you do not grow weary in doing good, in due season, you will reap if you do not lose heart.

We need to continue to pray consistently. Without a doubt, the most powerful weapon in the Christian's arsenal is prayer. Look at the Lord Himself, when He was in the Garden of Gethsemane on the night that they were going to arrest Him, He was praying. And when He was hanging on the cross, what was He doing? Matthew 27:46 tells us: "'Eli, Eli, lama sabachthani?' that is, 'My God, My God, why have You forsaken Me?'" Jesus was praying to His Father.

I heard a very powerful testimony once about a Chinese man who does a lot of work in the Far East. He said an old pastor, who had been arrested and put in solitary confinement for 25 years, was released. And when he was released, he was very emotional. The whole world (the Christian world)—media, television, radio, social media—were waiting to hear how he had managed to survive it. He said, very emotionally, that even though they had taken away everything, they could never take away his prayers.

I want to say to you today, it is the effective, fervent prayer of a righteous person that avails much. Pray today and God will answer your prayers.

HIS RETURN

"For as the lightning that flashes out of one part under heaven shines to the other part under heaven, so also the Son of Man will be in His day."
LUKE 17:24

Jesus is coming back like a flash of lightning. We don't have to look all over the place; we don't have to listen to this prophetic word or that prophetic word; or wait for this date or that date. No! When He comes back, we will all see Him in an instant. We need to be prepared for the coming back of our Savior. I can't wait!

We need to work like He is coming back in a thousand years but prepare as though He is coming back today. Peter said, "But, beloved, do not forget this one thing, that with the Lord one day is as a thousand years, and a thousand years as one day" (2 Peter 3:8). So time doesn't mean anything to God; He is no respecter of time because He is time.

Now I can hear somebody saying, "What are we to do, how should we live?" Well, Martin Luther said, "Even if I knew that tomorrow the world would go to pieces, I would still plant my apple tree." So, even if he knew that Jesus was going to come tomorrow, he would carry on living.

So be ready…enjoy your life and make plans for the future but always be ready for the coming of the Lord, because the kingdom of God is within you.

SOWN IN TEARS

Those who sow in tears shall reap in joy. He who continually goes forth weeping, bearing seed for sowing, shall doubtless come again with rejoicing, bringing his sheaves with him.

PSALM 126:5-6

I want to say to you today that if you are weeping because of a loved one who has maybe fallen by the way, who has maybe left home and said they are not coming back…whatever it might be, we can weep with tears and supplication to the Lord.

I once heard that tears are seeds and as we sow them, they will germinate and bring back a bountiful crop. I can relate to tears so easily folks. We have often gone out to pray in different areas in South Africa where drought has decimated the people. And when we go to those prayer meetings for rain, we see tears flowing openly. No one is shy, no one is ashamed, no one is fearful because they are needy. They are needing answers to their prayers and you know, every single time, God has answered their prayers because of a broken and contrite heart.

You know, a while ago, my grandson got up in church. No one even knew about it, not even his mom and dad. He went to the front to share something with the congregation and he started weeping. Well, I think every eye in that church was wet with tears, including mine. I went and stood with him, and put my arm around him as he delivered a beautiful testimony. But it was the tears that moved the hearts of the people. Don't be afraid to weep—Jesus wept, too.

NOTHING IS IMPOSSIBLE

He said, "The things which are impossible
with men are possible with God."
LUKE 18:27

Do you believe this Scripture verse today? I do. Mary also had her doubts at first as we can see in Luke 1:34-35, which says, "Then Mary said to the angel, 'How can this be, since I do not know a man?' And the angel answered and said to her, 'The Holy Spirit will come upon you, and the power of the Highest will overshadow you; therefore, also, that Holy One who is to be born will be called the Son of God.'" But then, in verse 37, the angel assures her again, "For with God nothing will be impossible."

People are reverting to their own efforts and trusting in their own abilities. It is time for us to get back to the Lord and to experience the miracles of God. I mean let's be honest, how can a beautiful young Jewish maiden conceive and bear a child without knowing a man? It is impossible. But nothing is impossible with God. So who are we trusting in today? We need to get back to believing in the miracle-working power of God.

I remember when thousands of South Africans came together in Bloemfontein to pray for the nation. Countless miracles happened after that because those people believed. We believe that God is the same yesterday, today and forevermore (see Hebrews 13:8). I want to exhort you today to start to believe, over this Christmas period, for the miracle-working power of a Lord, for whom nothing is impossible!

SPIRITUALLY FIT

"I discipline my body and bring it into subjection,
lest, when I have preached to others,
I myself should become disqualified."
1 CORINTHIANS 9:27

You and I need to look after our physical bodies better. We need to eat properly, sleep enough, and very importantly, we need to watch over our minds...what we take in, what we are watching on TV and on our devices. Look out for the lust of the flesh. We really need to discipline ourselves.

I hear a lot of people are suffering from anxiety, fear and stress. Philippians 4:6 tells us to "be anxious for nothing, but in everything by prayer and supplication, with thanksgiving, let your requests be made known to God."

What is even more important than physical fitness is spiritual fitness. We go to the gym regularly, but do we have a regular quiet time every morning with Jesus? How long do we spend exercising every day, and how long do we spend in the presence of God every day? First Timothy 4:8 says, "For bodily exercise profits a little, but godliness is profitable for all things..."

One of my heroes is Joni Eareckson Tada. When she was 17, she dove into shallow water, hit her head and broke her neck. But even though she is paralyzed, she has not let that physical disability hold her back. She became an author, a fantastic preacher, a singer and she even paints with a paintbrush held between her teeth. She is living life to the full and is spiritually extremely fit! Let us, too, get spiritually fit today.

ASK HIM

God said to Solomon, "Because...you asked for
wisdom and knowledge to properly govern my
people—I will certainly give you the wisdom and
knowledge you requested. But I will also give you
wealth, riches, and fame such as no other king has
had before you or will ever have in the future!"

2 CHRONICLES 1:11–12 NLT

We need to start asking Jesus for what we need. James 4:2 (NLT) says, "…Yet you don't have what you want because you don't ask God for it." And again, in John 14:14, Jesus says, "If you ask anything in My name, I will do it." Wow! What a promise from God! Why don't we use these opportunities that the Lord has given us?

How do we do that? If we look at John 14:15, the Lord says, "If you love Me, keep My commandments." We need to ask according to Jesus' will. It is no good just saying, "Lord, I want an airplane," or, "Lord, I want a Mercedes Benz." No. When you ask correctly, according to the Word of God, the Lord will answer your prayers. I am a testimony to that. God has answered my prayers so many times.

Another man who asked correctly was the wisest man who ever lived—Solomon. In a dream, the Lord asked him what he wanted and because Solomon was a godly man, he asked, "Give me wisdom so that I can govern my people." And the Lord's heart was moved because he had asked correctly, so He gave Solomon wisdom and so much more. If you ask correctly, the Lord will answer your prayers.

BE GENTLE

Always be humble and gentle. Be patient
with each other, making allowance for each
other's faults because of your love. Make every
effort to keep yourselves united in the Spirit,
binding yourselves together with peace.

EPHESIANS 4:2–3 NLT

We don't have to manufacture peace—we only have to maintain it. Now remember the Prince of Peace, in John 14:27, said very clearly, "Peace I leave with you, My peace I give to you; not as the world gives do I give to you. Let not your heart be troubled, neither let it be afraid."

You know with the extreme pressure that everyone around the world is under, it is easy for us to become extremely tense and sensitive. You and I need to be very careful how we talk to one another. We need to keep the unity, to bear with one another. We have to prefer each other and try to understand the other person's position.

I remember my late dad with great fondness. Early one morning, while I was in the field trying desperately to calibrate my seed planter, I got a message from my dad, who had been a heavy smoker, that he had run out of cigarettes and he needed a packet right now! I sent a message to say, "Dad, I will get to town at lunchtime. I am just battling with a critical situation." Of course, he replied, "Well then, I will just walk to town." Needless to say, I dropped everything and went to get a packet of cigarettes for my old dad. Although it isn't always easy, we need to do our best to keep the peace.

OUR WELL-SPRING

Keep your heart with all diligence,
for out of it spring the issues of life.
PROVERBS 4:23

We must not, in these troubled times, allow our hearts to become muddied by the issues of this world. I am talking about the issues of anger, bitterness, unforgiveness, fear, disappointment and revenge. These attitudes towards the issues of life will do us no good at all. In fact, it will probably make us very sick. We will stop the flow of life-giving water from that very delicate spring in the desert of life. If not managed correctly, we will stop the flow of life-giving water into our hearts. We need to manage the well-spring of life.

I had a good friend many years ago who worked for World Vision and he would go into arid areas where there was no water. He would help restore outlets of water where cattle, sheep and goats had trampled the trickling spring into a mud hole and stopped the flow of water. He would fence off the area when he arrived so that the animals couldn't get close to that muddy place. Then he would dig away and find the eye of the spring, gently removing the mud from around it to build a cement basin. Then the water would start to flow slowly and get stronger.

Guard your well-spring today. Let your beautiful heart not be obstructed whatsoever by the Evil One and by what is happening around you. Spend time with Jesus and He will continue to refresh you.

THE MINA

Therefore He said: "A certain nobleman went into a far country to receive for himself a kingdom and to return. So he called ten of his servants, delivered to them ten minas, and said to them, 'Do business till I come.'"

LUKE 19:12–13

We need to do business, Jesus says, until He returns. This is not a time for us to hold back. The best form of defense is to attack. That's right, do not become intimidated by the lies of the devil.

You know, in rugby they say, "Use it or lose it." When the ball is in the scrum you only have a few seconds to get that ball out to your team, otherwise the referee blows the whistle and it goes to the opposing team. I remember when I played rugby many years ago, we used to wrestle for that ball for what seemed like hours, but not today. Today, you have a few seconds; if you don't use it, you lose it.

Now Jesus goes on to say, at the end of this parable, that the nobleman gave the one mina, which came from the servant who hid the money instead of using it, and gave it to the servant who had ten minas. Now even the people said in verse 25: "Master, he has ten minas." But Jesus said, "For I say to you, that to everyone who has will be given; and from him who does not have, even what he has will be taken away from him" (Luke 19:26). We have got to keep on living; we have got to keep on doing business until the Lord returns.

DECEMBER 7

SPIRITUAL FRUIT

But the fruit of the Spirit is love, joy, peace,
longsuffering, kindness, goodness, faithfulness,
gentleness, self-control. Against such there is no law.
GALATIANS 5:22-23

If ever we needed to display the fruit of the Spirit, it is now in this season of Christmas. People are stressed out; they are tired and weary. As followers of Jesus Christ, we need to display the fruit of the Spirit.

Henry Morton Stanley was a journalist commissioned by the New York Herald to go to Africa to find the man of God, Dr. David Livingstone, who had gone missing. It was like trying to find a needle in a haystack but he eventually found Livingstone. Stanley stayed with him for five months and, even though he had plenty to complain about, not once did Stanley hear a complaint or an ugly word come out of Livingstone's mouth in all that time. Now, Stanley was not a Christian but his interaction with Livingstone changed him.

We need to display the fruit of the Spirit. It is not about preaching down to people, rebuking them or judging them. It is about loving people and displaying that fruit: Love and joy, peace, long-suffering and kindness, goodness, faithfulness, gentleness, and self-control.

Did you know that Dr. David Livingstone is known as the Good Man in Central Africa? He didn't lead thousands of people to Christ, yet he is one of the most famous missionaries. Why? Because he displayed the fruit of the Spirit.

NOT ASHAMED

But He answered and said to them,
"I tell you that if these should keep silent,
the stones would immediately cry out."
LUKE 19:40

We should not be ashamed to speak up and tell people that we are Christians! If we go to the Old Testament, Michal, who was David's wife, was so embarrassed because David was dancing, publicly, in front of the people because the Ark of the Lord had been returned. She said, "How glorious was the king of Israel today, uncovering himself today in the eyes of the maids of his servants, as one of the base fellows shamelessly uncovers himself!" (2 Samuel 6:20). In verse 22, David responded, saying, "And I will be even more undignified than this, and will be humble in my own sight…"

Romans 1:16 tells us, "For I am not ashamed of the gospel of Christ, for it is the power of God to salvation for everyone who believes, for the Jew first and also for the Greek." There is no such thing as a secret agent Christian. We either publicly admit that we follow Him or we don't.

Do the people you work with know that you are a Christian? Do the scholars where you study know that you are a Christian? We need to be unashamed of the Gospel of Christ—that is where the power lies.

Today, we need to ask God to give us the strength to speak up for the Lord. Go out today and tell three people that you are a follower of Jesus Christ.

PRACTICAL CHRISTIANITY

She extends her hand to the poor, yes, she reaches
out her hands to the needy. She is not afraid of snow
for her household, for all her household is clothed
with scarlet...She makes linen garments and sells them,
and supplies sashes for the merchants. Strength and
honor are her clothing; she shall rejoice in time to come.
PROVERBS 31:20-21, 24-25

It is time for practical Christianity. As churches continue to close down, it is time for the working man and woman to stand up so we can have church every single day in the workplace.

We need to be practical. You see, the woman in Proverbs 31 gave her husband tremendous honor because she worked hard with her hands for her family. Luke, who wrote the Gospel of Luke, was also a doctor. Jesus, the King of kings, was also a carpenter. Peter was also a fisherman, Paul a tentmaker, Dorcas a dressmaker and Joseph of Arimathea, a businessman. We have got to get into the workplace.

One Sunday morning, a bunch of cowboys were having a rodeo. Now you might say that they should have been in church. But you know what, they asked me to come and preach the Gospel in the rodeo arena. When Jesus used His illustrations, He spoke to the farmers about a sower and seed, which they could understand, and then He spoke of talents, which businessmen could understand.

Today you must understand one thing: Talk the language of the layman and he will come to Christ. And that's how you bring Christ into the workplace.

HOUSE OF PRAYER

Then Jesus went into the temple of God and
drove out all those who bought and sold in
the temple...And He said to them, "It is written,
'My house shall be called a house of prayer,'
but you have made it a 'den of thieves.'"

MATTHEW 21:12-13

Prayer is the engine room of the church. At Shalom farm, we have a thatched chapel next to the main church where we meet. And that little thatched chapel is open 24/7. People can come there and pray without any interruptions.

We need to have a place where we can go and be quiet before the Lord, and not allow it to be interrupted by a den of thieves. You don't need a chapel to pray in. You just need a quiet place where you can be alone with God. When you go to that place, whether it be a bedroom or quiet spot outside, those around you know that you are having a prayer time with your heavenly Father.

You cannot pray effectively to Jesus if you are multi-tasking. It is either God or the world, it can't be both. Now, we need to clear out that muddy temple today and we need to give the Lord priority. And I will tell you what, you will have a lot more time than you ever thought you had before because when you put Jesus first, He says, "Seek first the kingdom of God and His righteousness, and all these things shall be added to you" (Matthew 6:33).

OUR WEATHERMAN

And they feared exceedingly, and said to
one another, "Who can this be, that even
the wind and the sea obey Him!"

MARK 4:41

The Lord Jesus is our Weatherman; He is the Rainmaker! Every farmer studies the weather because it is so important to him and I am no exception. Very early one morning, I went out for a ride on my bike as I always do. Now, the sun was not quite up yet but I saw a cloud behind it and there was a rainbow. I have never seen a rainbow at 5 AM and it was beautiful.

Now, in Genesis 9:13, the Lord said, "I set My rainbow in the cloud, and it shall be for the sign of the covenant between Me and the earth." The Lord made a covenant with Noah that He would never, ever flood the earth again.

I don't know where you are today; I don't know what mountain you are facing. I don't know whether it is sickness or separation from family; whether it is a future that you don't know anything about; or maybe you don't have work for next year. Maybe your business has gone bankrupt or you have got a child that is sick. Know that the Lord Jesus Christ is firmly on the throne—nothing fazes Him.

It doesn't matter what the politicians say, it doesn't matter what the experts say, He is alive. And He loves you so much that He even died for you on a cross.

WORK HARD

"Thus says the LORD: 'Make this valley full of
ditches.' For thus says the LORD: 'You shall
not see wind, nor shall you see rain; yet that
valley shall be filled with water, so that you,
your cattle, and your animals may drink.'"
2 KINGS 3:16-17

You see, the Lord wants us to work hard with our hands.
When the Israelites said that they had no water for their cattle to drink, Jesus told them to dig ditches. Then He filled those
ditches with water. In 2 Kings 4:2-7, He instructed that widow,
who only had one jar of oil left, to borrow all the empty vessels
that she could find and keep pouring oil into every vessel. And
guess what? That one jar of oil filled all the vessels.

We must throw the nets into the water and God will fill
them with fish. He will, however, not throw the fish into the
boat. Remember, Jesus said to the disciples, "Cast the net on
the right side of the boat, and you will find some" (John 21:6).
So they did and they couldn't even draw the net back into the
boat because of how many fish there were.

There is no substitute for hard work. In fact, work is good for
the soul. God created you and me to work. If you don't put the
seed into the ground, you will not reap a crop. And I want to
say to the young people today, it is no good asking God to help
you with your exams when you don't do your part and study
hard. Let's work hard today and let's see God undertake for us.

ETERNITY IN YOUR HEART

"Praise the LORD, the God of our ancestors,
who made the king want to beautify the
Temple of the LORD in Jerusalem!"

EZRA 7:27 NLT

In Ezra 7, the Lord had put into the heart of the king of Persia a desire to beautify the temple in Jerusalem. In my Bible I've written this in the margin at this verse: "You cannot chain the Gospel!"

My dad used to tell me stories about the Salvation Army who would send young people into the ghettos of some of the cities of Britain. They would go and minister to people in the pubs, where even strong men would fear to go, and no one would harm them. Why, because those people knew that these young people were representatives of the living God. A man knows, in the depths of his soul, what is right and he knows what is wrong.

You can go into the jungle to speak to people who have never heard of the Gospel before but that person will tell you that he knows he has been created and that there is a Higher Being. He just hasn't been introduced to Him by name yet. The king of Persia knew that the God of Abraham, Isaac and Jacob was the Creator and that is why he wanted to beautify the temple in Jerusalem.

There is a God and His name is Jesus Christ and He loves you and me! All we need to do is pray and He will do the work for us.

THE LIVING GOD

"For He is not the God of the dead
but of the living, for all live to Him."
LUKE 20:38

He is not dead, He is alive. He is actually the God who raises the dead. You see, if we are in Christ, then we live forever. Remember the thief on the cross? Just before he died, he repented and he said, "Lord, remember me in heaven." And what did the Lord say? He said, "Assuredly, I say to you, today you will be with Me in Paradise" (Luke 23:43).

In Zulu, we say, "*Namuhla uzakuba Nami eParadisi.*" What a lovely promise! Now the thief wasn't a good man, that is why he was being crucified, but he acknowledged that Jesus Christ was the Son of the living God.

Luke 24:5-6 says, "Why do you seek the living among the dead? He is not here, but is risen!" I have been to Israel, to Jerusalem, and the tomb is empty! Why? Because Jesus is not dead! That is why Paul the Apostle could so boldly say in Philippians 1:21, "For to me, to live is Christ, and to die is gain."

You cannot frighten a Christian with heaven. If we live, we live for Christ. If we die, then we are going home. Now, remember, this is not our permanent home. We are just passing through. So make sure that your name is written in the Lamb's Book of Life. And how do we do that? By acknowledging Him as Lord and Savior.

FAITH CONNECTION

Without faith it is impossible to please Him, for he
who comes to God must believe that He is, and that
He is a rewarder of those who diligently seek Him.
HEBREWS 11:6

Charles Spurgeon said, "Faith is the telegraphic wire that links earth and heaven…But if that telegraphic wire of faith is snapped, how can we receive the promise?" Now, we all know that 2 Corinthians 5:7 says that we must walk by faith and not by sight. It is faith that links us with divinity. We need to look after our faith because that is the link between heaven and earth.

Now, remember, when people come to you and say, "This country is finished! There is no future. There is no hope," there are two words to answer them with: "But God!" So, when they say to you that it can't happen, or that it is impossible for you to do that, you say, "But with God all things are possible!" (see Matthew 19:26). I really want you to look after your supernatural cell phone, your faith. Spend time praying and believing the promises of God spoken over you.

When the devil attacks you with his lies and says, "You can't," answer with, "But God!" I will pass my examination because God will see me through. God will heal this body of mine. God will restore me. God has forgiven me. You speak life to yourself and you trust the Lord. The more you speak faith, the more faith you will receive.

FROM THE HEART

So He called His disciples to Himself and said
to them, "Assuredly, I say to you that this poor widow
has put in more than all those who have given to
the treasury; for they all put in out of their abundance,
but she out of her poverty put in all that she had."
MARK 12:43-44

Jesus saw the rich people coming up and showing everybody how much gold and silver they were putting into the treasury. Then this old widow came up, probably in rags, and she took out her two little coins and put them in. Then Jesus said, "She has given more than those other people because she gave out of her substance and they gave from their overflow." It's not how much you put in that counts, but rather whether you do it with the right heart.

I have some beautiful pictures of me with my horse Snowy that were drawn by little children and I will treasure these for the rest of my life. They mean more to me than a priceless painting from the Louvre because they were drawn with love from the heart.

Now today, you might be in a hospital or in an old age home; you might be bankrupt, or unemployed, and you say, "I have no gifts for my loved ones because I have no money." I want to suggest that you write a letter—a handwritten letter with loads of love. Write a letter today and you will bless somebody and that will be more than sufficient because it comes from the heart.

THE OTHER SIDE

Thomas said to Him, "Lord, we do not know where
You are going, and how can we know the way?"
Jesus said to him, "I am the way, the truth, and the life.
No one comes to the Father except through Me."

JOHN 14:5-6

A sick man once turned to his doctor as he was preparing to leave the examination room and said, "Doctor, I am afraid to die. Tell me what lies on the other side." The doctor replied, "I don't know."

So the patient said, "You don't know? You are a Christian man and you don't know what is on the other side?" The doctor was holding the handle of the door. On the other side came a sound of scratching and whining. As he opened the door a dog sprang into the room and lept onto him with an eager show of gladness and love.

Turning to the patient the doctor said, "Did you notice my dog? He's never been in this room before. He didn't know what was on the inside. He knew nothing except that his master was there. When the door opened, he sprang in without fear. I know little of what is on the other side of death but I know one thing: I know my Master is there and that is enough."

What a beautiful story. Maybe today you are mourning the loss of a loved one or you are battling an illness. I want to encourage you that Jesus Christ is on the other side and He is a friend who sticks closer than a brother. He will never leave you and He will never forsake you.

BUILDERS

"...Come and let us build the wall of Jerusalem, that we may no longer be a reproach." And I told them of the hand of my God which had been good upon me, and also of the king's words that he had spoken to me. So they said, "Let us rise up and build."

NEHEMIAH 2:17-18

We are builders; we are not demolishers. If we go to Matthew 16:18, Jesus said, "I will build My church, and the gates of Hades shall not prevail against it." Our God is in the building business; He is not a demolisher. He is a builder and as His children, we must do likewise.

We have to build people up, not break them down. If we have nothing good to say about someone, rather don't say anything at all. We might say that we don't have any building material to work with. Well, just like Nehemiah, let's use what we have—a kind word, a positive attitude.

I have often seen that when they build a new bridge, they will leave the old one standing. Now, I have spoken to some builders and I have asked them why they don't always take the old one down once they've built the new one. They told me that it takes more money to break down an old bridge than it does to build a new one.

Today, let's be builders and not destroyers. Let this Christmas time be a time of building up God's people.

LAUGHING STOCK

We have become a reproach to our neighbors,
a scorn and derision to those who are around us.

PSALM 79:4

Have you ever felt like a laughing stock? Have you ever been mocked by your neighbors? Have you ever felt that you are just no good? Well, let's go to Acts 4:13, which says, "Now when they saw the boldness of Peter and John, and perceived that they were uneducated and untrained men, they marveled. And they realized that they had been with Jesus."

We must never ever despise small beginnings. You know, William Carey stood up and said, "We need to go to India and tell the Indian people about Jesus Christ." And the theologians basically told him to sit down and shut up but he nevertheless went. Once a man made a mocking comment and said, "Was not William Carey once a shoemaker?" Carey replied, "No, Sir. I am not a shoemaker, only a cobbler." And yet, when the Holy Spirit came upon him, Carey translated the Bible into many languages.

I want to say to you that God is no respecter of persons. He will use any man who puts his hand up. We must not listen to those who mock us and become a laughing stock because if the Lord is with us, He becomes our Ultimate Teacher. We need to use what we've got and the Lord will do the rest.

This holiday time, take time out to see what the Lord has got prepared for you next year. Remember, if you aim at nothing, you are sure to hit it.

UNITED WE STAND

Behold, how good and how pleasant it is
for brethren to dwell together in unity...For there
the LORD commanded the blessing—life forevermore.

PSALM 133:1, 3

We need to get on together—there is strength in unity. There is no place for one-man shows. There are no lone rangers in the kingdom of God. We need to stand together, especially now in this holiday season. The Bible tells us, "A threefold cord is not quickly broken" (Ecclesiastes 4:12). It is quite easy to break a single cord or even a double cord, but not a threefold cord. That is what we always preach at the marriage ceremonies, don't we? Yes, it is the husband, it is the wife and in the middle is the Lord Jesus Christ. That is the marriage that will not be broken. Remember, the family that prays together, stays together.

In the days of the Roman Empire, they would say, "Divide and rule!" That is what they would do when they broke a country down. But we say, "United we stand!" We have got to stand together, mom and dad, boys and girls, brothers and sisters. This is the time for the family of God to stay in unity.

If you look at any team sport you will see, whether it is rugby or football, the team that normally wins is the team that plays together. It is not the team with individual stars in it—that team normally doesn't work. It is the team that plays together and we need to pray together.

This Christmas time, let's stand united in the love of God.

CONTENTMENT

"You shall not covet your neighbor's house; you shall not covet your neighbor's wife, nor his male servant, nor his female servant, nor his ox, nor his donkey, nor anything that is your neighbor's."
EXODUS 20:17

Jesus says that if you desire to be His disciple, you are to deny yourself, take up your cross and follow after Him (see Mark 8:34). But so often we look at the cross that our neighbor carries and we covet it. "Oh, he has got a much easier walk," or, "He has got such a wonderful business, or farm…"

The following is just a story but it illustrates a point about being content. The story goes that Jesus, the carpenter, was making crosses to fit every single person. But there was this man who didn't like his cross so he went and put it down on a heap of other crosses, and decided to choose another one.

He looked and saw a beautiful cross adorned with the most beautiful roses. But it was full of thorns that stuck into his hands. So he looked around and found another cross—a magnificent cross made out of pure solid gold. But when he picked it up, it was so heavy he could hardly put it on his shoulder. He looked around again and found a plain wooden cross. He decided that this was the one that he wanted, only to find out that that was the very one he had put down at the start.

Be content with your lot in life and thank Jesus for every day that He blesses you with.

THE OTHER CHEEK

"You have heard that it was said, 'An eye for an
eye and a tooth for a tooth.' But I tell you not to
resist an evil person. But whoever slaps you on
your right cheek, turn the other to him also."

MATHEW 5:38-39

You know, the Bushmen called the Baobab tree the upside-down tree because in winter the Baobab sheds all its leaves and it looks like its roots are in the air with the head of the tree under the ground. I've often heard people talk about the Gospel being the upside-down Gospel. In the world, they'll say, "An eye for an eye and a tooth for a tooth," but that's not what Jesus did. You and I are different from the world.

You see, it's very easy to love those who love us but it's not so easy to love those who hate us. It's very easy, also to rationalize our prejudices. But Jesus cuts through all of this by saying that we need to pray for our enemies. Remember, Jesus washed Judas Iscariot's feet just before he went out and betrayed the Master for 30 pieces of silver.

You see, we have to forgive for our own sakes. If we don't, that bitterness, that anger, that hurt, that unforgiveness, will eventually poison our whole system and consume us. Jesus, when He was dying on the cross, said to His Father, "Father, forgive them, for they do not know what they do" (Luke 23:34). Let us go out today and demonstrate the love of Christ by forgiving one another.

THE SPARROW

"...He makes His sun rise on the evil and on the good, and sends rain on the just and on the unjust."
MATHEW 5:45

Oh, my dear friend, we need to understand something very clearly: As believers, we are not exempt from the hardships and tribulations of this world.

In my humble opinion, the greatest man of faith in the whole Bible was a farmer named Job. Now, Job suffered more than anyone and yet he stood. He was not a fair-weather Christian. He trusted his God in the hardships and in the good times. Job 13:15 is one of my favorite verses and it says, "Though He slay me, yet will I trust Him."

The other day we had a devastating hail storm on this farm. We have a house with a flat roof and, of course, all the hail and the leaves from the trees around us packed onto the roof and the roof started to leak like a sieve. I got on the roof to shovel the hail and leaves so that the roof wouldn't collapse.

Suddenly I heard a noise. Folks, I heard a sparrow singing in the tree. Now, I didn't think there was a bird left alive as the hailstorm went on and on. I didn't think there would be a living creature left and there he was singing.

I want to tell you that Jesus Christ says, "If I can take care of a sparrow, I can take care of you" (see Luke 12:7).

KEEP WATCH

"Watch therefore, and pray always that you may be counted worthy to escape all these things that will come to pass, and to stand before the Son of Man."

LUKE 21:36

If ever we needed to be alert, it is in these days where there is so much going on. There is so much information being put out there, people don't know what to do or where to go. This is the time to watch and pray. First Thessalonians 5:6 says, "Therefore let us not sleep, as others do, but let us watch and be sober."

It is not a time just to throw caution to the wind. Like never before, we really need to be wide awake. I want to say to you today that the Lord Jesus Christ is on our side, He is looking after us and He is right with us. Watch and pray.

We need to be alert, we need to be awake and we need to hear from God. We need to spend time with the Lord. The early bird always catches the worm, and that is not a joke, it is a fact. We really need to be waiting on the Lord.

One of my uncles in Scotland was a shepherd. He was asthmatic from when he was a little boy. But you know what I saw in that old gentleman? I saw someone who was alert, patient and who watched his flock. We need to do the same. Let's take time to wait on the Lord and pray without ceasing.

MERRY CHRISTMAS

"For unto us a Child is born, unto us a Son is given;
and the government will be upon His shoulder.
And His name will be called Wonderful, Counselor,
Mighty God, Everlasting Father, Prince of Peace."
ISAIAH 9:6

Isaiah's prophecy came hundreds of years before Jesus was born. John 3:16 tells us: "For God so loved the world that He gave His only begotten Son, that whoever believes in Him should not perish but have everlasting life." I want to say to you today that that is the most incredible gift that anyone could give to a person—to give his own child to save another. And that is what our heavenly Father did.

Today you might be lonely, you might be sick, you might be mourning—but remember the little Baby who came into the world on this day many years ago to give you hope, to give you strength and to help you. His name is Jesus—the most beautiful name in our vocabulary. When I hear that name I want to weep with joy because He loves me so much, and He loves you so much, that He gave His life for us.

You never know whether this might be the last Christmas we have on this earth before the coming of the Lord. We need to be ready for the coming of the King. How can we get ready? Well, we need to believe that He is the Son of God. It is as simple as that. It is not about working your way to heaven, it is about acknowledging that the Baby in that manger is God made flesh, Immanuel.

PRINCE OF PEACE

"Peace I leave with you, My peace I give to you;
not as the world gives do I give to you. Let not
your heart be troubled, neither let it be afraid."

JOHN 14:27

This Scripture verse from our Lord is such a beautiful promise, isn't it? And so is John 16:33 where Jesus says, "These things I have spoken to you, that in Me you may have peace. In the world you will have tribulation, but be of good cheer, I have overcome the world."

My late dad was in the Second World War but he never spoke about his experiences. I think it was because they were too painful for him. He was captured in North Africa and spent three-and-a-half years in a prisoner of war camp.

My mom told us about one incident that impacted his life very greatly. It was on a cold frosty night in Germany at Christmas time. My dad was standing, looking through a barbed-wire fence. He was probably missing his family, wondering when the war was going to end, trying to deal with what he was going through.

All of a sudden, he heard the most beautiful singing from little children. He looked out through that barbed-wire fence and there were little children singing *Silent Night* in German. It gave him tremendous hope and peace in that turbulent time of his life.

The Prince of Peace is found everywhere—His name is Jesus. Cling to Him wherever you are today.

JEHOVAH JIREH

And Abraham called the name of the place,
The-LORD-Will-Provide; as it is said to this day,
"In the Mount of the LORD it shall be provided."
GENESIS 22:14

Jehovah-Jireh is our provider. One of my favorite Scripture verses is Philippians 4:19, which says, "And my God shall supply all your need according to His riches in glory by Christ Jesus."

We must be givers and not takers because the Lord is a giver. We say all the silver and gold belongs to our God and all the cattle on a thousand hills belong to Him. So why are we stressing? Numbers 23:19 says, "God is not a man, that He should lie, nor a son of man, that He should repent. Has He said, and will He not do? Or has He spoken, and will He not make it good?" He doesn't tell lies. Therefore, we need to trust Him going forward. Our confidence is not in our strength; our confidence is in the promises of God.

You know, one of my heroes is George Müller. He started the children's homes in Bristol, England. He started as an absolute rogue but he got gloriously saved and then he lived a life of extraordinary faith. He took care of no less than 10,024 children. He got no money from the government, only by faith could he help those children. He said, "My Lord is not limited. He knows my present situation, and He can supply all I need."

Put your trust in Jesus and He will take care of the rest.

FIND THE HONEY

So He said, "Come." And when Peter had come down
out of the boat, he walked on the water to go to Jesus.
MATTHEW 14:29

Peter is the only human being in the history of the world who has walked on water. I have been to the Lake of Galilee and it is very, very deep. There were no stepping stones underneath his feet—Peter walked on the water with Jesus.

Now I can hear someone saying, "Yes, but he failed. He started sinking." Better to have tried and failed than to have never tried at all. He took his eyes off Jesus for a moment; he looked at the waves, fear gripped his heart, and he started to sink, but at least he got out of the boat. I want to say to you today that fear is paralyzing many people in the world. The opposite of faith is fear.

I received the most beautiful diary from one of my family members and on the cover it says, "You can't find the honey if you are scared of the bees!" Isn't that right?

As a beekeeper, I can tell you that it is not fun to be stung, but you can't get the honey if you are scared of the bees. So, we have got to get out onto the water. If you want to taste that honey…you have to face the bees. If you want to walk on water…you have to get out of the boat. Once you have tasted that honey, a few stings won't even affect you. Let's go out and do what Mark 11:22 says, "Have faith in God."

FINISH IT

"I am doing a great work, so that I cannot come down. Why should the work cease while I leave it and go down to you?"

NEHEMIAH 6:3

You see, Nehemiah was rebuilding the wall of Jerusalem and the enemy was trying to confuse him and dissuade him. They kept calling him to come down for a meeting but he wanted to finish the work the Lord had given to him. Do not become distracted. Finish the work God has given you to do. Remember, it is not how well you start the race that counts, it is how well you finish the race that matters. We have got to complete the task.

God will not give us a new project until we complete the one He has set before us. We have got to finish the race. You have got to finish your university degree. It doesn't matter how tough it is, you made a commitment. Your apprenticeship, you must complete it so that you can get your papers.

The Lord Jesus finished His work here on earth. Remember, just before He died on the cross, He said, "It is finished!" (John 19:30). In Revelation 3:8, the Lord says very clearly to us, "I know your works. See, I have set before you an open door, and no one can shut it; for you have a little strength, have kept My word, and have not denied My name."

Don't try and break the door down. The Lord will open the one door as soon as you have completed the task and He will close the other door.

KEEP DIGGING

There the Israelites sang this song:
"Spring up, O well! Yes, sing its praises!"
NUMBERS 21:17 NLT

Are you going through a barren desert time in your life, my dear friend? Well, the Lord has a word for us. He says, "Keep digging your well." You say, "But, Lord, it's so dry, we're in the middle of the desert." No, keep digging your well. Jesus says in Matthew 5:6, "Blessed are those who hunger and thirst for righteousness, for they shall be filled."

When we first arrived on Shalom farm, it was just a piece of bush. There were no houses, no facilities and no electricity. There was nothing. It was just barren land. We had no water. I went looking and found a damp patch in a low-lying area. With a pick and shovel, and a couple of helpers, we started to dig right in that damp spot.

Eventually, we were lowering ourselves down with a rope, but we just kept on digging. I never thought we would get anything and then, all of a sudden, out of the side of a rock, a beautiful, clear spring started to trickle. The water gurgled up. We nurtured it lovingly and it grew stronger and stronger until we had a water supply for our little house. Today, we have no less than four small dams that originated from that little spring.

Today, the Lord says to you, "Keep digging your well and you will receive water to quench your thirst." Don't give up. Keep digging and the Lord will help you.

LOOKING FORWARD

Jesus said to him, "No one, having put
his hand to the plow, and looking back,
is fit for the kingdom of God."

LUKE 9:62

You and I are about to face a brand-new year and we need to implement the plowing principle. I was taught to plow in bonnie Scotland when I was a young man. It is critical that the first furrow is dead straight—that is the most important aspect of plowing.

We need to look forward. How you execute the first cut in that field with that plow will influence the rest of the field. As we are about to start the new year, the same principle applies. You get on that tractor, you put it in the correct gear and you set the plow correctly. Then, you pick a point on the horizon and you line that up with the nose of the tractor. Then by faith, you start plowing and you do not look behind you. That is a fatal mistake. As soon as you do that, you will pull the steering wheel, put a kink in the first furrow and that will be exaggerated every time you come down the next line. By the time you finish that large field, it will look terrible.

We need to keep our eyes fixed on Jesus, the Author and the Finisher of our faith (see Hebrews 12:2). Put the past behind you. This year is almost over and you are looking at a brand-new field with a brand-new plow and a brand-new tractor. Let's start plowing for Jesus.

May the Lord bless you in the year ahead!